Social Change in Modern India

M. N. SRINIVAS

Orient BlackSwan

SOCIAL CHANGE IN MODERN INDIA

ORIENT BLACKSWAN PRIVATE LIMITED

Registered Office
3-6-752 Himayatnagar, Hyderabad 500 029, Telangana, India
e-mail: centraloffice@orientblackswan.com

Other Offices
Bengaluru, Chennai, Guwahati, Hyderabad,
Kolkata, Mumbai, New Delhi, Noida, Patna

First published 1966 by the University of California Press
Berkeely and Los Angeles

Indian edition published by Orient Blackswan 1972
Reprinted 1977, 1980, 1982, 1984, 1985, 1987, 1988, 1989, 1990, 1991, 1992
Revised edition 1995
Reprinted 1995, 1997, 1998, 2000, 2001, 2002, 2003, 2004, 2005, 2006, 2007, 2008
First Orient Blackswan impression 2009
Reprinted 2009, 2010, 2011, 2012, 2013, 2014, 2015, 2016, 2017, 2018, 2019, 2020, 2021, 2022, 2023, 2024, 2026

ISBN 978-81-250-0422-6

Typeset by
Scribe Consultants
New Delhi

Printed in India at
B.B Press, Tronica City, Ghaziabad, U.P. 201 103

Published by
Orient Blackswan Private Limited
3-6-752 Himayatnagar, Hyderabad 500 029, Telangana, India
e-mail: info@orientblackswan.com

PREFACE

THE RABINDRANATH TAGORE MEMORIAL LECTURESHIP, which was inaugurated at the University of Chicago in October, 1961, was continued at the University of California, Berkeley, by lectures delivered in May, 1963. The lectures formed the kernel of this volume.

Rabindranath Tagore is justly known as India's greatest modern poet and one of its greatest modern thinkers. In these aspects he is celebrated by other holders of the Lectureship. He is less widely thought of as a traveller to the West and an observer of the West which had already in his time made so great an impact on his beloved country. His comments on his American and European travels showed him intensely interested in the relationship of India to the rest of the world and in the inter-influences that modern contacts would produce. If such influences have taken forms that might have surprised and perhaps even shocked him, it is unthinkable that he would have failed to be interested in an analysis by an ethnologist, and an Indian ethnologist at that, of what has happened and is happening.

This ethnologist, India's leading social anthropologist, is Mysore Narasimhachar Srinivas. In 1952 he first introduced the notion of Sanskritization as an underlying process of Indian social change, in his book *Religions and Society Among the Coorgs*. Since then there has been no more influential concept in the discussions on change in Indian society. In these lectures he has developed the idea both in itself and in its contrapuntal relations with that much more conspicuous process of change, Westernization. Both by training, as an Oxford social anthropologist, and by background, as a South Indian Brahmin, he is eminently fitted to give a sophisticated, yet intimate, expression to his themes, in a way that Tagore might well have appreciated highly. Not the least important part of the book, and an integral part of it by peculiarly intimate inner lines of connection, is Professor Srinivas' apologia for the anthropologist's role in the midst of the rapid change and "modern" development in his own society.

M.N. Srinivas' position since 1959 as Professor of Sociology in the Delhi School of Economics of the University of Delhi only enhances the reputation which he has earned by his notable series of writings in Indian ethnology. His Coorg book followed the earlier *Marriage and Family in Mysore* (1942), and was joined in 1962 by the collection of his articles, *Caste in Modern India, and Other Essays*. Acknowledgement of his outstanding position as an interpreter of India is to be seen in his Simon Senior Research Fellowship, Manchester University (1953–1954), his Rockefeller Fellowship in Great Britain and the United States (1956–1957), and his Fellowship at the Center for Advanced Study in the Behavioral Sciences, Stanford (1964–1965). He was awarded the Rivers Memorial Medal of the Royal Anthropological Institute of Great Britain and Ireland in 1955, and the Sarat Chandra Roy Memorial Gold Medal of the Asiatic Society (of Bengal) in 1958.

A great debt of gratitude must be acknowledged to the patrons who made the Lectureship possible, especially to Mr. and Mrs. Harvey Breit of New York and to the Asia Foundation. The administration of the Lectureship by the Committee for the Rabindranath Tagore Memorial Lectureship of the Association for Asian Studies has been immeasurably forwarded by the efficient and loving labours of Dean Richard L. Park of the Division of the Social Sciences, University of Pittsburgh. At the University of California, Berkeley, help was provided in connection with the lectures by the Committee for Arts and Lectures and, most especially, by the Center for South Asia Studies, Institute of International Studies.

M.B. EMENEAU
University of California,
Berkeley

AUTHOR'S PREFACE TO 1966 EDITION

THE COMMITTEE FOR THE RABINDRANATH TAGORE MEMORIAL LECTURESHIP of the Association for Asian Studies did me the honour of inviting me to give the Tagore Lectures for the academic year 1962–1963 at the University of California in Berkeley. I chose as my theme "Social Change in Modern India," and I gave four lectures on it during May, 1963. I did not have an opportunity to revise them for publication until September, 1964, when I came to the Center for Advanced Study in the Behavioral Sciences, Stanford, as a Fellow. I was very fortunate in that I was able to carry out the arduous task of replanning and rewriting the lectures in the *āshram*-like atmosphere of the Center. I take this opportunity to express my profound thanks to the Director of the Center, Dr. Ralph Tyler, and all members of the Center's staff, for their uniform courtesy and help to me during my stay there from September, 1964, to December, 1965.

In June, 1963, I was a Simon Visiting Professor in the Department of Social Anthropology and Sociology at the University of Manchester, and this appointment gave me an opportunity to hold a series of seminars with Professor Max Gluckman's class on the theme of the Tagore Lectures. I benefited greatly from the stimulating discussions which followed the reading of the papers, and I am thankful to Professor Gluckman and his colleagues for their critical and friendly interest in my work. I am indebted to my colleagues in the Department of Sociology in the University of Delhi, Drs. M.S.A. Rao, André Beteille, and Arvind Shah, who criticized the earlier drafts of the lectures and also provided me with information on points which I raised in my letters to them. Professors R. Bellah, D. Mandelbaum, and M. Singer have placed me in their debt by taking time from their own work to read my manuscript and make several suggestions for its improvement. I gratefully acknowledge the editorial advice and help of Miss Miriam Gallaher, research assistant at the Center for Advanced Study, and I am certain that the manuscript has gained in clarity as well as readability as a result of her efforts. I am also grateful to Mrs. Joan Warmbrunn for her patience and skill in typing the different drafts of the lectures and for much other secretarial help as well.

When I accepted the invitation to give the Lectures, I thought that I should choose an all-India theme though even then I had some idea of the risks I was running in so doing. The vastness and diversity of India and the lack of adequate data in many areas make generalization extremely hazardous. But that does not obviate the need to see cultural and social processes in an all-India perspective if only to locate some of the problems that need to be given priority in future research, and the areas where information is either totally lacking or very poor.

In the course of explicating my concepts regarding social change in modern India I have had to delve into nineteenth century history, a task for which I know only too well that I do not have the necessary qualifications. But I have gone to the works of well-known historians for my facts and interpretations, and it gives me pleasure to acknowledge the stimulus I have received from the writing of Drs. Percival Spear, Bernard Cohn, Donald Smith, Robert Frykenberg, and Arvind Shah. I have also benefited from reading the unpublished material of Drs. Eugene Irschick, Burton Stein, William Rowe and André Béteille. I thank them all, and many others to whose writings I have referred in the book.

I must express my apologies to the Committee for the Rabindranath Tagore Memorial Lectureship for making them wait for over two years for the manuscript of my lectures. They have shown great patience with me.

Finally, I dedicate this book to Professor E.E. Evans-Pritchard, my former teacher and colleague at Oxford, and friend, as a small acknowledgement of the stimulus and kindnesses I have received from him over the years.

M.N. SRINIVAS

Center for Advanced Study
in the Behavioral Sciences, Stanford

AUTHOR'S PREFACE TO 1977 REISSUE

SOCIAL CHANGE IN MODERN INDIA, originally delivered in May, 1963 as the Rabindranath Tagore Memorial Lectures in Berkeley, was published in 1966 by the University of California Press. The book was favourably if not generously reviewed in professional journals, and soon after publication, became prescribed or recommended reading for graduate students in sociology, anthropology and Indian studies.

At the risk of stating the obvious, I must make it clear that mine is only a social anthropologist's view of social change in modern India. An economist, political scientist, educationalist, lawyer or historian would certainly bring to bear a different perspective if not approach to the analysis of change. However, multiple perspectives are essential to balance the subjectivity inherent in an unidisciplinary approach. Indeed, the subject of social change is so vast that any specialist finds that he is poaching constantly on the preserves of others. Getting several specialists to write on their respective fields is a popular way out of this problem but not a satisfactory one: comprehensiveness is gained at the expense of a central focus which helps to organize the data. If the choice is between a single trained mind poring over a vast array of diverse facts and several scholars each of whom writes on a special area, it is not always best to opt for the latter. Inter-disciplinary research is advocated as a way out of the dilemma but its advocates are not always certain about what they mean by it. They refer to what they think has been achieved in the hard sciences and that too in some foreign institution, and do not seem to entertain any doubts that it can be replicated in the social sciences and anywhere. Instances of successful inter-disciplinary research in the social sciences are not easy to come by except when a scholar takes the trouble to learn two disciplines. Such a man is like an ambidextrous tennis or cricket player, and provision can be made in our academic system to train scholars who are specialists in two disciplines with the full knowledge that over the years one of the specialisms is likely to rust. But this is different from inter-disciplinary research involving several specialists all of whom are engaged in tackling a single problem and are continually engaged in a creative dialogue.

Since this book was first published radical changes have occurred in the Indian polity, economy and society. The events which find place in the newspapers seem to be too violent, anarchic and unpredictable to be susceptible to analysis in terms of known and predictable patterns. I have often asked myself whether my analysis does not err on the side of order, regularity and predictability. In some sense, any analysis of processes gives the impression of arresting their flow but that does not render the analysis wrong. If I were analysing social change in India today, I would probably restate the nature of the relation between such processes as Sanskritization, Westernization and Secularization, and also emphasize the increasing dominance of politicization in Indian social and cultural life. The relationship of dominant caste to other castes is perhaps beginning to change as also the role of the dominant caste in local, regional and state politics. Finally, and most important of all, are the changes which are occurring in the caste system such as to herald a systemic change?

A short reading list has been added at the end of the book for the benefit of those interested.

M.N. SRINIVAS
Bangalore
18 May, 1977

CONTENTS

1

SANSKRITIZATION

1

THE SUBJECT of social change in modern India is vast and complex, and an adequate understanding of it will require the collaboration, for many years, of a number of scholars in such diverse fields as economic, social and cultural history, law, politics, education, religion, demography and sociology. It will have to take account of regional, linguistic and other differences. My aim, however, is much more limited: I shall try to consider here, somewhat more systematically than before, two concepts—Sanskritization and Westernization—which I put forward some years ago to explain some features of religious, cultural and social change in India.[1] Of the two processes to which the concepts refer, Sanskritization seems to have occurred throughout Indian history and still continues to occur. Westernization, on the other hand, refers to changes introduced into Indian society during British rule and which continue, in some cases with added momentum, in independent India. Westernization, unlike Sanskritization, is not confined to any particular section of the Indian population and its importance, both in the number of people it affects and the ways in which it affects them, is steadily increasing. The achievement of independence has in some ways quickened the process of Westernization, and it is not unlikely that independence was a necessary precondition of such acceleration. The complex and intricate interrelation between Sanskritization and Westernization, on a short-term as well as long-term basis, offers a fertile field for analysis and speculation.

When the concepts of Sanskritization and Westernization were first put forward they aroused a certain amount of interest among sociologists and anthropologists working in the Indian field.[2] Sanskritization was found to be a widespread cultural and social process among Hindus in different parts of India. It is also reported to be occurring among some tribal groups such as the Bhils and Oraons. The relation of these two processes to changes in the caste system in different parts of the country also needs to be properly understood.

The opportunity to find out for myself whether and how far these concepts were still useful for the analysis of social changes, and whether any further clarifications, refinements, elaborations and modifications were needed, was presented to me when the Rabindranath Tagore Memorial Lectureship Committee invited me to give the Tagore Lectures for 1963. I have embarked on this task with some hesitation, nevertheless, as I am acutely aware of the difficulties and hazards involved in making statements claiming to hold good for Hindus all over India. I now appreciate the advantages that I enjoyed in much of my previous work: the topics were more specific, and they concerned a small region and particular sections of the people in it, and I had myself collected a great deal of the data. I am glad, however, that I chose the topic of social change in modern India, inasmuch as it forced me out of my micro-shell. The limitations of micro-studies are only too obvious in a country like India, which has great regional diversity and whose people are divided into hundreds of castes. On the other hand, macro-studies are apt to miss the nuances, refinements and subtleties which can be reached only by detailed micro-studies. At the risk of giving expression to a truism, I would say that the Indian sociologist has to be temperamentally and methodologically ambidextrous, resorting to either type of study as the occasion demands. Micro-studies provide insights while macro-studies yield perspectives, and movement from one to the other is essential.

Before discussing Sanskritization I shall examine briefly the manner in which the influential concept of *varna* successfully obscured the dynamic features of caste during the traditional or pre-British period.[3] The fact that the concept continues to be relevant for understanding some aspects of caste has only helped to perpetuate the misconceptions and distortions implicit in it. Let me briefly recount the main features of caste as embodied in *varna*:

(1) There is a single all-India hierarchy without any variations between one region and another; (2) there are only four *varnas* or, if the Harijans, who are literally "beyond the pale" of caste, are included, five; (3) the hierarchy is clear; and (4) it is immutable.

Caste is undoubtedly an all-India phenomenon in the sense that there are everywhere hereditary, endogamous groups which form a hierarchy, and that each of these groups has a traditional association with one or two occupations. Everywhere there are Brahmins, Untouchables, and peasant, artisan, trading and service castes. Relations between castes are invariably expressed in terms of pollution and purity. Certain Hindu theological ideas such as *samsāra, karma* and *dharma* are woven into the caste system, but it is not known whether awareness of these concepts is universal or confined only to certain sections of the hierarchy. This depends on the degree to which an area is Sanskritized.

But the existence of some universal features should not lead us to ignore the significant regional differences. It is not merely that some castes—for example, the *bhārbujha* or grain parcher, *kahār* or water carrier, and the *bārtos* or genealogists—are to be found only in some parts of the country, or that the position of a few occupational castes varies from one part of the country to another, but that caste mainly exists and functions as a regional system. In fact, all the Brahmins speaking the same regional language, let alone all the Brahmins in India, do not form a single endogamous group. There may be a dozen or more endogamous groups among them. Again, even within a small region a caste normally interacts with only several other castes and not with all. (However, a few castes are found spread over a wide area, and this usually means that there are cultural differences between its various sections.) To the average peasant, moreover, the names of castes in other linguistic areas are pure abracadabra. They make sense only when they are fitted into the Procrustean frame of *varna*.

There are hundreds of *jātis* or endogamous groups in each of the linguistic areas of modern India. The four or five *varnas* represent only broad all-India categories into which the innumerable *jātis* can be grouped for some very limited purposes. According to the *varna* model, the Harijans or Untouchables are outside the caste system and contact with Harijans pollutes members of the other four *varnas*. But if economic, social and even ritual relations between the castes of a region are taken into account, Harijans are an integral part of the system. They perform certain essential economic tasks in agriculture, they are often village servants, messengers and sweepers, and they beat the drum at village festivals and remove the leaves on which people have dined at community dinners.

In the *varna* model, there is no doubt whatever as to the place occupied by each caste category. Certainty of position in the ranked order of castes is not, however, a characteristic of caste at the existential level. Actually, even the two ends of the caste system are not as firm as they are made out to be. Some Brahmin groups are regarded as so low that even Harijans will not accept cooked food from them.

It is clear that vagueness or doubt regarding mutual position is not accidental or unimportant, but is an essential feature of caste as an ongoing system. Two castes each of which claims superiority to the other should not be regarded as exceptional in their behaviour but as the typical product of a dynamic system in which there is some pushing and jostling in the attempt to get ahead. In pre-British India, disputes regarding caste rank occasionally reached the king, whose verdict was final.

Thus the position of castes in the hierarchy as it actually exists is liable to change, whereas in the *varna* model the position of each *varna* is fixed for all time. It is really a matter for wonder that, in spite of the distortions of the reality implicit in the *varna* model, it has continued to survive.

Finally, the *varna* model of caste is really a hierarchy in the sense that the priestly *varna* is placed at the top and the criterion of ranking is derived from religious considerations. The ordering of different *varnas* is clearly intended to support the theory of Brahminical supremacy and only partially overlaps with the actualities of caste ranking in different parts of the country. What is more noticeable, however, is the fact that the possession of secular power by a caste is either reflected in its ritual ranking or leads, sooner or later, to an improvement of its position.

The *varna* model of the caste system seems to have evolved gradually during the Vedic period of Indian history, and the early Brahmin writers seem to have accepted it as providing a rough description of caste system as it existed then. These writers laid down the rights and duties of the first three *varnas*, which were regarded as "twice-born" (*dwija*) on account of their undergoing the ritual of donning the sacred thread (*upanayana*).

According to Ghurye; the "*varna dharma*" or code governing

the conduct of the different *varnas* seems to have received a high degree of elaboration in the post-Vedic period (circa 600 B.C.–A.D. 300):

> This period sees a great consolidation of the position of the Brahmin class, while the degradation of the Shūdras comes out in marked contrast to the growing superiority of the Brahmins. The discomfiture of the Kshatriyas is complete, and the Vaishyas, at least the general mass, have progressively approximated to the Shūdras.... The three lower castes are ordered to live according to the teaching of the Brahmin, who shall declare their duties, while the king is exhorted to regulate their conduct accordingly.[4]

The Brahmin writers on law propounded a model of the caste system which placed them at the top and gave them the privilege of declaring the duties of the other castes, including the King's. The claims which the Brahmins made for themselves and their view of the caste hierarchy are understandable, but not so the fact that many scholars, Indian as well as foreign, have regarded them as representations of the historical reality. One wonders how many dominant peasant castes in rural India had even heard of the rules governing different *varnas* or, having heard of them, paid heed to them. One is also at a loss to understand how people living in villages were made to obey the rules or punished for violating them. Even today, with all the facilities and resources at the disposal of the Government of India, it has been found very difficult to ensure that the rights which the Indian Constitution confers on the Harijans are actually translated into practice in India's 560,000 villages. The situation in ancient or medieval India can be left to the reader's own inferences.

There is no doubt, however, that the *varna* model has been regarded by urban and educated Indians as providing a more or less true picture of caste as an ongoing system. It is my hunch that the *varna* model became more popular during the British period as a result of a variety of forces: the institution, which prevailed till 1864, of attaching Brahmin Pandits to British-established law courts, the presence in every town of a body of Western-educated lawyers who tried to apply Brahminical law to all Hindus,[5] the translation of a vast mass of sacred literature from Sanskrit into English, the rise everywhere of caste *sabhas* who tried to introduce reforms by Sanskritizing the way of life of their respective castes, and the growth of a vigorous anti-Brahmin movement which attempted to displace Brahmins from the positions of power and influence which they occupied in some parts of the country. The list is obviously incomplete and tentative, and a full explanation of the popularity of the *varna* model can only be arrived at after study.

2

Sanskritization is the process by which a "low" Hindu caste, or tribal or other group, changes its customs, ritual, ideology and way of life in the direction of a high, and frequently, "twice-born" caste. Generally such changes are followed by a claim to a higher position in the caste hierarchy than that traditionally conceded to the claimant caste by the local community. The claim is usually made over a period of time, in fact, a generation or two, before the "arrival" is conceded. Occasionally a caste claims a position which its neighbours are not willing to concede. This type of disagreement between claimed and conceded status may be not only in the realm of opinion but also in the more important realm of institutionalized practice. Thus Harijan castes in Mysore will not accept cooked food and drinking water from the Smiths who are certainly one of the touchable castes and therefore superior to Harijans even if their claim to be Vishwakarma Brahmins is not accepted. Similarly peasants (Okkaligas) and others such as shepherds (Kurubas) do not accept cooked food and water from Mārka Brahmins, who are certainly included among Brahmins. I remember talking to a Lingāyat in north Coorg who referred to the Coorgs as "jungle people [kādu jana]," and this contrasted with the Coorg claim to be true Kshatriyas and even "Aryans". The above instances are all from Mysore State, but parallels can be cited from every part of India.

Sanskritization is generally accompanied by, and often results in, upward mobility for the caste in question; but mobility may also occur without Sanskritization and *vice versa*. However, the mobility associated with Sanskritization results only in *positional changes* in the system and does not lead to any *structural change*. That is, a caste moves up above its neighbours and another comes down, but all this takes place in an essentially stable hierarchical order. The system itself does not change.

As I have already stated, Sanskritization is not confined to

Hindu castes but also occurs among tribal and semitribal groups such as the Bhils of Western India, the Gonds and Oraons of Central India and the Pahādis of the Himalayas. This usually results in the tribe undergoing Sanskritization claiming to be a caste, and therefore, Hindu. In the traditional system the only way to become a Hindu was to belong to a caste, and the unit of mobility was usually a group, not an individual or a family.

I now realize that in both my book on Coorg religion and my "Note on Sanskritization and Westernization", I emphasized unduly the Brahminical model of Sanskritization and ignored the other models—Kshatriya, Vaishya and Shūdra. Even the Brahminical model was derived from the Kannada, Tamil and Telugu Brahmins, and not from Brahmin castes in other regions. D.F. Pocock has pointed to the existence of a Kshatriya model in addition to a Brahminical model:

> Just as the Kshatriya or King stands with the Brahmin as superior to the Vaishya and Shūdra *varna*, so we may also speak of the Kingly model in Hindu society which is complementary to, though dependent in certain respects upon, the Brahminic. At any given time or place the Kingly model is represented by the dominant political power in any area, and is mediated by the local dominant non-Brahmin caste or castes of that area. Thus in secular matters the Moghuls and the British at various times have provided a standard by which secular prestige is gauged.[6]

I would like to add here that not only the kingly model but also the other models are mediated by the locally dominant caste, and the concept of the dominant caste supplements in some ways the concept of Sanskritization.

Milton Singer has also drawn attention to the fact that there exist not one or two models of Sanskritization but three if not four:[7]

> The local version [of Sanskritic Hinduism] may use the four *varna* labels—Brahmin, Kshatriya, Vaishya and Shūdra—but the defining content of these labels varies with locality and needs to be empirically determined for any particular locality. It has also been discovered that the relative prestige and rank of these different *varnas* tend to vary with locality, time and group. In many areas, e.g., the kingly or martial, life-style has a rank equal with or sometimes higher than that of the Brahmin. Groups in these areas who wish to improve their

> status do so by adopting some of the stigmata of the Rājpūt life-style, i.e., by "Rājpūtizing" their way of life (Sinha). Even the life-style of the merchant and peasant have been taken as models in localities where these groups are dominant.[8]

The first three *varnas* are called *dwija* or "twice-born" as only they are entitled to don the sacred thread at the ceremony of *upanayana* which is interpreted as a second birth. Only members of the first three *varnas* are entitled to the performance of Vedic ritual at which hymns (*mantras*) from one or other of the Vedas (excluding the Atharva Veda) are chanted. Among the "twice-born" *varnas* the Brahmins are the most particular about the performance of these rites, and they may therefore be regarded as "better" models of Sanskritization than the others. The cultural content of each *varna*, however, varies from one area to another and from one period of time to another; and the diversity is generally far greater at the lower levels of the *varna* hierarchy than at the highest.

Let me begin with a brief consideration of the diversity in the Brahmin *varna*.[9] In the first place, some elements of the local culture would be common to all the castes living in a region, from the highest to the lowest. Thus the Brahmin and Harijan (Untouchable) of a region would speak the same language, observe some common festivals and share certain local deities and beliefs. I have called this "vertical solidarity", and it contrasts with "horizontal solidarity" which members of a single caste or *varna* have.

Some Brahmin groups such as the Kāshmiri, Bengāli and Sāraswat are non-vegetarians, while Brahmins elsewhere are traditionally vegetarians. Some Brahmin groups are more Sanskritized in their style of life than others, and this is quite apart from the differences between *vaidika* (priestly) and *loukika* (secular) Brahmins. There is also considerable occupational diversity between different Brahmin groups.[10] Brahmins in some areas such as the Punjab and parts of Western Uttar Pradesh and Rajasthan have a low secular status,[11] and several Brahmin groups in Gujarat (for example, Tapodhan), Bengal and Mysore (Mārka) are regarded as ritually low.[12]

By and large it would be true to say that Kshatriya, Vaishya and Shūdra *varnas* would draw more of their culture from the local area than the Brahmins, and it follows from this that profound cultural differences exist between castes claiming to be Kshatriya and Vaishya in different parts of the country. In fact, while there seems to be some agreement in each area in India as to who are Brahmins and who Untouchables, such consensus is absent with regard to Kshatriyas and Vaishyas. Kshatriya and Vaishya status seems to be claimed by groups who have traditions of soldiering and trade respectively. Neither Kshatriyas nor Shūdras in different parts of the country have a common body of ritual. Many of them do not undergo the essential sacraments (samskāras) characteristic of the twice-born *varnas*.

The historian K.M. Panikkar has maintained that there has been no such caste as the Kshatriya during the last two thousand years of history. The Nandas were the last "true" Kshatriyas, and they disappeared in the fifth century B.C. Since then every known royal family has come from a non-Kshatriya caste, including the famous Rājpūt dynasties of medieval India.[13] Panikkar also points out that "the Shūdras seem to have produced an unusually large number of royal families even in more recent times. The Pālas of Bengal belonged undoubtedly to that caste. The great Marātha Royal House, whatever their function today, could hardly sustain their genealogical pretensions connecting them with Rājpūt descent."[14] (One of the most important functions of genealogist and bardic castes was to legitimize mobility from the ranks of lower castes to the Kshatriya by providing suitable genealogical linkage and myth.)

That lack of "fit" between the *varna* model and the realities of the existing local hierarchy is even more striking in the case of the Shūdra. Not only has this category been a fertile source for the recruitment of local Kshatriya and Vaishya castes, as Panikkar has pointed out, but it spans such a wide cultural and structural arch as to be almost meaningless. There are at one extreme the dominant, landowning, peasant castes which wield power and authority over local Vaishyas and Brahmins, whereas at the other extreme are the poor, near-Untouchable groups living just above the pollution line. The category also includes the many artisan and servicing castes such as goldsmiths, blacksmiths, carpenters, potters, oil pressers, basket makers, weavers, barbers, washermen, watermen, grain parchers, toddy tappers, shepherds and swineherds.

Again, some castes in the omnibus category of Shūdra may have highly Sanskritized style of life whereas others are only minimally

Sanskritized. But whether Sanskritized or not, the dominant peasant castes provide local models for imitation; and, as Pocock and Singer have observed, Kshatriya (and other) models are often mediated through them.

3

A feature of rural life in many parts of India is the existence of dominant, landowning castes.[15] For a caste to be dominant, it should own a sizable amount of the arable land locally available, have strength of numbers and occupy a high place in the local hierarchy. When a caste has all the attributes of dominance, it may be said to enjoy decisive dominance. Occasionally there may be more than one dominant caste in a village and over a period of time one dominant caste may give way to another.[16] This happened occasionally even in pre-British India,[17] and has been an important aspect of rural social change in the twentieth century.

New factors affecting dominance have emerged in the last eighty years or so. Western education, jobs in the administration and urban sources of income are all significant in contributing to the prestige and power of particular caste groups in the village. The introduction of adult franchise and *panchāyati rāj* (local self-government at village, *tehsil* and district levels) since independence has resulted in giving a new sense of self-respect and power to "low" castes, particularly Harijans, who enjoy reservation of seats in all elected bodies from the village to Union Parliament. The long-term implications of these changes are probably even more important, especially in those villages where there are enough Harijans to sway the local balance of power one way or the other. In the traditional system it was possible for a small number of people belonging to a high caste to wield authority over the entire village when they owned a large quantity of arable land and also had a high ritual position. Now, however, in many parts of rural India power has passed into the hands of numerically large, landowning peasant castes; it is likely to remain there for some time, except in villages where Harijans are numerically strong and are also taking advantage of the new educational and other opportunities available to them. Endemic factionalism in the dominant caste is also another threat to its continued enjoyment of power.

No longer is dominance a purely local matter in rural India. A caste group which has only a family or two in a particular village but which enjoys decisive dominance in the wider region will still count locally because of the network of ties binding it to its dominant relatives. What is equally important is that others in the village will be aware of the existence of this network. Contrariwise, a caste which enjoys dominance in only one village will find that it has to reckon with the caste which enjoys regional dominance.

The vast improvement in communications during the last fifty years has contributed to the decline in prestige of purely local styles of living. Rural leaders, or at least their sons, now tend to borrow items from prestigious, urban ways of living, and the long-term effects of this process are a decrease in cultural diversity and an increase in uniformity.

Landownership is a crucial factor in establishing dominance. Generally, the pattern of landownership in rural India is such that the bulk of the arable land is concentrated in the hands of a relatively small number of big owners as against a large number who either own very little land or no land at all.[18] The small number of big owners wield a considerable amount of power over the rest of the village population, and this situation is only made worse by rapid population growth. The big landowners are patrons of the bulk of the poor villagers. Each household from artisan and servicing castes provides goods and services to a certain number of landowning households; traditionally these ties have been stable, continuing from generation to generation. The former are paid in grain and straw during harvests. Ties between landlord and tenant or agricultural servant are also of an enduring kind, though in recent years they have become weaker. Tenants, labourers, artisans, and members of servicing castes stand in a relation of clientship to the landowning patron, and clientship involves a variety of duties.[19]

Similar disparities in the pattern of landownership perhaps exist in other developing countries, but what is unique to the Indian situation is that owners, tenants, landless labourers, artisans, and those who provide services form permanent and hereditary caste groups. Landowners generally come from the higher castes while 35 per cent of Harijans are landless labourers, and the bulk of those who own land "have such small holdings that their condition is hardly better than that of agricultural labourers."[20]

Landownership confers not only power but prestige, so much so that individuals who have made good in any walk of life tend to invest in land.[21] If landownership is not always an indispensable passport to high rank, it certainly facilitates upward mobility. The existence of a congruence between landownership and high rank in the caste hierarchy has been widely observed, but it is important to remember that it is only of a general kind and admits of exceptions in every area.

The power and prestige which landowning castes command affect their relations with all castes, including those ritually higher. This is true of parts of the Punjab where the landowning Jāts look upon the Brahmins as their servants, and of Madhopur village in eastern Uttar Pradesh where formerly the dominant Thākurs refused cooked food from all Brahmins except their *gurus* or religious teachers.[22] In Rāmpura village in Mysore State, the Brahmin priest of the Rāma temple was a figure of fun; when, at a temple festival, he tried to distribute *prasāda* (food consecrated by being offered to the deity) to the congregation, the peasant youths gathered there teased him by asking for more, and tugged at his *dhoti* when he did not comply. The priest complained to the headman, and the latter arranged for a representative from one of the dominant peasant lineages to be present in the temple whenever the priest distributed *prasāda*. On one occasion, a young peasant boy who was walking with the priest and me criticized the priest's over-attentiveness to agriculture and his "indifference" to temple ritual. The embarrassed priest only made a few unsuccessful efforts to change the subject.

But important as secular criteria are, ritual superiority has an independent existence and power of its own. Beidelman remarks rightly:

> At the risk of inconsistency I must emphasize that there are many areas in which ritual rank seems to operate independently of economic determinants. In Senapur and Rampur the Brahmins were not the powerful or economically superior caste, but were subordinate to the Jāts and Thākurs. But by consensus the village would probably agree that these same Brahmins are ritually supreme. The village would not even find it paradoxical that Brahmins may refuse certain cooked foods and sometimes other social gestures from other

> castes, even from the economically powerful ones. They would recognize that these castes are all ritually impure to Brahmins.[23]

The inconsistency stressed by Beidelman, of which the people themselves are aware, is an important aspect of caste ranking in which there is occasionally a hiatus between secular and ritual rank. On secular criteria alone a Brahmin may occupy a very low position, but he is still a Brahmin and as such entitled to respect in ritual and pollution contexts. A millionaire Gujarati Bania will not enter the kitchen where his Brahmin cook works, for such entry would defile the Brahmin and the cooking utensils. Not only is there contextual distinction, but Brahmins are also distinguished from the religion with which they are so closely bound up, a fact which has helped in the modern reinterpretation of Hinduism. This has enabled Hinduism to survive the powerful anti-Brahmin movement of South India. It is true that rationalism and atheism are a part of the ideology of the Dravida Munnetra Kazhagam (Dravidian Progressive Federation), but it is doubtful how far the Tamil non-Brahmin castes subscribe to it.

The mediation of the various models of Sanskritization through the local dominant caste stresses the importance of the latter in the process of cultural transmission. Thus if the locally dominant caste is Brahmin or Lingāyat, it will tend to transmit a Brahminical model of Sanskritization, whereas if it is Rājput or Bania, it will transmit Kshatriya or Vaishya models. Of course, each locally dominant caste has its own conception of Brahmin, Kshatriya or Vaishya models.

Two distinct tendencies are implicit in the caste system. The first is an acceptance of the existence of multiple cultures, including moral and religious norms, in any local society. Such acceptance is accompanied by a feeling that some institutions, ideas, beliefs and practices are relevant to one's group while others are not. A peasant takes a great deal of pride in his agriculture, and talks about its importance and difficulty and the skill and patience required. An artisan or a member of a servicing caste has a similar attitude toward his hereditary occupation. Occasionally, a man is heard making slighting remarks about the hereditary occupations of other castes.

The other tendency inherent in the caste system is the imitation of the ways of higher castes. Not any particular caste is imitated, or even the highest caste. Pocock is essentially right when he observes:

> A non-Brahmin caste of relatively low status does not (or did not before the advent of books) imitate an *idea* of Brahminism nor did it have *general* notions of secular prestige. For it the models of conduct are the castes higher than itself with which it is in the closest proximity. Properly speaking, we may not even speak of one caste imitating another but rather *one local section of a caste imitating another local section* (Italics mine).[24]

It is necessary, however, to caution against treating the local, village system as completely independent from the wider, all-India system. Ideals of behaviour may be derived from sources of Great Tradition such as pilgrimages, *harikathas* and religious plays. The Sanskritization of the Pātidārs, for instance, owes much to these sources and to the influence of Vallabhachāri and Swāminārāyan sects.

The elders of the dominant caste in a village were the watchdogs of a pluralistic culture and value system. Traditionally, they prevented the members of a caste from taking over the hereditary occupation of another caste whose interests would have been hurt by an inroad made into their monopoly, the only exceptions being agriculture and trade in some commodities. The dominant caste probably ignored minor changes in the ritual and style of life of a low caste, but when the latter refused to perform the services, economic or ritual, which it traditionally performed, or when it appropriated an important high-caste symbol, then punishment followed swiftly.[25] Pocock narrates an incident from his field area in Kaira district in Gujarat State in Western India:

> A story is told in Mōtāgām which relates events only thirty years old. At that time a Bāriā from Nānugām was seen walking through Mōtāgām wearing his *dhoti* in the distinctive Pātidār style, sporting a large handle-bar moustache which Pātidār of the period cultivated, and smoking a portable *hookah*. A leading Pātidār had him caught and forcibly shaved, and he was ordered, under pain of a beating, never to try to look like a Pātidār again and to carry his *hookah* behind his back whenever he walked through a Pātidār village. Today the lack of power to enforce such distinctions has made for a greater uniformity of dress, but distinctive dress is no longer stressed by the Pātidār. This indifference to a

> once valued custom is the equivalent of repudiating it, and today the middle-class Bāriā models his formal or ceremonial appearance upon the old Pātidār style of some thirty years ago.[26]

Similar incidents have been reported from other parts of rural India during the last fifty years or so. William Rowe mentions that when, in 1936, the Noniyas ("low" caste of salt-makers now employed in digging wells, tanks and roads, and in making tiles and bricks) of Senāpur village in eastern Uttar Pradesh donned *en masse* the sacred thread,

> the affronted Kshatriya landlords beat the Noniyas, tore off the sacred threads and imposed a collective fine on the caste. Some years later the Noniyas again began to wear the sacred thread but were unopposed. Their first attempt had been a direct, public challenge, but on the second occasion the Noniyas assumed the sacred thread quietly and on an individual basis.[27]

We learn from *Census of India Report for 1921* that when the Ahīrs (cowherds) of North India decided to call themselves Kshatriyas and donned the sacred thread, their action roused the wrath of the dominant higher castes. In North Bihar, for instance, the high-caste Rājpūts and Bhumihār Brahmins tried to prevent the Ahīrs from assuming the symbols of twice-born status, this resulted in violence and resort to the law courts.[28] Hutton has described a similar conflict between the Kallar, a dominant caste in Rāmnād district in the extreme south of India, and Harijans:

> In December 1930 the Kallar in Rāmnād propounded eight prohibitions the disregard of which led to the use of violence by the Kallar against the exterior Harijan castes, whose huts were fired, whose granaries and property were destroyed, and whose livestock was looted. The eight prohibitions were as follows:
>
> 1. that the Ādi-Drāvidas shall not wear ornaments of gold and silver;
> 2. that the males should not be allowed to wear their clothes above the hips;
> 3. that their males should not wear coats or shirts or *baniyans*;

4. no Ādi-Drāvida shall be allowed to have his hair cropped;

5. that the Ādi-Drāvidas should not use other than earthenware vessels in their houses;

6. their women shall not be allowed to cover the upper portion of their bodies by clothes or *ravukais* [blouses] or *thāvanis* [upper cloths worn like togas];

7. their women shall not be allowed to use flowers or saffron paste;

8. the men shall not use umbrellas for protection against sun and rain, nor shall they wear sandals.[29]

The dominant castes, then, maintained the structural distance between the different castes living within their jurisdiction. Many of the rules they upheld and enforced were local rules while a few—such as the ban on the donning of the sacred thread by a low caste—were the rules of the Great Tradition. However, it was likely that in those areas where the peasant castes enjoyed decisive dominance they had only a perfunctory knowledge of the Great Tradition. Since, in the traditional system, only the Brahmin priest was the repository of knowledge of the Great Tradition, the dominant caste was able to prevent cultural trespass by ensuring that the priest served only the high castes. Understandably enough, the priest had a healthy respect for the susceptibilities of the dominant caste and of his own caste-fellows.[30]

The role of the dominant caste was not, however, restricted to being the guardian of a pluralistic culture. It also stimulated in lower castes a desire to imitate the dominant caste's own prestigious style of life. The lower castes had to go about this task with circumspection—any attempt to rush things was likely to meet with swift reprisal. They had to avoid imitating in matters likely to upset the dominant caste too much, and their chances of success were much better if they slowly inched their way to their goal.

D.R. Chanana has discussed the spread of Sanskritization and Westernization in an area which, until the Partition of 1947, was markedly influenced by Islam and by certain West Asian cultural forms.[31] Sikhism, itself the result of the fusion of Hindu and Islamic religions, enjoyed a secondary dominance while the Hindus in the area revealed the impact of both Islam and Sikhism. Among Hindus, the trading castes of Khatri, Arora and Agarwāl were important whereas the Brahmin was economically backward and not distinguished for learning.

> The first thing to note is the historic fact of the relative weakness of the Brahmin influence in this region. Ever since the large-scale conversions of the artisans, craftsmen and peasants to Islam, the Hindus living in these areas have been relatively few in number, and instead of exercising dominating influence on the Muslims, they have themselves been influenced by the latter. As proof thereof may be noted the relative scarcity of temples in these parts, the non-existence of Brahmins well-versed in the *shāstras* (except in Jammu and other Hindu-ruled hill states), the total absence of any Sanskrit schools till very recently, and the relative laxity in the enforcement of prohibitions regarding eating, etc.[32]

While Hindu women did not take to the veil (*burka*) as did Muslim women, they did not appear in public in overwhelmingly Muslim areas. The Hindus did not recite any Sanskrit *mantras*, and they sent their children to *madrasas* (Muslim schools) run by *maulvis* (Muslim divines). They donned the sacred thread only at the time of marriage. The wedding rites included the essential Vedic sacraments with a Brahmin officiating as priest. Very little of the Great Tradition of Hinduism was known. Chanana states that in the sphere of religion Hindus were "deeply influenced by Islam, especially by the teachings of Sufi saints."[33]

The picture that emerges from Chanana's description is that throughout the former Punjab and North-West Frontier Provinces, Muslims enjoyed primary dominance while Sikhs exercised a secondary dominance in certain selected areas of this region. Among Hindus, the trading castes were important while the Brahmins had neither wealth nor learning. They were also influenced by Sikhism and "therefore the very group which could have helped Brahminize, Sanskritize the Hindu masses was in no position to do so."[34]

The minimal Sanskritization of nineteenth-century Punjab reveals how the style of life of a dominant group is impressed on the local region. Only the complex forces brought into existence by British rule were responsible for the increased Sanskritization of Punjabi Hindus. The Ārya Samāj and its rival, the Sanātan Dharma Sabha, along with the educational institutions, both traditional (*gurukuls* and *rishikuls*) and modern (Dayānand, Anglo-

Vedic and Sanātan Dharma Sabha schools and colleges), started by them, spread traditional as well as modern learning among the Hindus of the Punjab.

The influence of the dominant caste seems to extend to all areas of social life, including so fundamental a matter as the principle of descent and affiliation. Thus the two patrilineal Tamil trading castes, the Tarakans (of Angadipuram) and Mannadiyārs (of Pālghāt *tāluk*), gradually changed, in about 120 to 150 years, from patriliny to matriliny. Tarakan women had husbands from Nambūdri Brahmin or Sāmanthan families while Tarakan men married Kiriyam Nāyar women. Some Tarakan women had connubial relations with men of the royal Vellāttiri lineage, and this was a source of wealth for the lucky Tarakan lineages. The immigrant, weaving caste of Chāliyan follow matriliny in parts of Ponnāni *tāluk*, and patriliny elsewhere. Some Chāliyans in Ponnāni *tāluk* assumed the caste name of Nāyar (dominant, matrilineal caste of Kerala) in the 1940s.[35] Patrilineal Kurukkals working in temples in Travancore became matrilineal toward the end of the eighteenth century, and after that Kurukkal women began to have hypergamous relations with Nambudri men while Kurukkal men married women from the matrilineal Marans. The Kurukkal seem to have been forced to switch over to patriliny by the powerful Pottis.[36]

S.L. Kalia has described the process of "tribalization" occurring in Jaunsar-Bawar in Uttar Pradesh and in the Bastar region of Madhya Pradesh, according to which high-caste Hindus temporarily resident among tribal people take over the latter's mores, ritual and beliefs, which are in many respects antithetical to their own. Kalia's examples illustrate the radical changes which may come about in the style of life and values of people when they move away from their reference groups. The ease with which the high-caste Hindus took over the new culture was perhaps due to the temporary nature of their stay, and some of them at least were aware of this. Thus Uttar Pradesh Brahmins who ate meat, drank liquor and consorted with hill women in the Jaunsar-Bawar area told Kalia, "We have to do it because of the climate. There is nothing available here except meat. We will purify ourselves the day we cross the Jumna and return to our homes in Dehradun."[37] Such a situation is, however, different from that in a multi-caste village dominated by a single caste. Each caste in the village knows the rules it has to obey and the punishment that follows violation. The elders of the concerned or dominant caste punish violation with fine, infliction of physical pain, or outcasting. But even the threat of punishment does not seem to deter the non-dominant castes from developing an admiration for the style of life of the dominant caste and gradually trying to imitate it. Thus small numbers of Brahmins or other high castes may gradually assimilate elements from the culture of a locally dominant caste. They may "go native," and instead of being agents of Sanskritization become themselves the imitators of local Rājpūt, Jāt, Ahīr, Reddi, Kamma, Marātha or Okkaliga culture. This is especially likely to happen when communications are poor, and there is no regular contact with towns, centers of pilgrimage and monasteries. The representatives of the Great Tradition may, in short, succumb to the Little Traditions, and this seems to have happened occasionally.

It is not correct, however, to assume that the culture of the Brahmin is always highly Sanskritized. The style of life of the Sanādh Brahmins of Western Uttar Pradesh, for instance, is only minimally Sanskritized. In 1951–1952, when Marriott made a study of Kishan Garhi, a village in Western Uttar Pradesh, about a hundred miles southeast of Delhi, they were the locally dominant caste. Marriott writes:

> *The relatively slight Sanskritization of the Brahmins in this area contains a clue to the general slowness of Sanskritization and to the relatively small proportion of great-traditional contents in the religion of the rest of the castes in Kishan Garhi.* Brahmins are, by their position in the caste hierarchy, and by their association with priesthood, the best potential local agents of the great tradition. Since their religious forms are in large part little-traditional, what filters down from the Brahmins to lower castes in Kishan Garhi must also be in large part little-traditional. Thus the festival Pitcher Fourth, whose lack of Sanskritic reference is described above, is explicitly identified in Kishan Garhi as a festival of Brahmin wives, who may not remarry if they are widowed; this festival is said to have been taken up in recent generations by the lower castes of Kishan Garhi. So, too, the priesthood of the village site, which descends in the most influential Brahmin lineage of Kishan Garhi, is the priesthood of the non-Sanskritic mother-godling called by the untranslatable name of "Cāmeṛ." When persons

> of lower caste would propitiate this powerful mother-godling of the Brahmins, they must take their offerings, not to any temple of the great tradition, but to Cāmeṛ's rude mound of stones and mud.[38] (Italics mine)

In most parts of rural India there exist landowning peasant castes which either enjoy decisive dominance, or share dominance with another caste drawn from the categories of Shūdra, Kshatriya or Brahmin. The changes that have occurred in independent India have been generally such as to increase the power and prestige of the peasant castes, and usually at the expense of the higher castes such as Rājpūts and Brahmins.

It is possible to prepare a map of rural India showing the castes dominant in each village, but it would require a great investment of labour. In the absence of a systematic map, the names of some of the more prominent dominant castes may be mentioned here. Villagers in North India speak of the *Ajgar*, which literally means "python" and testifies to the fear which the dominant castes rouse in the oppressed minority castes. "*Ajgar*" is an acronym in Hindi standing for the Ahīr (cattle herder), Jāt (peasant), Gujar (peasant) and Rājpūt (warrior). The Sadgop is a dominant caste in parts of West Bengal; Pātidār and Rājpūt in Gujarat; Marātha in Maharāshtra; Kamma and Reddi in Andhra; Okkaliga and Lingāyat in Mysore; Vellāla, Goundar, Padaiyāchi and Kallar in Madras; and finally, Nāyar, Syrian Christian and Izhavan in Kerala.

Dominant castes set the model for the majority of people living in rural areas including, occasionally, Brahmins. Where their way of life has undergone a degree of Sanskritization—as it has, for instance, among the Pātidārs, Lingāyats and some Vellālas—the culture of the area over which their dominance extends experiences a change. The Pātidārs have become more Sanskritized in the last hundred years or so, and this has had effects on the culture of all other groups in Kaira district in Gujarat including the Bāriās. The Lingāyats and the Vellālas of South India also have a Sanskritized style of life, and from a much older period than the Pātidārs. The Lingāyats have been a potent source of cultural and social change in Mysore State, especially in the region to the north of the Tungabhadra river. They have been able to do this because of their use of the popular language of Kannada instead of Sanskrit for the spread of their ideas, and the existence of a network of wealthy and prestigious monasteries. The monasteries have converted—and are still converting—people from different castes to the Lingāyat sect.

The Marāthas and Reddis, and in more recent years the Padaiyāchis (who have changed their name to Vanniya Kula Kshatriyas), have laid claim to Kshatriya status. In pre-British times a claim to Kshatriya status was generally preceded by the possession of political power at the village if not higher levels, and a borrowing of the life-style of the Kshatriyas. This set off a chain reaction among the low castes, each of which imitated what it considered to be the Kshatriya style of life. Thus present-day Bāriās in Kaira district don the red turban and sword in imitation of Pātidārs of thirty years ago.[39] The Pātidārs themselves seem to have wanted to be classed as Kshatriyas until recently, when they changed their preference to Vaishya status.[40] A variety of castes in modern Gujarat seek to be recognized as Kshatriyas. According to Pocock, "almost every caste in Charōttār, including the Untouchable Dedh, has in its caste stories and legends a history of warrior and kingly origin; these claims can only become effective when supported by wealth suitably invested in Brahminic and secular prestige."[41]

Brahmins, like Kshatriyas, have exercised dominance in rural as well as urban India. In strength of numbers they have rarely been able to compete with the peasant castes, but they have enjoyed ritual pre-eminence, and that in a society in which religious beliefs were particularly strong. In pre-British and princely India, a popular mode of expiating sins and acquiring religious merit was to give gifts of land, house, gold and other goods to Brahmins. The gifts were given on such occasions as the birth of a prince, his marriage, coronation and death. In their roles as officials, scholars, temple priests (*pujāris*), family priests (*purohits*), and in some parts of the country, village record-keepers (*shānbhog, kulkarni, karnam*) also, they came to own land. Ownership of land further increased the great prestige Brahmins already commanded as members of the highest caste.

Centers of pilgrimage and monasteries were also sources of Sanskritization. Each pilgrimage center had its own hinterland, the most famous of them attracting pilgrims from all over India, while the smallest relied on a few neighbouring villages. Even when a pilgrim center had an all-India following, it probably attracted more pilgrims from one or a few areas than uniformly from every part of India. In the case of centers drawing from a small region, however, there were perhaps more pilgrims from particular castes or villages than from others. In spite of such limiting factors, a pilgrim center as well as a monastery managed to influence the way of life of everyone in its hinterland. When a section of a dominant caste came under the influence of a center or monastery, Sanskritization spread vertically to nondominant castes in the area and horizontally to members living elsewhere. Such spreading has been greatly facilitated in recent years by a variety of forces, technological, institutional and ideological.

Sanskritization has been a major process of cultural change in Indian history and it has occurred in every part of the Indian subcontinent. It may have been more active at some periods than at others, and some parts of India are more Sanskritized than others; but there is no doubt that the process has been universal.

4

As I stated earlier, there has been not one model of Sanskritization but three or four, and during the early period of Indian history there was some rivalry between the different models. The later Vedic texts, for instance, record instances of conflict between Brahmins and Kshatriyas:[42] The Brāhmana claim to supremacy was now and then contested by the Kshatriya, and we have declarations to the effect that the Kshatriya had no superior and that the priest was only a follower of the king."[43]

Jainism and Buddhism also show traces of conflict between Kshatriyas and Brahmins for supremacy. According to Ghurye:

> Whatever be the express statements about caste in the original preachings of Mahavira and Buddha, a close student of the early literature of these religious movements will feel convinced that the chief social aim of the writers was the assertion of the pre-eminence of the Kshatriyas. It is a well-known fact that no Jain Tirthankara was ever born in any but a Kshatriya family. In Buddhist literature there are several examples where the enumeration of the four castes is headed by the Kshatriya, the Brahmin coming next. Many a

> time the Kshatriyas aggressively put forward claims for prior recognition over the Brahmins.[44]

The new faiths also attracted large numbers of traders who, like the Kshatriyas, resented Brahminical dominance, and sought a way out of the disabilities imposed on them in the caste system.[45]

But, as seen earlier, in the *varna* model of the caste hierarchy there is no doubt as to the place of each *varna* and, furthermore, the hierarchy is immutable. The sacred literature of the Hindus, largely a creation of Brahmins throughout the ages, naturally lent support to the idea of Brahminical supremacy and the benefits that would flow to the king and country if the Brahmins were kept happy and prosperous. But how far such a picture corresponded to the existential situation at different periods of Indian history and in different parts of the Indian subcontinent is another question which can only be answered after we have detailed regional histories—assuming, of course, that materials are available for the writing of such histories. In the meanwhile it will be reasonable to postulate that the wielders of secular power, political or economic, were everywhere important and that the Brahmin was aware of their importance, and that they, in turn, had use for the Brahmin, as a means of legitimizing their mobility. In a word, there existed in Brahmins, along with a desire to establish their supremacy, a lively appreciation of the power wielded by the others. It should be stressed here that as recipients of gifts from rich Kshatriyas and Vaishyas, Brahmins were more likely to be appreciative of political and economic power than other groups. Moreover, not all Brahmins were priests or unworldly ascetics.[46] As Daniel Ingalls has observed, "There were in the first place those Brahmins who sought wealth. The pathway to wealth was education, a Sanskrit education, specifically the education of what is now called a *Sāstri*. It is hard for us few Sanskritists nowadays to realize what material pleasures could once be attained by our discipline."[47]

The early Brahminical way of life underwent important changes during the Vedic period. Beef-eating came to be tabooed: "The use of animal food was common, especially at the great feasts and family gatherings. The slaying of the cow was, however, gradually looked upon with disfavour as is apparent from the name *aghnyā* (not to be killed) applied to it in several passages."[48] The consumption of liquor, a feature of Vedic ritual as well as a part of Brahmin diet, also disappeared in post-Vedic India. Today liquor is not traditionally consumed by any Brahmin group, and only a few Brahmin groups are non-vegetarian.

This change in the mode of life of the Brahmins is important, as the Brahminical model followed by the other castes is that of the post-Vedic Brahmins. The Kshatriya and Vaishya models are indeed important but not as influential as the Brahminical, as a few Kshatriyas and almost all Vaishyas follow the Brahminical model regarding diet, ritual and certain important religious ideas. Only with the increasing impact of the Western model in the last several decades has the Brahminical model begun to lose ground among some sections of the Hindus.

Ingalls notes that toward the end of the Vedic period there appeared "traces of ascetic orders recruiting members from the Brahmin class. There is evidence that such orders had existed among the non-Brahmin indigenous population from a much earlier period. The Brahmin ascetics become more numerous as one passes into the Christian era."[49] It is more common, however, to attribute the change which came over the life of the post-Vedic Brahmins to the influence of Buddhism and Jainism.[50]

It would be fascinating to trace the gradual emergence over the centuries of a puritanical style of life as a dominant feature of Hinduism, and the association of that style of life with Brahmins and with certain sects such as the Jains, Lingāyats and others, but that is not my task here. I shall rest content with pointing out that the powerful Bhakti movement of medieval India, an all-India movement involving the low castes and the poor, deepened and extended the earlier puritanism by its insistence on love of God as the most important thing in religion, rather than ritualism or caste. The Bhakti saints "preached the fundamental equality of all religions and the unity of Godhead, held that the dignity of man depended on his actions and not on his birth, protested against excessive ritualism and formalities of religion and domination of the priests, and emphasized simple devotion and faith as the means of salvation for one and all."[51] Thanks to the Bhakti movement some individuals from low castes, including Harijans, became religious leaders.[52] The movement also ignored the distinction between the sexes, and there were women saints such as Āndāl, Akkamahādevi and Meera. It is indisputable that the net effect of the movement was to strike a blow for equality and prepare the higher castes for the more massive assault that came during British rule. Unfortunately, no history has yet been written of the Indian attacks on the concept of hierarchy.

The Bhakti cults are significant in yet another way. They employed regional languages instead of Sanskrit for purveying to a vast and unlettered populace the contents of Sanskritic Hinduism. V. Raghavan not only confirms the occurrence of this process but also points out how there was eventually a feedback into the Great Tradition from the literature in the regional languages:

> Where the local religious movement developed under Sanskrit inspiration but the linguistic vehicle of consolidation was the regional tongue, there was a second attempt at Sanskritization which produced Sanskrit back-formations.... Sanskrit devotional literature was also increased by reabsorbing into Sanskrit garb, material which was originally given to the people in their own local tongues. In Tamil Saivism, for instance, the story of the greatness of Madurai Hālāsya Māhātmya and the hagiology of the sixty-three Saiva saints were done into Sanskrit; and in Tamil Vaishnavism, Vedāntadeśika composed Sanskrit resumés of the Tamil psalms of the Vaishnava Ālvārs.[53]

The Brahminical and on the whole, puritanical, model of Sanskritization has enjoyed an over-all dominance, and even meat-eating and liquor-consuming Kshatriya and other groups have implicitly conceded the superiority of this model to the others. Thus among non-vegetarians, fish-eaters regard themselves as superior to the consumers of the flesh of sheep and goats, while the latter look down upon the consumers of fowl and pig who, in turn, regard beef-eaters with great contempt. Not all meat-eaters are traditionally consumers of liquor. It is again, except in some areas such as Rajasthan, a mark of the low castes.

In southern Mysore, for instance, the vessels in which meat is cooked are usually kept separate and are not used for cooking rice or vegetables. In villages meat is customarily cooked outside the main kitchen and on a separate stove. No meat may be cooked on any festival day as it is sacred for worshipping one or another deity, but only on the day following. Even at weddings, a non-vegetarian dinner is cooked only on the day following the completion of the wedding ritual.

In the Delhi-Punjab area meat-eating is often characteristic of the male members of the caste, women being restricted to a vegetarian diet. Again, even in castes where both sexes consume meat, individuals who are priests are often vegetarians. One of my neighbours in Rāmpura was a priest from the meat-eating shepherd (Kuruba) caste, and he cooked his own vegetarian food apart from the members of his family. This was also true of the headman of the Harijan caste in Rāmpura, who was a hereditary priest at a local temple belonging to his caste, and who was respected for his vegetarianism and teetotalism.

Even among Brahmins an orthodox person, as distinct from the Sanyasi who has renounced the world, may decide to practise extreme exclusiveness in personal life as part of his religion. Such exclusiveness cuts him off from social contact with his fellow beings, from his kindred outside the nuclear family and sometimes, even from his children. Among the Shri Vaishnava Brahmins, for instance, a man may decide, under the advice of the religious head of his sect, to eat food cooked only by his wife or himself. Such a man is expected to spend a good deal of his time in prayer, fasting, meditation, visiting temples and listening to the narration of religious stories (*harikatha*). He is recognized by his castefolk to be leading a pure life (*maḍi āchāra*) which endears him to God. These ideas have lost much of their force in recent years among educated and urban Indians, but they have not disappeared altogether. For instance, in the summer of 1964, I met in Mysore City an elderly Shri Vaishnava Brahmin clerk who told me proudly that he had taken *sharaṇāgati* (surrender) from the *guru* of his sect, and that he would not accept even coffee from his relatives. This evoked from one of those present the irreverent comment, "He will now ascend directly to heaven."

5

I have commented at some length on the ways in which the *varna* model of the caste system distorts our understanding of traditional Indian society. I have stressed the point that the traditional system did permit of a certain amount of mobility, and I shall pursue this further in this section.

There is, first of all, the process of Sanskritization itself. One of its functions was to bridge the gap between secular and ritual rank. When a caste or section of a caste achieved secular power it usually also tried to acquire the traditional symbols of high status, namely the customs, ritual, ideas, beliefs and life-style of the locally highest castes. It also meant obtaining the services of a Brahmin priest at various *rites de passage*, performing Sanskritic calendrical festivals, visiting famous pilgrimage centers and finally, attempting to obtain a better knowledge of the sacred literature.

Ambitious castes were aware of the legitimizing role of the Brahmin. Even a poor Brahmin priest living in a village dominated by peasants had to be treated differently from poor people of other castes. Burton Stein, a student of medieval India, pointed out that even the powerful rulers of the Vijayanagar kingdom (1336–1565) in South India had to acknowledge and pay a price for the legitimizing role of the Brahmin:

> These rulers identified and justified their own power in terms of the protection of Hindu institutions from Islam. The maintenance of proper caste duties and relationships (*varnāshrama dharma*) was frequently cited as an objective of state policy in Vijayanagar inscriptions. The new warriors, then, did come to terms with the Brahmin elite of South India. *On the basis of their continued support of Brahmin religious prerogatives and high ritual rank—though not support of the earlier almost complete socio-political autonomy of landed Brahmin communities—they won recognition from the Brahmins for their own ascendant military and political power.*[54] (Italics mine)

In the traditional setup, the desire to possess the symbols of high rank assumed that the aspiring caste was aware of a wider social horizon than the purely local one.[55] This, in turn, implied contact with centers of pilgrimage and urban capitals, or the presence locally of an influential body of Brahmins. When, for instance, the dominance of a caste extended only to a few neighbouring villages, there was frequently no opportunity for it to seek to legitimize its position by resort to Sanskritization. But when that power extended over a wider area, it was likely to come up against the might of the Great Tradition of Hinduism.

All over North India the bardic castes were traditionally a fruitful source of legitimization of the acquisition of political power. Thus Shah and Shroff observe:

> The Vahīvancā is important to the Rājpūt not only as genealogist but also as mythographer. Anyone who wants

> to call himself a Rājpūt should show that he is descended from an ancient Rājpūt dynasty, and it is only the Vahīvancā who is believed to be able to show this authoritatively. A Rājpūt's existence as a member of his caste depends upon the Vahīvancā. Moreover, some of the most vital social and political institutions of the Rājpūts are based on the belief that these have existed since time immemorial. The Vahīvancā's records are, to the Rājpūt, proof of the antiquity of the institutions.[56]

The Vahīvancā provided the means of legitimization not only for the Rājpūt but also for others, including the tribal Koḷīs. In Central Gujarat Rājpūts marry girls from the lineages of the Koḷī chiefs, and this has provided the latter with a rope to pull themselves up with. Building upon the fact of the hypergamous marriage of Koḷīs with Rājpūts, the Vahīvancās are able to provide a charter to Koḷī mobility.[57]

A caste group is generally endogamous, but occasionally endogamy is found to coexist with hypergamy. The caste considered to be lower has a one-sided relationship with the higher by which it gives its girls in marriage to the latter. This results in a scarcity of girls in the lower group, and of boys in the higher. Hypergamy occurs in several regions of India—Kerala, Gujarat, Bengal and parts of Uttar Pradesh. And it provides evidence of the upward mobility of castes. In Pocock's terminology hypergamy corresponds to the "inclusive" aspects of caste while endogamy corresponds to its "exclusive" aspect. A caste would like to include itself with those it considers superior, and the existence of hypergamy provides an institutional basis for such inclusion. Similarly the practice of caste endogamy is an implicit repudiation of the claims of lower castes to equality.

Hypergamy may occur among different sections of the same caste or *jāti* when such sections are more or less clearly distinguishable. This type of hypergamy occurs, for instance, among the Pātidārs of Kaira district in Central Gujarat and the Anāvil Brahmins of coastal, South Gujarat. But sometimes, as in the Koḷī-Rājpūt case, hypergamy may cross wide structural gulfs. In Bengal, hypergamy occurs among ranked Brahmin castes among whom the Kulins are the highest.

The giving of girls in marriage to boys from a higher caste or higher section of the same caste added to the prestige of the wife-giving lineage and caste. In some cases it also enabled the lower group to claim, eventually, equality with the higher group.

Hypergamy was significant for mobility in yet another way. A caste or section of a caste would Sanskritize its way of life and then claim to be superior to its structural neighbours or to the parent section. Amma Coorgs, a section of the main body of the Coorgs, came under strong Brahminical influence in the first half of the nineteenth century and became vegetarians and teetotalers and donned the sacred thread. In course of time they became a distinct endogamous group even though they numbered only 666 individuals at the 1941 census. It may be presumed that throughout the history of caste new caste groups arose as a result of such fission from the parent body.

6

It is necessary to stress that the mobility characteristic of caste in the traditional period resulted only in *positional* changes for particular castes or sections of castes and did not lead to a *structural* change. That is, while individual castes moved up or down, the structure remained the same. It was only in the literature of the medieval Bhakti (literally, devotion to a personal god) movement that the idea of inequality was challenged. A few sects even recruited followers from several castes in their early, evangelical phase, but gradually either the sect became an endogamous unit, or endogamy continued to be an attribute of each caste within the sect.

It is not my aim in this section to marshal systematically evidence to support the view that there was social mobility in every period of Indian history. I shall cite a few instances of mobility from ancient and medieval India while paying more attention to the period immediately prior to the establishment of British rule.

The institution of *varna* evolved gradually during the Vedic period (*circa* 1500–500 B.C.), the earliest period for which any literary evidence is available. The Purusha Sūkta, one of the later hymns of the earliest of the four Vedas, Rig Veda, gives a mythical account of the origin of the four *varnas*, Brāhmana, Rājanya (that is, Kshatriya), Vaishya and Shūdra, and this is the first mention of the *varna* hierarchy as we know it today. The Brahmin's position began to strengthen during the latter part of the Vedic period, and this was linked up with the increasing importance and elaboration of the institution of sacrifice. By the end of the Vedic period the Brahmin's position had become impregnable, and his rival from an earlier period, the Kshatriya, had been pushed to a secondary place. Ghurye has stated that Jainism and Buddhism were both started by "Kshatriyas of exceptional ability preaching a new philosophy which was utilized by their immediate followers for asserting the social superiority of the Kshatriyas over the Brahmins. The Brahmin has a fresh cause for grudge. He comes forward as the saviour of the Vedic Brahminic culture."[58]

The Vaishya occupied a low place in the hierarchy during the Rig Vedic period and indeed, this *varna* figures singularly little in Vedic literature. The term Vaishya, in its earliest usage, referred to ordinary people, and Basham thinks that the caste "originated in the ordinary peasant tribesman of the Rig Veda."[59] The conversion of Vaishyas to Buddhism and Jainism probably resulted in an improvement in their position.

> Though the Brāhmaṇa literature gives Vaiśya few rights and humble status, the Buddhist and Jaina scriptures, a few centuries later in date and of more easterly provenance, show that he was not always oppressed in practice. They mention many wealthy merchants living in great luxury and powerfully organized in guilds. Here the ideal Vaiśya is not the humble tax-paying cattle-breeder but the *asītikoṭivibhava*, the man possessing eight million *paṇas*. Wealthy Vaiśyas were respected by kings and enjoyed their favour and confidence.[60]

Apart from the rise and fall of particular *varnas* over the centuries, the system seems to have enjoyed a degree of "openness." This is pointedly seen in the case of Kshatriyas who seem to have been recruited in ancient times from several ethnic groups including Greeks (*Yavana*), Scythians (*Shaka*) and Parthians (*Pahlava*).[61] Panikkar has been quoted earlier as saying that in historical times there was no such caste as the Kshatriyas, and ever since the fifth century B.C. ruling families have come from a wide variety of castes.

Burton Stein considers the medieval period to be characterized by "widespread and persistent examples of social mobility." He emphasizes the contrast between theory and practice:

> When the rank of persons was in theory rigorously ascribed

> according to the purity of the birth-group, the political units of India were probably ruled most often by men of very low birth. This generalization applies to South Indian warriors and may be equally applicable for many clans of "Rajputs" in northern India. *The capacity of both ancient and medieval Indian society to ascribe to its actual rulers, frequently men of low social origins, a "clean" or "Kshatriya" rank may afford one of the explanations for the durability and longevity of the unique civilization of India.*[62] (Italics mine)

A potent source of social mobility in pre-British India was the fluidity of the political system. Such fluidity was not limited to any particular part of India, but characterized the system everywhere. It constituted an important, though not the only, avenue to social mobility. In order to capture political power, however, a caste or its local section had to have a martial tradition, numerical strength, and preferably also ownership of a large quantity of arable land. Once it had captured political power it had to Sanskritize its ritual and style of life and lay claim to being Kshatriya. It had to patronize (or even create) Brahmins who would minister to it on ritual occasions, and produce an appropriate myth supporting the group's claim to Kshatriya status. The establishment of *Pax Britannica* resulted in freezing the political system and blocked this avenue to mobility. That eventually British rule opened other avenues to mobility does not concern us here.

We are able to have a clearer understanding than before of the process of social mobility through the achievement of political power, thanks to the excellent studies of pre-British India by Bernard Cohn and Arvind Shah. Cohn has studied the Banaras region in Eastern Uttar Pradesh, and Shah, the Central Gujarat region.

Cohn distinguishes four levels of the political system in eighteenth century India—imperial, secondary, regional and local. The Mughals occupied the "imperial" level, and incidental to their efforts at ruling the entire subcontinent they had to have a loyal army and a bureaucracy. They succeeded so completely in monopolizing the symbols of legitimacy that in the eighteenth century even those groups "which were trying to free themselves of actual imperial control nonetheless turned to the remnants of the imperial authority for legitimizing their power ..."[63] The "secondary" level consisted of successor states such as Oudh which emerged after dissolution of Mughal power, and which exercised suzerainty over a major historical, cultural or linguistic region. Each "secondary" system was made up of several "regional" systems, and at the head of the latter was an individual or family which had the status of hereditary official or ruler, a status conferred on it by the imperial or the secondary authority. "The leaders [of regional systems] were loosely incorporated through rituals of allegiance and financial obligation to the national power and were in competition with potential regional leaders."[64] At the bottom of the power structure was the "local" system represented by lineages, an indigenous chief, a tax official turned political leader or a successful adventurer. The heads of the local system were subordinate to the regional leader although they often derived their positions from the secondary authority. These heads controlled the local peasants, artisans and traders, and offered them protection from outside interference. They collected from their subjects money or a share of the crop in return for their services.[65]

In the Banaras region the Nawāb of Oudh was nominally the political overlord and he derived his authority from the Mughal Emperor in Delhi. The Nawāb ruled this area through his officials from 1720 to 1740, and through his partially independent subordinate, the Raja of Banaras, from 1740 to 1775.

> The Raja of Banaras in turn had to control, extract revenue or tribute from, and on occasion get military help from a large number of localized lineages, petty chiefs, and *jāgīrdārs* (holders of revènue-free lands from the Nawab of Oudh or the Emperor of Delhi). Feuds within lineages, warfare between lineages, or warfare between lineages and the Raja of Banaras were frequent. Disputes often were settled by the direct use of force.[66]

At the base of the social and political pyramid were the lower castes who actually cultivated the land as tenants, sharecroppers, serfs and slaves. Above them were the members of the dominant castes, either Rājpūt or Bhumihār Brahmin, organized into corporate lineages controlling the land. The founders of the lineages were either conquerors or recipients of royal or other grants. By the end of the eighteenth century the lineages were large, corporate bodies often including over a thousand families related to each other by agnatic links. The corporate lineages realized from the actual tillers of land a share of the produce, a part of which they were forced to surrender to "superordinate political powers."

> By the end of the eighteenth century still another interest had insinuated itself into the situation. These were men who agreed with the superordinate political power, the Raja of Banaras, to pay a fixed amount of tax each year to the Raja's treasury. They in turn extracted what they could, on the basis of tradition and what force they had at their disposal, from the lineages or in a few instances from local chiefs and in even fewer instances directly from the cultivators.[67]

Cohn traces the rise of Mansa Rām, a member of the landholding, dominant Bhumihār caste in a village in Jaunpur district, who worked for a local *āmil* or tax collector, and eventually replaced the latter. His ability and lack of scruples enabled him to obtain from Safdar Jang, who succeeded his uncle to the Nawābship of Oudh, a royal grant making Mansa Rām's son, Balwant Singh, the Raja of Banaras and the Zamindār of the three districts of Banaras, Jaunpur and Mirzapur.[68]

The Raja of Banaras had to pay tribute to the Nawāb of Oudh, and also provide him with troops when necessary. The Raja had a dual role. He did not have the necessary administrative machinery to collect revenue directly from the people, by passing the local chiefs and lineages. He was also dependent upon the latter for his troops without which he could not be independent from the Nawāb of Oudh. In fact, he made a continuous effort to be completely independent from the control of the Nawāb. He also needed to keep in check lineages and local chiefs who wielded power within his province. The more powerful of the chiefs posed a threat to his existence.[69]

Cohn characterizes the political system of eighteenth century Banaras region as one of "balanced oppositions, each element in competition with the other, each dependent on the other, cultivator, corporate lineage, tax farmer and Raja."[70] The conflicts between lineages and between them and the local Raja or *jāgīrdār*, between the latter and the Raja of Banaras, enabled leaders of dominant groups to acquire political power, and through it a higher position in the hierarchy.[71] In other words, the political system favoured social mobility.

Arvind Shah's description of the political system of eighteenth century Gujarat—or more correctly, central Gujarat—also emphasizes its fluidity.[72] The central plains, the most fertile part of Gujarat, are inhabited by caste Hindus such as Brahmins, Banias, Rājpūts, Pātidārs and Koḷīs. The Pātidārs, originally called Kunbis, are the traditional peasant caste while the Koḷīs are the largest single ethnic group, forming more than a quarter of the Hindu population in Gujarat.

Between the eleventh and thirteenth centuries the Solanki kings in Pāṭaṇ were the overlords of Gujarat, Saurashtra and Kutch. Under them were the Rājpūt princes and chiefs ruling over smaller areas. The rigid rule of clan exogamy among Rājpūts resulted in the forging of affinal ties between princes ruling in different areas. The rule of primogeniture was followed in the matter of succession to office, the younger sons being granted land in different parts of the princedom.

Rājpūt princes also ruled over the tribal areas of Gujarat, Rajasthan and Madhya Pradesh; this meant the imposition of the Rājpūt political system over the tribal, with the tribal chiefs acting as links between the two.

With the establishment of Muslim hegemony in Gujarat toward the end of the thirteenth century, a movement to displace the Rājpūt princes and chiefs in the central plains and bring the area under the effective control of the Sultan of Delhi began. During the entire period of Muslim rule the Koḷīs were referred to as marauders and dacoits, and they joined the irregular armies of political adventurers who were a perennial source of trouble to the rulers.

Like Cohn, Shah also discerns several levels in the political system of eighteenth century Gujarat. There was the imperial level, occupied by the Mughals until the beginning of the eighteenth century and by the Peshwas of Poona after 1768. Below the imperial was the "regional" or "provincial" level; here too the Marātha rulers, the Gāikwāds of Baroda, replaced Mughal governors by about 1730. At a still lower level was the territory ruled by tribute-paying princes—Rājpūt, Muslim, Koḷī or Pātidār—as well as the territory administered by the regional authority through either officials called *Kamāvisdārs*, or grantee of land called *jāgīrdārs*. At the bottom of the administrative system was the village, and it was by no means a passive unit. There was a "continuum of power relations between the various levels."

The period between the death of the Mughal emperor Aurangazeb (1707) and the establishment of Peshwa authority over Gujarat (1768) was one of strife and confusion. There were three main contenders for power: high Muslim officials and nobles who wanted to found independent principalities; several conflicting cliques among the Marāthas; and finally, Rājpūt chiefs in highland Gujarat, Saurashtra and Kutch. There was a shifting pattern of alliances among the different contenders. A few Muslim officials and nobles in plains Gujarat succeeded in establishing petty kingdoms such as Cambay, Balasinor, Palanpur and Radhanpur. They maintained their position by playing one Marātha clique against the others, and paying tribute to whoever troubled them the most. The Rājpūt princes also did the same. A few Koḷī leaders took advantage of the prevalent confusion and established small kingdoms. The bulk of plains Gujarat, however, came directly under the authority of the Marāthas.[73]

A *pargana*, including between forty and seventy villages, was the basic administrative entity; it was usually under a *Kamāvisdār* except for two *parganas*, which were under the control of *jāgīrdārs* who were members of the Gāikwād's family. The *jāgīrdār's* twin obligations to the Gāikwād were to pay him an annual tribute and to provide him with troops when called upon to do so. With his position in the local system, and with troops at his disposal, he was always a potential source of trouble to the Gāikwād. This was why a *jāgīr* was liable to be withdrawn or one *jāgīr* substituted for another.

A *Kamāvisdār* was an official appointed by the Gāikwād for a specific period of time; he was in charge of one, and occasionally more than one, *pargana*. He had a body of troops to help him in his administrative tasks, which included maintenance of law and order, collection of taxes, and seeing that the Muslim, Rājpūt and Koḷī princes in his neighbourhood did not make trouble. The Gāikwāds did not supervise administration at the local level as they had neither the leisure nor the inclination to do so.[74]

Every *pargana* had one or more hereditary headmen called *Desais*. When there was more than one *Desai*, the villages included in the *pargana* were distributed among them. The *Desais* were local men from one of the high castes, Brahmin, Bania or Pātidār. Each *Desai* had his own accountants (*majumdārs*), clerks (*mehtas*) and servants (*rāvaṇiyās*).

There were three types of villages—the law-abiding (*rāsti*), the unruly (*mewāsi*), and the mixed (*rāsti-mewāsi*). Either Rājputs or

Koḷīs predominated in the *mewāsi* villages. The Rājpūts in the *mewāsi* villages were descendants of those princelings who had lost much of their land to Muslim rulers, and who were now left with a village or two each. They could not forget that they were Kshatriyas and continually tried to assert their independence. The Koḷīs also claimed to be Rājpūts by virtue of their marriage alliances with Rājpūt lineages. The *rāsti-mewāsi* villages alternated between quite and turbulent periods.

The *mewāsi* villages were generally situated near the deep ravines of rivers or in the jungles bordering the plains. Some of them had forts built around them. During the heyday of Mughal rule a network of village police stations kept order in the *mewāsi* villages, but with the decline of Mughal power, they began making trouble. They paid tax only when threatened with force, and every year the *Kamāvisdār* or *Desai* had to go to them accompanied by his troops. They also exacted payments from *rāsti* villages and from highway travellers. Many *rāsti* villages bought peace from them by permanent grants of land or annual cash payments.

The eighteenth century also saw the rise of the famous peasant caste of Gujarat, the Pātidārs. In central Gujarat there were many *rāsti* villages dominated by landowning Kunbi lineages. The latter were jointly responsible for the payment of tax which was assessed in a lump sum. Each lineage paid its share of tax to the village headman. Those Kunbis who paid tax were called by the prestigious term of Pātidār. In course of time, however, Pātidār became a caste name and Kunbi disappeared from use.

The Pātidārs grew cash crops such as indigo, cotton and tobacco for export. They had become a wealthy caste by the end of the Mughal rule, and their wealth enabled them to dominate over the others in the villages. The declining importance of Rājpūts under the Mughals also favoured the Pātidārs. The political importance of the Pātidārs seems to have been acknowledged by both the Mughals and Marāthas. "Folklore refers to the friendship between Pātidārs had taken to arms, and a couple of them had established petty principalities. All this had led the Pātidārs to claim the status of Kshatriya *varna*, and to adopt many 'kingly' customs and manners."[75]

The situation in the Banaras and Gujarat regions in the eighteenth century may be summed up by saying that the political system favoured mobility for the leaders of the dominant local groups such as the Bhumihār Brahmins, Rājpūts, Pātidars and

Koḷīs. It also favoured a few officials (for example, Mansa Rām in Banaras and Muslim officials in Gujarat) who drew on their official authority to establish principalities. (I suspect, however, that at some point their individual mobility became linked up with that of their castes.) The fact that the Mughal power was on the wane in the eighteenth century made the period particularly favourable to mobility, but the difference between it and earlier periods was only one of degree. Considering that pre-British India was characterized by primitive technology and poor communications, peripheral areas of large kingdoms were always likely to have considerable autonomy from the central power.

I shall now briefly consider my third and last example, Kerala in Southwest India, several hundred miles away from both Gujarat and Uttar Pradesh. Kerala has been studied in recent years by two British anthropologists, Kathleen Gough and Eric Miller, and I shall be mainly relying on their writings in my discussion of the region. Of Central Kerala (an area comprising the former kingdoms of Calicut, Walluvanād, Pālghāt and Cochin) Gough writes:

> The traditional period was one of perpetual wars between adjacent kingdoms, interrupted only in the rainy seasons. A royal lineage's strength lay in its monopoly of gunpowder, coinage and customs dues, its ability to use foreign and Muslim ships for naval warfare and its control of the royal domains both as a source of produce and of Nayar retainers as soldiers. Through its superior wealth and military power a royal lineage could force feudatory princes and vassal nobles to muster soldiers throughout the kingdom in periods of large-scale war. Each district and each village was classified according to the number of Nayar soldiers it could customarily muster for war.[76]

In North Kerala (comprising the southern part of South Canara, and the northern part of Malabar districts), ever since the sixteenth century, local rulers sought the aid of rival foreign powers, European and Arab, in their mutual struggles for supremacy. Gough comments that in the struggles of the seventeenth and eighteenth centuries some new Nāyar chiefs "arose with mushroom rapidity on the basis of European support and gained partially autonomous sway over small groups of villages. Political and social mobility among Nāyar aristocrats was more marked in North Kerala than in the more stable central kingdoms. Indeed, a North Kerala proverb remarks that 'When a high caste Nayar becomes ripe, he turns into a king'."[77]

In his paper, "Caste and Territory in Malabar,"[78] Miller has discussed the relationship between caste and territory in northern, and parts of central, Kerala in the context of the pre-British political system. The *dēsam* or village has always been a fundamental unit of Malayāli society, though its importance was even greater in the pre-British period than subsequently. The traditional *dēsam* was largely self-sufficient, and caste ranking bore a relationship to differential rights in land. Pre-British Malabar society was martially oriented, each unit in the system being defined by the number of troops it could muster. Villages were grouped into *nāds* or chiefdoms, and the chieftain of the *nād* led his troops in war. The chiefdom was not only a political unit but also a social, cultural and even religious unit.

Warfare was endemic between rival chieftains.

> Although the boundaries of the chiefdoms were relatively stable, the history of Malabar is the rise and fall of individual chieftain families. Neighbouring chieftains were defeated and became feudatories or allies. During the last 500 years of the traditional period, three chieftain families who secured wider realms in this manner were the Rajas of Walluvanad (in the center of South Malabar), the Maharajas of Cochin, and above all the Zamorins of Calicut.... There were thus several centers of power. *Nāds* closest to these centers were absorbed into the kingdoms and ruled directly. Those further away were feudatory. Peripheral chiefdoms, as allies, were largely autonomous and transferred their support from one king to another.[79]

The pre-British political system of Kerala was then very fluid, and as Gough emphasizes, it was more fluid in the north than in the central, and probably southern, regions. Political fluidity resulted in social mobility, especially for the dominant castes. Some Nāyars "ripened" into Sāmanthans and Kshatriyas. The royal matrilineages of Calicut, Walluvənād, Pālghāt and Cochin, for instance, although of Nāyar origin, considered themselves superior in ritual rank to their Nāyar subjects.

> Between kingdoms, royal lineages disputed for rank and would not intermarry. Although exogamous, therefore, each

> royal lineage considered itself a separate caste. The Cochin lineage claimed descent from the Perumals and ranked as Kshatriyas.... The Walluvanad, Palghat and Calicut lineages, once vassals of the Perumals, were not strictly recognized as Kshatriyas in Brahmin theory and held the title of Samanthans.[80]

Disputing for rank was not confined to the royal lineages but extended to the lower chiefly lineages as well, each of which "tended to regard itself as a separate caste acknowledging no peers."[81]

It is not necessary to labour further the point that the political system of pre-British India favoured mobility for some strategically situated individuals and groups. I shall now turn briefly to a secondary source of mobility in that system—the king or other acknowledged political head of an area. The latter had the power to promote or demote castes inhabiting his kingdom. The Maharaja of Cochin, for instance, had the power to raise the rank of castes in his kingdom, and the final expulsion of anyone from caste required his sanction.[82] He is, in fact, reputed to have raised some "Charmas" [Cherumans?] to the status of Nāyars for helping him and his allies, the Portuguese, against his traditional enemy, the Zamorin of Calicut.[83] The power to raise the rank of castes living within their jurisdiction seems to have been enjoyed in South India by even some big *Zamindārs*. During the British period, when their accounts were examined for the purposes of revenue assessment, they were found to include receipts on account of the privilege conferred by them on certain persons to wear the sacred thread.[84]

The power to promote or demote castes stemmed from the fact that the pre-British Indian king, Hindu or Muslim, stood at the apex of the caste system. In the last analysis, the ranking of castes within the kingdom had the king's consent, and an individual who had been outcasted by his caste council for an offense had always the right of appeal to the king. The latter had the power to re-examine the evidence and confirm or alter the verdict. H. J. Maynard, a British official who served in the old Punjab area at the turn of the century, had the good fortune to witness the Rājpūt chief of a large region actually exercising his authority in caste matters. According to Maynard, "It appears that, even under the Mughal emperors, the Delhi Court was the head of all the Caste

Panchayats, and that questions affecting a caste over a wide area could not be settled except at Delhi, and under the guidance of the ruler for the time being."[85]

In settling disputes with regard to rank and in deciding the appropriate punishment for an offense, learned Brahmins were consulted by the king. But they only declared or expounded the law; it was the king who enforced their decision.

7

So far I have considered only mobility arising from the political system and ignored mobility resulting from the pre-British productive system. In this connection it is necessary to emphasize that pre-British India did not suffer from over population; Kingsley Davis, for instance, has argued that India's population was stationary between 1600 and 1800, and that it numbered about 125 million in 1800.[86] In many parts of the country there existed land which, with some effort, could be rendered arable. This in turn meant that tenants and agricultural labourers enjoyed an advantage in their relations with their landowning masters. If the master was unusually oppressive and cruel, the tenants could move to another area and start new farms or work for another master. The fear of labourers and other dependents running away was a real one, and it served to restrain masters somewhat.[87] It is relevant to point out here that all agriculture, especially agriculture involving irrigation, requires large and concentrated inputs of labour at certain points in the agricultural cycle such as sowing, transplanting, weeding, harvesting and threshing. The greater the quantity of land owned by a family, the greater the input of labour required; and the labour resources available within the family will not be enough to meet the demand even during normal times—and this on the highly unlikely assumption that all members of the family work on the land. It is a mark of low status to do physical work on land, and the bigger the landowner the greater is the force of this prohibition. Besides, the existence of a certain amount of congruence between caste rank and the agricultural hierarchy would mean that generally landowners belonged to high castes while tenants, and more especially, landless labourers, belonged to low castes. Considerations of prestige as well as caste would, therefore, prevent landowners from actually working on their land, thus greatly increasing the demand for labour. In my field village of Rāmpura, in many ways favourably with regard to the availability of agricultural labour, even the wealthiest and most prestigious families had difficulty assuring themselves of necessary labour, and had to use all their power, contacts and ingenuity to see that their farming did not suffer.[88]

If during 1948-1952, in a relatively favoured area such as Rāmpura, wealthy landowners were experiencing difficulties in finding enough labour, the situation must have much worse in pre-British India when there was a scarcity of labour. It is well known that the number of agricultural labourers has been rapidly increasing since the beginning of this century. Thus while 12 per cent of the agricultural population were landless labourers in 1900, in 1956 they comprised 24 per cent of the total rural households.[89]

Burton Stein has argued cogently that the availability of "marginally settled lands suitable for cultivation which permitted the establishment of new settlements and even new regional societies" imposed limitations

> on the amount of tribute in the form of agricultural surplus, which local warriors could extract from peasant villages under their control, as well as on other forms of arbitrariness. ... Different branches of the Vellāla community of Tamil-speaking South India, a respected and powerful cultivating caste, seem to have developed in this manner. This "looseness" in the agrarian order of medieval South India has been noted by historians, but there has been no systematic study of it. If a developing social system, characterized by such "openness" is seen as typical in many parts of South India during the medieval period, then the model of the contemporary competition of ethnic units for enhanced rank within a narrow, localized ranking system appears inappropriate for understanding the process of mobility in an earlier period. Much of the evidence we have on the nature of the medieval social order indicates that there was considerable opportunity for individual mobility in an earlier period.[90]

According to Stein, then, social mobility in medieval India was closely bound up with spatial mobility; and the availability of potentially arable land along with other factors such as floods, droughts, epidemics and excessive tribute demands stimulated migration. There were also obstacles to movement, but they were not insuperable. His mention of the existence of subdivisions among the agrarian Veḷḷālas is peculiarly apt, and subdivisions have similarly proliferated among other peasant castes such as Nāyar, Kamma, Reddi, Okkaliga and Marātha. A section which moved out became a separate endogamous *jāti* after the lapse of several years, and true to caste tradition, each such *jāti* claimed to be superior to the others. One division may change its occupation ever so slightly, or adopt a new custom, or become more or less Sanskritized in its style of life than the others. The forces released during British rule, and subsequently, have led to these *jātis* coming together to form large castes. The process is still active, and different sections of a *jāti* are differently affected by it. I have called this an increase in "horizontal solidarity," but the *jātis* subsumed in the emergent entity are not, strictly speaking, equal.

Stein's other point—that "the model of the contemporary competition of ethnic units for enhanced rank within a narrow, local ranking system is inappropriate" for understanding social mobility in pre-British India—is also important in that it helps to account for cultural variations between sections of the same caste living in different areas. A family or group of families would have greater freedom to adopt the Sanskritic style of life in a new area where they were unknown than in their natal area where the locally dominant caste knew them. In other words, migration made "passing" possible, and the mobile group was able to assume new and prestigious cultural robes. But even within a narrow region the dominant caste of political chief did not have unlimited power, and this allowed low castes a certain amount of elbowroom. This is not to deny, however, that mobility within a localized ranking system, such as that described by Pocock, is the result of British rule.

Stein thinks that opportunities for "individual family mobility were great" in medieval India; also there was little need then for corporate mobility. Facilities such as the printing press which modern "corporate mobility" movements appear to require, as well as the political need for them, came into existence only recently.[91] I presume that Stein is using "corporate" in the sense of "collective," and if I am right in so thinking, it is certainly true that collective movements are characteristic of modern times while "individual family movements" were characteristic of the medieval period. *But the latter have to be translated at some point into collective movements, and this necessity is forced on them by caste.* Where will the mobile family find brides for sons and grooms for daughters? Even in South India where the marriage of cross cousins and cross uncle and niece are preferred, a few families would be essential for the recruitment of spouses. Hypergamy also would enable a small group to be mobile, but that group must be much larger than an individual family.

NOTES

1. See my *Religion and Society Among the Coorgs of Southern India*, Oxford, 1952; and "A Note on Sanskritization and Westernization," in *Far Eastern Quarterly*, vol. 15, no. 4, August 1956, pp. 481–496. The latter essay has been included in my book, *Caste in Modern India*, Bombay, 1962, pp. 42–62.
2. See section I of the Reading List for papers and books in which the concepts of Sanskritization and/or Westernization are discussed.
3. See my essay "Varna and Caste" in *Caste in Modern India*, pp. 63–69; and also D.G. Mandelbaum's "Social Perception and Scriptural Theory in Indian Caste", in S. Diamond (ed.), *Culture in History, Essays in Honour of Paul Radin*, New York, 1960, pp. 437–448.
4. G.S. Ghurye, *Caste and Class in India*, Bombay, 1950, p. 57.
5. Marc Galanter has recently stated that "the British period may be seen as one in which the legal system rationalized the intricacies of local customary caste relationships in terms of classical Hindu legal concepts like *varna* and pollution. To borrow and slightly distort Srinivas' terms, we can think of the British period as a period of 'Sanskritization' in legal notions of caste. In independent India, as *varna* and pollution gave way to the notion of groups characterized by economic, educational, political and religious characteristics, we may think of this not as the abolition of caste, but as the 'Westernization' of notions of caste." ("Law and Caste in Modern India", in *Asian Survey*, vol. III, no. 11, November, 1963, p. 558.) In this connection, see also William McCormack's paper, "Lingayats as a Sect" (*Journal of the Royal Anthropological Institute*, vol. 93, Part I, January–June, 1963, pp. 57–59), in which he discusses the effects of the application of British law and Westernization generally on Lingayatism in the twentieth century.
6. D.F. Pocock, "The Movement of Castes", *Man*, May, 1955, pp. 71–72.
7. M. Singer, "The Social Organization of Indian Civilization", *Diogenes*, vol. 45, Winter, 1964, pp. 84–119.

8. *Ibid.*, p. 101.
9. According to Sir Athelstane Baines the Brahmins are "perhaps the most heterogeneous collection of minute and independent subdivisions that ever bore a common designation." (*Ethnography*, Strassburg, 1912, p. 26.)
10. *Ibid.*, pp. 26–29.
11. See P. Tandon, *Punjabi Century*, London, 1961, pp. 76–77; M. Darling, *Wisdom and Waste in a Punjab Village*, London, 1934, p. 264; T.O. Beidelman, *A Comparative Analysis of the Jajmani System*, New York, 1959, p. 19; and Baines, *op. cit.*, p. 28.
12. "In every linguistic group, moreover, there are certain classes which though called Brahmans by the public, and enlisted to perform some of the ceremonial functions of the Brahman, are either not recognized by other Brahmans, or are relegated by them to a degraded position, inferior, in reality, to that to which many of the non-Brahman castes are admitted." (Baines, *op. cit.*, p. 26.)
13. K.M. Panikkar, *Hindu Society at Crossroads*, Bombay, 1955, p. 8.
14. *Ibid.*, p. 9.
15. For an analysis of the kind of roles played by a dominant caste in rural society and culture see my essay, "The Dominant Caste in Rāmpura", *American Anthropologist*, vol. 61, February, 1959, pp. 1–16.
16. In my field village Rāmpura, for instance, Brahmin dominance had given way to Okkaliga (peasant caste) dominance. This seems to be part of a peninsula-wide phenomenon.
17. See Bernard S. Cohn, "Political Systems in Eighteenth Century India: the Benares Region", *Journal of the American Oriental Society*, vol. 82, no. 3, July–September, 1962, p. 314; and A.M. Shah, "Political System in Eighteenth Century Gujarat", *Enquiry*, vol. 1, no. 1, Spring, 1964, pp. 83–95.
18. "According to a study conducted by the National Sample Survey in 1953-54, '... of the 66 million rural households in the country, nearly 15 million or 22 per cent, do not own any land at all, another 25 per cent hold less than one acre each, while at the other end, 13 per cent of the total households exercise permanent ownership rights over 65 per cent of the total area.'" Quoted by R. Benedix in *Nation-Building and Citizenship*, New York, 1964, p. 254.
19. See McKim Marriott (ed.), *Village India*, Chicago, 1955, pp. 26–31, 56, 121, 154, 165 and 225.
20. V.K.R.V. Rao. "Employment of Scheduled Castes and Scheduled Tribes", *Tribal Research Institute Bulletin*, Udaipur, vol. 1, no. 1, October, 1964, p. 10.
21. This was also true, until recently, of urban Indians. Recent land reform legislation has made land unattractive as a form of investment for absentee landowners, and for very big resident owners.

22. M. Darling, *op. cit.*, p. 264, and T.O. Beidelman *op. cit.*, p. 19.
23. Beidelman, *op. cit.*, pp. 18–19.
24. D.F. Pocock "Inclusion and Exclusion: A Process in the Caste System of Gujarat", *Southwestern Journal of Anthropology*, vol. 13, no. 1, Spring, 1957, pp. 24–25.
25. M.N. Srinivas, see *supra* note 15, pp. 3–4.
26. Pocock, *op. cit.*, p. 26.
27. W.L. Rowe, "The New Chauhans: A Caste Mobility Movement in North India", in J. Silverberg (ed.), *Social Mobility in Caste in India*, special issue of *Comparative Studies in Society and History* (to be published).
28. *Census of India Report for 1921*, pp. 231–232.
29. J.H. Hutton, *Caste in India*, Oxford, 1961, pp. 205–206.
30. See in this connection L.S.S. O'Malley, *Bengal Census Report*, 1911, p. 441.
31. D.R. Chanana, "Sanskritization, Westernization and India's North-West", *Economic Weekly*, vol. XIII, no. 9, March 4, 1961, pp. 409–414.
32. *Ibid.*, p. 409.
33. *Ibid.*
34. *Ibid.*, p. 410.
35. Information kindly given by Dr. K. Raman Unni, Reader in Sociology in the School of Planning and Architecture, New Delhi.
36. *Travancore Census Report*, vol. I, 1901, p. 269.
37. S.L. Kalia, "Sanskritization and Tribalization", *Bulletin of the Tribal Research Institute*, Chindwara (M.P.), vol. 2, no. 4, April 1959, pp. 33–43.
38. M. Marriott, "Little Communities in an Indigenous Civilization", in *Village India*, p. 211.
39. Pocock, see *supra* note 24, p. 26.
40. A.M. Shah and R. G. Shroff, "The Vahivancā Bārots of Gujarat. A Caste of Genealogists and Mythographers", in Milton Singer (ed.), *Traditional India: Structure and Change*, American Folklore Society, Philadelphia, 1959, pp. 62–63.
41. Pocock, see *supra* note 24, p. 24.
42. R.C. Majumdar, H.C. Raychaudhari and K. Datta, *An Advanced History of India*, London, 1963, p. 44.
43. *Ibid.*, p. 46.
44. Ghurye, see *supra* note 4, p. 71.
45. D.D. Kosambi, *An Introduction to the Study of Indian History*, Bombay, 1956, pp. 156–162.
46. Ghurye, *op. cit.*, pp. 16–17, 84–85, 103 and 109.
47. D. Ingalls, "The Brahman Tradition", in M. Singer (ed.), *Traditional India: Structure and Change*, p. 7.

48. R.C. Majumdar *et al., op. cit.,* pp. 31–32. Professor Hutton writes, "The first prohibition of cow-killing seems to be found in the comparatively late Atharvaveda and to be applied specially, if not exclusively, to Brahmans, while elsewhere we learn that the cow, although a fit offering for Mitra and Varuna, should not be sacrificed because such sacrifice is opposed to public feeling. ..." (*Caste in India,* Oxford, 1963, p. 228).
49. Ingalls, *op. cit.,* p. 7.
50. Majumdar *et al., op. cit.,* p. 8.
51. *Ibid.,* pp. 403–404.
52. V. Raghavan has stated recently, "As extensive as the regional spread of the devotional movement, was the spread of the social standing of its leaders. If Meera was a princess of Rajasthan and Manikkavācaka was a minister of the Tamil court of Madurai, Nāmadeva was a tailor, Tukārām was a shopkeeper, Akho of Gujarat was a goldsmith, and Sādhana, a butcher. Dadoo was a cotton-ginner, and Sena, a barber. Deriving the brotherhood of man from the fatherhood of God, these saint-singers could recognize no differences in social status. Rāidās, a cobbler, and Kabīr, a Muslim weaver, were accepted by the great Brahmin teacher and philosopher, Ramānand. Throughout the centuries the devotional movement has been a great solvent for the exclusive and separatist feelings stemming from the consciousness of social status." (From the summary of Professor Raghavan's Patel Lectures, "Vision of the World Family—Message of Saint Singers of India" in *Indian and Foreign Review,* January 1, 1965, pp. 14–15).
53. V. Raghavan, "Variety and Integration in the Pattern of Indian Culture", *Far Eastern Quarterly,* vol. XV, no. 4, August, 1956, pp. 500–501. See also his "Methods of Popular Religious Instruction in South India", in M. Singer (ed.), *Traditional India: Structure and Change,* p. 136. It is only fair to add, however, that another Sanskrit scholar, J.F. Staal, is very critical of identifying material in regional languages as "Sanskritic": "Both the Hindi and the Tamil Ramayana are based upon the Sanskrit Ramayana, but both contain numerous new elements. Do these belong to Sanskrit culture? What about further transformations of the Ramayana, e.g., in Kathakali? The Alvars composed Tamil hymns which are in many respects similar to Sanskrit devotional literature, but are they based upon it? The Sanskrit sources in other cases are based upon vernacular sources, while serving themselves again as a source for vernacular literature: Buddhism offers examples of this. Is Buddhism to be called part of Sanskrit culture only where a Sanskrit intermediary had been found? An attempt at analysis of the expression 'material content' would encounter similar difficulties. We can accept the term Sanskritization

only if it is made clear that its relation to the term Sanskrit is extremely complex." ("Sanskrit and Sanskritization", *Journal of Asian Studies*, vol. XXII, no. 3, p. 265). Staal will find a reference not only to the "complexity" of Sanskritization but also to its "looseness" in my "Note on Sanskritization and Westernization", *Far Eastern Quarterly*, vol. XV, no. 4, August, 1956, p. 482. I have also envisaged the spread of Sanskritic ideas through the use of regional language in my references to Lingayatism and *harikathas* (p. 482 and p. 486). There is also a clear recognition in my essay of the weaving of local elements into Sanskritic Hinduism (p. 494).

54. B. Stein, "Social Mobility and Medieval South Indian Hindu Sects", in J. Silverberg (ed.), *Social Mobility in Caste in India*, special issue of *Comparative Studies in Society and History*. See *supra* note 27.
55. See McKim Marriott, "Changing Channels of Cultural Transmission in Indian Civilization", in V.F. Ray (ed.), *Intermediate Societies*, Seattle, Wash., 1959, p. 71.
56. Shah and Shroff, see *supra* note 40, p. 57.
57. *Ibid.*, p. 60.
58. Ghurye, *op. cit.*, pp. 70–71. Ghurye has also made the point that the movements started by Kshatriyas also made an appeal to Vaishyas. A.L. Basham, however, thinks that it was Vaishyas rather than Kshatriyas who chiefly favoured the unorthodox religions of Buddhism and Jainism. See *The Wonder That Was India*, New York, 1959, p. 143.
59. Basham, *op. cit.*, p. 142.
60. *Ibid.*, pp. 142–143.
61. *Ibid.*, p. 142.
62. Stein, see *supra* note 54.
63. B.S. Cohn, "Political Systems in Eighteenth Century India: The Banaras Region", *Journal of the American Oriental Society*, vol. 82, no. 3, July–September, 1962, p. 313.
64. *Ibid.*
65. *Ibid.*, pp. 313–314.
66. B.S. Cohn, "From Indian Status to British Contract", *Journal of Economic History*, December, 1961, p. 616.
67. *Ibid.*, p. 619.
68. Cohn, see *supra* note 63, p. 314.
69. B.S. Cohn, "The Initial British Impact on India: A Case Study of the Benares Region", *Journal of Asian Studies*, vol. XIX, no. 4, August, 1960, p. 422.
70. Cohn, see *supra* note 66, p. 619.
71. For a description of the conflict between the lineages, chiefs and *jāgīrdārs* on the one hand and the Raja of Banaras on the other, see Cohn, *supra* note 63, pp. 313–318.

72. A. M. Shah, "Political System in Eighteenth Century Gujarat", in *Enquiry*, vol. 1, no. 1, Spring 1964, pp. 83–95.
73. *Ibid.*, p. 87.
74. *Ibid.*, p. 88.
75. *Ibid.*, p. 94.
76. K. Gough, "Nayar: Central Kerala", in D.M. Schneider and K. Gough (eds.), *Matrilineal Kinship*, Berkeley and Los Angeles, 1961, pp. 317–318.
77. K. Gough, "Nayar: North Kerala", in *supra* note 76, 386–387.
78. E. Miller, *American Anthropologist*, vol. 56, no. 3, June 1954, pp. 410–420.
79. *Ibid.*, pp. 414–415.
80. Gough in *supra* note 76, pp. 306–307.
81. *Ibid.*, p. 307.
82. Hutton, *Caste in India*, p. 94.
83. H. J. Maynard, "Influence of the Indian King upon the Growth of Caste", *Journal of the Punjab Historical Society*, vol. 6, p. 93.
84. *Ibid.*
85. *Ibid.*, pp. 98–99.
86. K. Davis, *The Population of India and Pakistan*, Princeton, 1951, pp. 23–26.
87. See in this connection my *Religion and Society Among the Coorgs of South India*, pp. 20–23.
88. See my "The Social System of a Mysore Village", in M. Marriott (ed.), *Village India*, Chicago, 1955, pp. 1-36; and A. Baines, *op. cit.*, pp. 72–73.
89. Mrs. D. Kumar, "Caste and Landlessness in South India", in *Comparative Studies in Society and History*, vol. IV, no. 3, April 1962, p. 337. Mrs Kumar says, "Differences in definition may exaggerate the growth of landless labour, but the fact of this growth is undeniable" (p. 337, n. 2).
90. Stein, see *supra* note 51.
91. *Ibid.*

2

WESTERNIZATION

1

BRITISH rule produced radical and lasting changes in Indian society and culture. It was unlike any previous period in Indian history as the British brought with them new technology, institutions, knowledge, beliefs and values. The new technology, and the revolution in communications which this brought about, enabled the British to integrate the country as never before in its history. I have pointed out how the establishment of *Pax Britannica* put an end once and for all to local wars which were endemic in pre-British India and which were a most important source of social mobility for individuals as well as groups.

During the nineteenth century the British slowly laid the foundations of a modern state by surveying land, settling the revenue, creating a modern bureaucracy, army and police, instituting law courts, codifying the law, developing communications—railways, post and telegraph, roads and canals—establishing schools and colleges, and so on. The British also brought with them the printing press, and the profound and many-sided changes this brought about in Indian life and thought deserve a volume in itself. One obvious result was that books and journals, along with schools, made possible the transmission of modern as well as traditional knowledge to large numbers of Indians—knowledge which could no longer be the privilege of a few, hereditary groups—while the newspapers made people in different parts of the far-flung country realize they had common bonds, and that events happening in the world outside influenced their lives for good or ill.

Christian missionaries from Europe knew India long before the British arrived there. However, during the early days of the East India Company the entry of European missionaries into India was banned; this ban was lifted in 1813 when the British Parliament permitted them to enter the country under a new system of licensing. This eventually threw the entire subcontinent open to missionary activity.

In the first half of the nineteenth century the British, often with the support of enlightened Indian opinion, abolished such institutions as *suttee* (1829), female infanticide, human sacrifice and slavery (1833). It is not my aim, however, to list all the changes introduced by the British; in a word, the Indo-British impact was profound, many-sided and fruitful. I have used elsewhere the term "Westernization" to characterize the changes brought about in Indian society and culture as a result of over 150 years of British rule, and the term subsumes changes occurring at different levels—technology, institutions, ideology, values.[1] I shall discuss later the appropriateness of the term, but meanwhile I would like to state that I am using it deliberately in spite of its vagueness and omnibus character. There is need for such a term when analyzing changes that a non-Western country undergoes as a result of prolonged contact with a Western one. When the entities involved, as well as the emergent processes, are extremely complex, it is hardly realistic to expect that a simple, unidimensional and crystal-clear concept will explain them fully.

It is necessary to distinguish conceptually between Westernization and two other processes usually concomitant with it—industrialization and urbanization. On the one hand, there were cities in the preindustrial world, though they differed significantly from the cities of the Industrial Revolution in the West. For one thing, they needed large rural populations for their support, so that ancient and medieval countries remained dominantly agricultural in spite of a few great cities. Again, while the Industrial Revolution resulted in an increase in the rate of urbanization and "highly urbanized areas are generally highly industrialized areas, urbanization is not a simple function of industrialization."[2] Finally, while the most Westernized groups are generally found in the big cities, a caution must be uttered against equating Westernization with urbanization. Even in a country such as India, it is possible to come across groups inhabiting rural areas which are more Westernized in their style of life than many urban groups.

The former are to be found in areas where plantation or commercial crops are grown, or which have a tradition of supplying recruits to the Indian army.

Westernization results not only in the introduction of new institutions (for example, newspapers, elections, Christian missions) but also in fundamental changes in the old institutions. Thus while India had schools long before the arrival of the British, they were different from British-introduced schools in that they had been restricted to upper-caste children, and transmitted mostly traditional knowledge—to mention only two of the most important differences.[3] Other institutions such as the army, civil service and law courts were also similarly affected.

Implicit in Westernization are certain value preferences. A most important value, which in turn subsumes several other values, is what may be broadly characterized as humanitarianism, by which is meant an active concern for the welfare of all human beings irrespective of caste, economic position, religion, age and sex. Equalitarianism and secularization are both included in humanitarianism. (I am aware that expression of concern for the welfare not only of all mankind but also of all sentient creatures occurs, and occurs frequently, in Sanskritic ritual and thought, but I am now thinking only of the embodiment of such concern in legal, political, educational and other social institutions.)

Humanitarianism underlay many of the reforms introduced by the British in the first half of the nineteenth century. The introduction of British civil, penal and procedural law put an end to certain inequalities that were part of Hindu and Islamic jurisprudence. In pre-British Hindu law, for instance, punishment varied according to the caste of the person committing the offense as well as to that of the victim. In Islamic law the evidence of non-Muslims was inadmissible; and both Hindus and Muslims regarded their codes as divine, though early Hindu jurists gave considerable importance to customary law.[4]

According to O'Malley, two revolutionary results of introducing the British judicial system were the establishment of the principle of equality and the creation of a consciousness of positive rights: "The last was a plant of slow growth owing to the object submissiveness of the lower classes which prevented them from taking advantage of the system of equal laws and vindicating their rights by legal action."[5] However, not only their "abject submissiveness", but also their illiteracy, extreme poverty and the intricacies of a highly complex, expensive, cumbersome and slow system of law made it very difficult for most villagers to resort to the courts to have their rights enforced and grievances redressed. Spear has aptly said, "the courts were to the public a great penny in the slot machine whose working passed man's understanding and from which anything might come except justice."[6]

The principle of equality found expression in the abolition of slavery, in the opening of the new schools and colleges—in theory at least—to all irrespective of religion, race and caste. The new economic opportunities were also; in theory, open to all, though castes and other groups who traditionally lived in the big towns and coastal areas enjoyed a considerable advantage over the others.

The introduction of reforms and the British legal system involved the changing or abolition of customs claiming to be a part of religion. This meant that religious customs had to satisfy the test of reason and humanity if they were to be allowed to survive. As British rule progressed, rationality and humanitarianism became broader, deeper and more powerful, and the years since the achievement of Independence have seen a remarkable increase—a genuine leap forward—in the extension of both. The attack on untouchability which Independent India has launched provides a striking example of such extension. No alien government would have dared to declare the practice of Untouchability in any form an offense, or to enforce the right of Harijans to enter Hindu temples and draw water from upper caste wells in villages.

Humanitarianism resulted in many administrative measures to fight famine,[7] control epidemics, and found schools, hospitals and orphanages. Christian missionaries played a notable part in humanitarian activity, especially in providing education and medical aid to sections of Indian society most in need of them—Harijans, women, orphans, lepers and tribal folk. Equally important were their criticisms of such Hindu institutions as caste, untouchability, the low position of women, child marriage and polygamy. The British-Western attack resulted in a reinterpretation of Hinduism at both the ideological and institutional levels, and the conversion of the lower castes (especially Harijans) to Islam and Christianity was an important factor in producing a changed attitude among the Hindu elite toward caste and Untouchability.

2

A popular term for the changes brought about in a non-Western country by contact, direct or indirect, with a Western country is "modernization". Daniel Lerner, for instance, after considering the suitability of "westernization" as well as "modernization", has opted for the latter.[8] According to him, "modernization" includes a "disquieting positivist spirit" touching "public institutions as well as private aspirations". But the positivist spirit is not enough a revolution in communications is essential.[9] Modernization is also marked by increasing urbanization which has, in turn, resulted in the spread of literacy. The latter again has tended to enhance "media exposure", and finally, enhanced media exposure is associated with wider economic participation (per capita income) and political participation (voting). Modernization also implies social mobility: "A mobile society has to encourage rationality for the calculus of choice shapes individual behaviour and conditions its rewards. People come to see the social future as manipulable rather than ordained and their personal prospects in terms of achievement rather than heritage."[10]

"Westernization" is unsuitable for several reasons: It is too local a label, and the model which is imitated may not be a Western country but Russia, Turkey, Japan or India. An important reason for Lerner's preferring modernization to Westernization is that educated people in the Middle East, which is Lerner's area of interest, while wanting "the modern package" "reject the label 'made in U.S.A.' (or, for that matter, 'made in U.S.S.R.')."[11] The allergy to "Westernization" is the result of Middle Eastern "ethnocentrism, expressed politically in extreme nationalism, psychologically in passionate xenophobia. The hatred sown by anti-colonialism is harvested in the rejection of every appearance of foreign tutelage. Wanted are modern institutions but not modern ideologies, modern power but not modern purposes, modern wealth but not modern wisdom, modern commodities but not modern cant."[12] The passionate urge to repudiate the West prompts some Middle Eastern leaders to ignore "certain behavioural and institutional compulsions common to all [Europe, America and Russia]" countries which have achieved modernization, and to try "instead new routes and risky bypasses."[13]

One of the results, then, of prolonged contact with the West is the rise of an elite class whose attitude to the West is ambivalent.

The hostility aspect of the ambivalence may express itself in a variety of forms, and in several areas of culture and social life. It is indeed a potential source of anti-rational, and even self-destructive, action. One reason for the enormous appeal of Communism to non-Western countries is its hostility to the West, expressed in Communistic anti-imperialism and anti-capitalism. Communism is seen as a humanitarian creed in its espousal of the cause of the underdogs, the workers and the subject nations; and its forecast that capitalism and imperialism are doomed to disappear and give way to a classless society wears the mask of science. It also enables the non-Western intellectual to reject, in the name of science and humanity, not only the aggressive West but also his own society and its traditions. It enables him to identify himself with the future, with progress, science and humanitarianism.

How can the sociologist be certain that a particular change is part of the process of modernization? Such a difficulty is not merely logico-philosophical, but is inescapable in the actual analysis of empirical processes of change. Robert Bellah rightly observes, "Where modernization means only an increased effectiveness in goal attainment with no increase in the rationalization of the goal-setting process very serious pathologies can result. Empirically such pathologies of modernization have occurred, but they are the product of partial or disturbed modernization, not the inevitable result of modernization itself."[14] Modernization thus involves the "rationalization of ends", according to Bellah, which means that the goals chosen by a society should be "rational" and the subject of discussion.[15] It needs to be pointed out, however, that social goals are in the final analysis the expression of value preferences, and therefore, non-rational. The public discussion of goals can in no way guarantee their rationality. Rationality can only be predicated of the means but not of the ends of social action.

The term "Westernization", unlike "modernization", is ethically neutral. Its use does not carry the implication that it is good or bad, whereas modernization is normally used in the sense that it is good. But there are other difficulties in Westernization; as we have seen, it often involves, on the part of Westernized individuals, political or cultural hostility to the West. Moreover, not all the elements of Western culture in the eighteenth and nineteenth centuries originated in Western Europe. Some important components of Western technological superiority in the eighteenth and nineteenth centuries were derived from the ancient Far East, and from medieval India. Gunpowder, printing types and paper were all invented in China. Lynn White, Jr. has stated that "the symptom of a conscious and generalized lust for natural energy and its application to human purposes is the enthusiastic adoption by thirteenth-century Europe of an idea which had originated in twelfth-century India—perpetual motion."[16] The Arabs transmitted the idea of perpetual motion from the Indians to the Europeans just as they passed on Hindu numerals and positional reckoning. What distinguished medieval Europeans from Indians and Arabs was their intense interest in the idea of perpetual motion, "the attempt to diversify its motors, and the effort to make it do something useful."[17]

Again, evangelical Christianity is regarded as characteristically Western, and it is indisputable that Christian missionaries played a crucial role in India's "modernization". But Christianity, like all other world religions, had its origin in Asia.

While there are certain common elements in Westernization, each European country, along with the United States, Canada, Australia and New Zealand, represents a particular variant of a common culture, and significant differences exist between one country and another. In the analysis of social and cultural change in India the British model of Westernization is obviously the most important one, though since 1947 the American and Russian models have become increasingly relevant. I have treated the British model as a static one, as complete, ready and gift-packed for delivery to India by the middle of the nineteenth century. I am aware that such an assumption is historically untenable, but it is heuristically unavoidable.

Westernization is an inclusive, complex and many-layered concept. It covers a wide range from Western technology at one end to the experimental method of modern science and modern historiography at the other. Its incredible complexity is seen in the fact that different aspects of Westernization sometimes combine to strengthen a particular process, sometimes work at cross-purposes, and are occasionally mutually discrete. I shall try to make clear what I mean by reference to a few examples.

Traditionally Indians ate their meals sitting on the floor. The food was served either on leaves or on metal (brass, bronze or silver) plates. Among the upper castes, and especially among Brahmins, eating was a religious act. The food had to be cooked while the women were in a ritually pure state, since it was offered first to the domestic deities before being served to the members of the family. The men and children ate first, adult men being in a ritually pure state while eating. This meant removing their shirts and changing into a silk *dhoti* (silk is ritually superior to cotton) and upper cloth, or a freshly washed cotton *dhoti* and upper cloth. At the end of the meal the dining leaves became impure and were thrown out. The places where the leaves had rested were purified with a solution of cow-dung.

Now, in the larger towns and cities, the educated and Westernized groups increasingly prefer to eat at tables.[18] The most obvious feature of the change is the new technology—chairs and table, stainless steel utensils, spoons—but it also has other implications. It means a degree of secularization, and the deliberate adoption of a style of life different from the traditional, because it is prestigious or convenient or both. The point I wish to stress is that the new mode of eating contributes to an increase in secularization, as the table is not likely to be purified with cow-dung solution after meals, and the ritual acts traditionally performed before and after meals tend to be dropped.

In urban areas school and office schedules determine the times of eating, and all members of the family, except the senior woman of the house who serves or supervises the serving, sit together for dinner. The weakening of customary dietary restrictions leads to the consumption of hitherto forbidden vegetables such as tomatoes, beetroot, carrots, onion and radish. Eggs are slowly becoming a part of the diet of urbanized, middle class, vegetarian castes.

In short, education, high income and urbanization result in a secularization of the style of life, which includes a radical change in the technology of eating as well as in the timing of meals and the dietary. Eating at a table, a product of secularization, also furthers secularization; in other words, there is a feedback from the new technology to secularization. A new attitude toward food begins to emerge; it is looked at more from the point of view of whether it promotes health and efficiency and less from whether it is traditionally permitted or prohibited.

In other instances, unlike the one above, Westernization in one area or level of behaviour does not result in Westernization in another related area or level. The two remain "discrete". In the summer of 1952, in my field village of Rāmpura in Mysore, I came across the driver of a government bulldozer who was levelling a few acres of land in one of the fields of the headman. The driver was a Tamil-speaker from Bangalore, the biggest city in the state, and his recreation in the village was giving demonstrations of traditional black magic. He saw no inconsistency between driving a bulldozer for his livelihood and indulging in displays of black magic for his pleasure. It is only fair to remark that the foregoing instance, egregious as it is, is not unique or even unusual. Indian workers in factories, generally men with low education, carry over religio-magical attitudes to the technology they work with. Thus, a printer may decorate the machinery in his shop with vermilion before beginning the day's work. All over India, during the annual festival of Dasara (September–October), it is customary for the tools of one's trade to be cleaned, and venerated with vermilion, incense and flowers. This holds not only for the village carpenter, goldsmith and potter, but also for urban workers in mills and factories. Motor cars are washed, marked with vermilion, and festooned with flower garlands. Sewing machines, typewriters, and books receive similar attention. (Books traditionally represent Saraswati, the Goddess of Learning.)

Thus the manipulation of Western technology does not mean that the manipulators have accepted a rationalistic and scientific world view. Far from it. The bulldozer driver in Rāmpura had mastered the mechanical motions necessary to drive it, and could even do minor repairs; but he was not only traditional in his religious beliefs, he had even picked up some black magic, a knowledge usually confined to small groups. He did not perceive any incompatibility between driving a bulldozer and practising black magic. The two sectors were kept completely "discrete". The veneration of tools and machines at the Dasara festival, however, is more than "discreteness"; it represents a carry-over of traditional magico-religious beliefs into the new world of modern technology.

There are instances, moreover, where Westernization has given birth to forces which are mutually at cross-purposes. This is perhaps more evident in its earlier than in later stages, though there is no guarantee that all short-term discordances will disappear in the long run. The introduction of printing, for instance, made possible the transmission of not only modern knowledge but also knowledge of the traditional epics, mythology, the lives of saints and other religious literature. Shanti Tangri records that:

> By 1877 there were 3064 titles published in the vernaculars, another 729 in classical languages, and 544 in English; 2451 of these were original, 2003 republications and 436 translations. Alternately 1138 of these were educational and 3752 general. And though *a great deal of this general literature was poor in quality and dealt with mythology or religion from a traditional-conservative viewpoint*, the revolution of communication was on.[19] (Italics mine)

In the political and cultural field, Westernization has given birth not only to nationalism but also to revivalism, communalism, "casteism", heightened linguistic consciousness and regionalism. To make matters even more bewildering, revivalist movements have used Western-type schools and colleges, and books, pamphlets and journals to propagate their ideas.

When the links between the Western stimulus and the Indian response are few, there is no doubt as to the identification of the process. But doubts may arise when the links are numerous or not visible on the surface. Thus it is easy to perceive increased literacy as the result of printing and the development of towns, but it is difficult to perceive the connection between Westernization and the Backward Classes Movement, or the Ārya Samāj or linguistic consciousness in the twentieth century. I think it will be increasingly necessary to qualify "Westernization" by the prefix "primary", "secondary" or "tertiary"; in primary Westernization, unlike secondary and tertiary, the linkage is simple and direct.

3

The foregoing may convey some ideas of the complexity as well as the diversity of the process involved in Westernization. I have also made the point that each Western country represents only a particular model of Westernization, and that significant differences exist between the different models. Moreover, within each country various sections of its population carry or embody particular aspects of its culture in addition to sharing certain others which are common to all. A knowledge of the social background of the different sections of the population—both of the "model" country and the "borrowing" country—will greatly further understanding of the different facets of Westernization, the way particular elements have been transmitted, and the changes they may have undergone during transmission. While I shall refer only briefly to the different sections of the British population, I will have more to say on the Indian sections. It is patently absurd to assign a purely "blotting-paper role" to the Indians; they did not merely absorb everything they came into contact with—though this has no doubt happened in the case of a few individuals—and transmit to others what they had absorbed. Some elements were borrowed from the West while others were rejected, and the borrowed elements in turn underwent a transformation in India. While some elements of British culture and style of life appealed to all Indians, different aspects of British culture were especially attractive to different sections of the Indian population. Thus the Coorgs, with their catholic dietary which included practically all meat except beef, and their love of liquor, dancing, sports and hunting, found it easy to emulate the style of life of the European planter in Coorg, whereas the South Indian Brahmin or Lingāyat would have found it very difficult. As it happened, South Indian Brahmins took to English education in considerable numbers and entered professions and government service at all levels. In the first phase of their Westernization, their professional life was lived in the Western world while their domestic and social life continued to be largely traditional. (The term "cultural schizophrenia" naturally comes to one's mind, but a caution must be uttered against viewing it as pathological.) Only South Indian Brahmins who had prolonged exposure to Western life outside India, either as students or as members of the defense services, found it possible to switch over to British diet, drink and dance.

While selection, elaboration and transformation of the elements of British culture do occur, it is essential to add that it is not a deliberate process, with rational choice operating at every stage. There is a seeming spontaneity in borrowing, and elaboration has the appearance of organic growth. But at this juncture it is well to remind ourselves of the historical background of Indo-British contact. By the beginning of the nineteenth century the British were masters of a great part of India, and they had at their disposal overwhelming and organized force with which to impose their will on the Indian population. This gave them a sense of superiority to Indians. As rulers they had their goals and policies which at every stage they attempted to implement through their British representatives in India. The personalities of the local implementers of policy, the men on the spot, were of critical importance in this connection as great distance and poor communications gave them considerable latitude, especially before steam-powered ships became popular, and prior to the cutting of the Suez Canal.

The British in India fell into several distinct occupational and social categories. Bernard Cohn has observed:

> Even in an outstation like Banaras, there was not one British society but several British societies. The basic cleavage was official versus non-official. In terms of its impact on India and England and in terms of power and status, the official community far outweighed the unofficial community in the first half of the nineteenth century. The official civilian had a generally higher status and pay than did the military official. The head of the Government was usually a civilian. And the owners of the East India Company were civilian.[20]

After the civilians came the merchants and traders who, except for some wealthy and powerful ones in the Presidency Towns, tended to be socially separate from the officials. The planters were somewhat distinct from other commercial groups, and lived near their plantations or in towns where their crops (indigo, jute, tea) were processed. Finally, in the port cities there were the European artisans, servants and floaters, often recruited from the enlisted ranks of the military and from the sailors of East Indiamen. This group shaded into the Eurasians, who were at the bottom of the White hierarchy.

The occupational categories overlapped to some extent with the social divisions in British society. The military and civilian officers were drawn from more or less the same strata of English life: landed gentry, substantial merchants of London, and the professions.[21] The military outnumbered the civilians, and usually lived separately from the latter. Though fewer in number, the civilians were "the dominant class in the British colonial society".[22] They were connected by kinship and affinity, by a common social background, and by the old school tie to Haileybury.[23]

The merchants, traders and planters, on the other hand, hailed from lower social orders; they were the sons of merchants and officials. The planters considered themselves a cut above the traders and merchants, and their greatest ambition was to gain entry into the society of civilian officials.[24]

The missionaries as a group were small and insignificant in the beginning of the nineteenth century and, as mentioned earlier, they were only permitted to work in British Indian territory from 1813 onward, and that, under a system of licensing. Their importance, however, increased steadily during the subsequent years of the century.[25] Of the several class affiliations of British missionaries in India, we can only speak with certainty regarding the Baptists and Methodists, many of whom were lower class, being the children of artisans and traders.[26]

Students of Indian society may be forgiven if they see the British in India in a *varna* idiom. At the top of the social pyramid were the officers of the civil service, the higher ranks of the military, and the biggest and wealthiest among the merchants and bankers. They corresponded to Brahmin, Kshatriya and Vaishya categories respectively. Below them were the European artisans, servants and "floaters" corresponding to the Shūdras. To the bulk of Indians, however, the Europeans were an undifferentiated mass of people standing above Indians as far as purely secular criteria of rank were considered, but occupying an extremely low ritual rank.[27]

Frykenberg notes that the English in India underwent a process of Indianization, and lived like one of the many Indian castes. "Guntur [headquarters of a district in Andhra Pradesh in South India], like the country in general, possessed anything but a homogeneous society. Its population was communally dissected and stratified. The British in Guntur were one among many self-contained and semi-isolated communities."[28] However, the British civilians in the course of their official work came into close contact with the Deshasthas, Marāthi-speaking Brahmins, who had for nearly three centuries administered Guntur district, and who supplied the British with a number of lower officials. The British rulers also had close contact with the previous Muslim rulers of the area, and with several other castes and communities.[29]

The close official contact between British civilians and Deshasthas led in many cases to the establishment of intimate friendships between them. "British businessmen contacted local business communities (*Komatis, Chettis*, Armenians and Muslims); and missionaries, by their very work, found themselves often among the poorest and lowliest of communities (e.g., Mālas and Mādigas)."[30]

There was also contact between Indians and the British across the lines of occupation, income, and class; for example, the British civilian and judge came into contact with a variety of Indians in the course of their official work. In fact, Cohn argues conclusively that the Briton's view of India and Indians varied according to his occupation and the particular period of Indo-British history during which he worked in India. Thus after 1840, as a result of the British officials' experience with settlement work, there began to develop an admiration for the peasant and contempt for the educated, urban, middle class Indian, and this continued until Independence.[31]

4

I shall now turn to the Indian side in order to identify the sections of the traditional society which led the others in Westernization, and shall also describe some of their aims, ideas and conflicts. I shall call them the "New Elite"' as there is no doubt that they were an elite group, and their role was seminal in the ushering in of new India. I shall not call them the "middle class" inasmuch as the term is used in different senses by different scholars, and I am not certain that the new elite—for example, Rām Mohan Roy, the Tagores and Swāmi Vivekānanda—always hailed from, or formed the "middle class".

Only a tiny fraction of the Indian population came into direct, face-to-face contact with the British or other Europeans, and those who came into such contact did not always become a force for change. Indian servants of the British, for instance, probably wielded some influence among their kin groups and local caste groups but not among others. They generally came from the low castes, their Westernization was of a superficial kind, and the upper castes made fun of their pidgin English, their absurd admiration for their employers, and the airs they gave themselves. Similarly, converts to Christianity from Hinduism did not exercise much influence in Indian society as a whole because, first, these also generally came from the low castes, and second, the act of conversion alienated them from the majority community of Hindus. Finally, conversion to Christianity often only changed the faith but not the customs, the general culture or the standing of the converts in society.

As far as the bulk of the people were concerned, Westernization began to occur indirectly and gradually; the process has become greatly intensified, in many ways, since 1947 when India became independent. The first and most critical step in Westernization was the establishment of *Pax Britannica*, and the revolution in communications that followed. The extension of the administration and trading frontiers broke the centuries-old isolation of groups inhabiting the forested mountains, and provided them with new contacts and opportunities. The development of communications, and the removal of internal customs barriers, integrated the economy of the various regions in the country into a single one. The introduction of steam-powered ships and the building of the Suez Canal (1869) enabled Britain not only to increase her control of India and other parts of her Eastern empire but also to link up the Indian economy with the economy of the world outside. Indigo, jute, cotton, tobacco, tea and coffee began to be grown in India by European planters for consumption abroad. World prices for these products assumed significance for the living standards of thousands of people in different parts of the country. The advent of plantations marked the beginning of migration of labourers to the two plantation areas—one formed by the mountain regions of Assam and Bengal, the other in the southern parts of the Western Ghats. The Assam area was by far the more important, in terms of the number of workers employed and the value of the crops. Assam attracted labourers not only from neighbouring states but also from modern Madhya Pradesh, Maharāshtra and Madras, whereas the Western Ghats attracted labourers only from the surrounding densely populated areas. Tea plantations were started in 1840, and importation of labourers for work on them began thirteen years later. The movement of labour was greatly facilitated by the abolition of slavery in 1843, which cut the legal knot binding the serfs and slaves, generally from very low or Harijan castes, to the landowners from the higher castes. It is interesting to note in this connection that the labourers on the South Indian plantations came mostly from the Harijan castes, whereas those on the Assam plantations came from "clean" castes, Harijans and tribes such as Mundas and Santals.[32]

The increasingly close integration of India with the world outside is seen, from 1850 on, in the migration of Indian labourers, under the "indenture system", to other British overseas dependencies such as Ceylon, Malaysia, Fiji, South Africa,

Mauritius, the Caribbean and British Guiana. During the period 1834 to 1908, when there were no restrictions on the emigration overseas of Indian labourers, some fourteen million left India; ten million returned subsequently because of the harshness of the indenture system, of working conditions and the racial discrimination.[33]

In a word, the political and administrative integration of India—a process continuing well into the sixties of the twentieth century—involving as it did the development of communications, the beginnings of industrialization and agricultural development, increased spatial and social mobility not only for the elite but also for the rural poor, and laid the foundation for subsequent nation-wide Westernization.

My main concern here, however, is with those who participated in Westernization processes in a more immediate sense, who attended the new educational institutions, entered the professions, took up jobs in the bureaucracy, and engaged themselves in trade, commerce and industry in the big and developing towns. A much larger number underwent Westernization in a secondary sense—for example, patients in the hospitals, litigants in law courts,[34] and readers of newspapers and books in the Indian languages.

From a geographical point of view the inhabitants of coastal areas, especially those close to the fast-growing port towns, were favourably situated to undergo primary Westernization. The areas immediately around Calcutta, Bombay and Madras experienced Westernization for a hundred or more years before interior areas such as the Punjab Again, people in princely states were generally more sheltered from the new winds of change than people in British India; in a few exceptional states such as Mysore, Travancore and Baroda, however, the Westernization process or some aspects of it, made greater headway mainly owing to the power, prestige and initiative of enlightened though autocratic rulers.

The three presidency towns of Calcutta, Bombay and Madras attracted elements of the Indian population who quite early showed a sensitivity to the new commercial, educational and other opportunities. Merchants and bankers found in the British-administered areas not only security of life and property but also freedom from the arbitrary exercise of political power. According to Tangri, "The growing middle class in port towns was thus primarily non-Muslim. Western education gave to them opportunities for associating with the ruling elites, prospects for jobs in government and business, enhanced social status and better commercial contacts with the growing foreign firms."[35]

It is necessary, however, to caution against a purely geographical approach to the location of elites. For instance, though the Punjab came under the impact of Westernization much later than the littoral areas, some caste groups there such as the Khatri, Arora and Agarwāl have traditionally engaged in trade and commerce and shown a high sensitivity to the profit incentive. The arid, inland region of Rajasthan is famous for its trading caste of Mārwāris who are to be found in trade, banking or industry in every big city in India. During British rule, these various groups took advantage of trading and commercial opportunities not only in their home regions but also outside. Some even went abroad to other British colonies and established themselves in trade and commerce there.

5

Generally speaking, people living in towns are more exposed to Western influences than are rural folk. The bigger the town the greater is the chance of such exposure, while in the smaller villages such chances are, even today, minimal, though greater than before Independence. But urbanism does not always result in Westernization. Tangri points out that in 1842 schools had to be closed for lack of students in the two North Indian towns of Chaprah and Arrah, with populations of 50,000 each. According to him it was not urbanism as such, but the greater contact with foreign influences in the coastal areas, that was crucial. He also notes that in 1931 Hindus with 10.5 per cent of their population in urban areas had 8.4 per cent literates, whereas Muslims with 13.5 per cent in urban areas had only 6.4 per cent literates.[36]

Members of the minority religions are more urbanized than Hindus or Muslims. If we consider figures for 1931, we see that 89 per cent of Pārsis, 69.2 per cent of Jews, 34.6 per cent of Jains, and 20.2 per cent of Christians are urban. (The Sikhs, however, provide an exception to the general rule with only 7.8 per cent of their population living in urban areas.) But the overall strength of the Hindu and Muslim population is so great that, in 1931, Hindus formed 66.46 per cent and Muslims 27.68 per cent of the total urban population, with Christians (3.22 per cent), Jains (1.16),

Sikhs (0.91), Jews (0.04) and Pārsis (0.03) trailing well behind them.[37]

As far as the Hindus are concerned, there was—and to a very limited extent still is—a very broad and general correlation between traditional caste hierarchy and the new Western-occupational hierarchy. Thus the members of the higher castes dominated the professions, the higher level posts in the government—in fact, all white-collar jobs—while the lower castes provided certain essential services and goods. A traditional-modern continuum did exist; Brahmins, Baidyas, Kāyasthas and Banias sought Western education and reaped its rewards, whereas members of the low artisan, servicing and landless labour castes became launderers, barbers, domestic servants, peons, basket makers, oilmen, potters and sellers of vegetables, milk and fruits. I would like to caution, however, that it is only too easy to exaggerate the scope of this continuum. There were breaches in it from the beginning, and as the years passed the breaches became wider and more significant.

It is doubtful whether such a continuum exists in industry, although earlier generalizations, which were not based on carefully conducted empirical studies, helped to spread the idea that at the lowest levels of the industrial workforce Harijans and other low castes preponderated.[38] As a careful student of Indian labour problems, Morris D. Morris has remarked, "Despite the ubiquity of caste and the intense interest the phenomenon has generated among scholars, virtually no attention has been paid to the relationship of caste to the process of industrialization in India. Certain generalizations have been made about the caste groups that flow into industry, about the impact of industrial employment on caste coherence and about the caste composition of industrial entrepreneurship. Although some widely-held notions exist, it is rather startling to discover that these conclusions have no detailed empirical support whatever."[39] After a critical examination of current generalizations he concludes, "Very generally speaking, however, the available evidence suggests that Hindus of all castes will seek and accept all jobs in the industrial sector and that this has been true historically."[40] History apart, a recent survey by Richard Lambert of five factories in Poona city confirms Morris's conclusion. Lambert found that 15 per cent of the workforce was Brahmin, 35.2 per cent Marātha, 8.5 per cent "Intermediate Castes", 6.8 per cent village servants, 16.8 per cent "Backward Castes". The fact that some members who should have gone into the last category returned themselves as Buddhists is responsible for the low percentage of Backward Castes. ("Other religions" accounted for 9.3 per cent.) Lambert concludes, "Another presumption—that Brahmins are reluctant to enter so physical an enterprise as factory work—finds no support here. Nor do the Backward Castes seem to be either excluded from or disproportionately attracted to the factories."[41] The factories attracted workers from all levels of traditional society as they offered comparatively high wages.[42]

Of the nature of the relation obtaining between caste hierarchy and factory hierarchy in the Poona factories, Lambert has written that

> Brahmins are disproportionately represented in the clerical and supervisory classes and hold the highest ranking positions within those classes. Their relative position among the P & M [non-clerical workers below the supervisor level] workers depends upon the factory, and in most factories it is not substantially higher. The Backward Classes are hardly represented at all among the supervisors and clerks and are either absent or lower in mean wages in all factories. Aside from Brahmins and Backward Classes, the general ranking of castes does not seem to be reflected in significant differences in hierarchical positions within the factories.[43]

It is not unlikely that this pattern is common to the whole of peninsular India except probably in factories run by the state governments, where appointments at all levels, especially the higher levels, until very recently gave preference to the non-Brahmin castes.

Looking at the urbanization process from the rural end, Harold Gould has argued that in Uttar Pradesh it is only high castes such as Brahmins and Rājpūts who are undergoing Westernization, including urbanization, and that the lower castes lack the means as well as the motivation to move into the modern world. They are poor, uneducated and lack kin connections in towns, and all these hamper their mobility.[44] And when a low-caste family became rich, as it very rarely did, it invested much of its money in building up its "traditional status", whereas the Brahmins and Rājpūts had a positive urge to invest in Westernization in their effort to seek new means of distinguishing themselves from the swiftly Sanskritizing low castes. Gould has cited evidence from two other villages in Uttar Pradesh besides his own in support of his view that it is the high castes such as Brahmins, Rājpūts (Thākurs) and Jāts who are undergoing Westernization and urbanization, and not the lowest and poorest: "reality appears to be at wide variance with classical expectations concerning mobility in modernizing societies, where it is held that the landless and the impoverished are compelled to move towards the city in search of cash employment while the landed and the well-off are content to remain proportionately longer in their rural habitat."[45]

Gould includes Brahmins, Rājpūts and Jāts (landowning peasant caste) among the high castes, and the Ahīr, Murau, Kūrmi, Kori and Chamār among the low. But one of his "low" castes, the Ahīrs, have shown since at least the beginning of this century considerable dynamism and are present in some strength in the Indian army.[46] And they are now demanding the formation of an Ahīr regiment. Another "low" caste of Uttar Pradesh, the Noniyas, have become wealthy by taking advantage of new economic opportunities since the latter part of the nineteenth century, and they now call themselves Chauhans, in an effort to claim Kshatriya status.[47] The well-known Harijan caste of North India, the Chamārs, are to be found in some strength in cities such as Agra, Aligarh, Lucknow, Kānpur and Delhi, and they too have shown a desire to move up not only along the traditional Sanskritic axis but also along the modern, Western axis. Bernard Cohn, who made an intensive field study of the Chamārs of Senāpur in Eastern Uttar Pradesh, a particularly depressed area of Uttar Pradesh if not of India as a whole, has written that in 1952, 36 Chamārs out of a total of 636 were employed out of the village. Extra-village employment was not, however, new to them, but familiar since the middle of the nineteenth century.

> The figure of thirty-six Camārs working out of the village does not give an adequate picture of their experiences out of the village. The majority of adult male Camārs have at one time or another worked away from the village in a city. Urban employment is not, however, a way of life for these people. ... A few younger men work in the cities through choice, some even say they like it, but the older men, i.e., those over thirty, seem to prefer the village.[48]

In 1952, 72 Chamārs (71 men and one woman) were literate out of a population of 583 who were above five years of age.[49]

Taking an all-India view, it is impossible to maintain that Harijan castes, let alone the "low" castes, have failed to be drawn into the urbanization process. I agree with Morris when he says:

> While there have been village studies that give us evidence that caste status and income are somewhat correlated, there is no evidence to my knowledge that will show us that the migration out of rural areas is disproportionately high for special castes. While it is certainly true that the low castes together with Untouchables constitute an overwhelmingly large proportion of migrants to urban areas, on the face of it this is merely the result of the fact that God[!] has put so many Indians into these categories in the rural sector.[50]

Translated into lay language this means that since the low castes so greatly outnumber the high castes, there are more of them everywhere, including the cities.

6

It is generally assumed by writers on India that the modern Indian elite draws disproportionately on certain sections of the population. Edward Shils, for instance, comments on the predominance of Brahmins among the new elites:

> Just as the *pandits* acclaimed the British, even though they no longer occupied the highest positions which had been theirs when they were in power under the pre-British rulers, Brahmins with modern education served the British in the Civil Service. For a long time the Madrasi and Bengali Brahmins led the way in the service of the British and they were predominant among the Indians in the Indian Civil Service. Likewise, when the current began to turn toward independence and toward modernizing social reforms, the Brahmins took the lead there too.[51]

Others such as B.B. Misra[52] and Selig Harrison[53] have written in similar terms on the dominance of Brahmins in the administration, professions and the political movement. The Brahmins referred to by these writers are an all-India category and not a localized, endogamous *jāti*. Brahmin, as an all-India *varna*, refers to a congeries of *jātis* which differ from each other in language, diet, dress, occupation and style of life. Thus in some places Brahmins are not only not priests or scholars, but are poorer and socially more backward than castes which are ritually below them. In parts of Uttar Pradesh and Rajasthan, they are occasionally found working as tenants of Rājpūt or Jāt landowners. The low position and lack of learning of Brahmins in the Punjab has been commented upon by Prakash Tandon.[54]

Even the Brahmins in a single linguistic region, let alone Brahmins all over India, are split up into several endogamous *jātis*, and inter-*jāti* differences cannot be ignored. Thus in Gujarat, until recently, Nāgar and Anāvil Brahmins were prominent in secular-Western contexts while the others such as the Audich Sahasra were not. And, as we have seen earlier, even within a local section of a single *jāti* there may be much cultural and economic diversity, and this sometimes provides a basis for the fissioning-off of the "superior" section from the rest.

The point I wish to make is that an entire *varna* category is rarely found occupying only a particular stratum or a few strata in the new hierarchy. What happens is that in certain strata and occupations, members from certain local *jātis* are found much more frequently than are other similar *jātis*. Sometimes a cluster of roughly equal and allied *jātis* may preponderate in certain occupations. Translating *jāti* into *varna* terms has its hazards, though it is unavoidable when discussing India as a whole. Listing all the *jātis* involved in a given process would not only detract from readability but would also assume that we have the necessary information. Vague terms have their uses.

The composition of the new elite varies not only regionally but also over a period of time. Thus the Indian elite in 1964 contained elements that would have been regarded as "backward" in 1904, and even in 1934. Over the years, sections of the population labelled "backward" have undergone Westernization in increasing measure; this is more true of some parts of the country, such as South India, than of the others. In my discussion of the elite I shall, however, keep in view the period just before World War I when the character of the new elite began to alter radically. I shall refer to some of these changes later.

I have already noted that there is a certain amount of continuity between the traditional elite and the new or Westernized elite. Such continuity exists in a double sense: first, some members or sections of the traditional elite transformed themselves into the new elite, and second, there is a continuity between the old and new occupations.[55] A simple instance of continuity is provided when the sons of a Brahmin *pundit* enter the professions, or when a chieftain's son achieves a high position in the Indian army, or a Bania's son becomes a leading exporter and importer of goods. It is only natural that during the first phase of Westernization each section of the Indian elite should choose a model of Westernization traditionally closest to it. This is only true, however, in very broad terms, and there were exceptions. The Pārsis of Bombay,[56] for instance, were one of the first groups to take advantage of the new opportunities; they entered the professions, government service, industry, commerce and trade, especially trade in liquor, and finally, were also prominent in civic and national life. But a section of rural Pārsis living near Surat remained—and continue to remain—backward, economically, educationally and socially. Again, Marāthi Brahmins not only entered the professions and government service, but also the army.

I shall now take note of some of the castes that took the lead in undergoing Westernization—though when a caste is mentioned this does not mean that all its members became Westernized to the same degree, or that other groups not mentioned have not undergone any Westernization. Brahmin groups in most parts of India, Kāyasthas (writers and government officials) in North India,[57] Baidyas in Bengal,[58] Pārsis and Banias in Western India, some Muslim groups in Uttar Pradesh and Western India, and Nāyars and Syrian Christians in Kerala, took to Western education and the new careers which it led to. Various Brahmin *jātis* in different parts of the country—South Indian Brahmins excepting Nambūdris, Nāgar and Anāvil Brahmins in Gujarat, and Kashmīri, Bengali and Marāthi Brahmins—were prominent in the professions and government service. The new opportunities for trade and commerce which British rule opened up were taken advantage of by trading castes such as Khatris and Aroras from the Punjab; the trading castes of Rājasthan, and Hindu and Jain Banias, and Muslim Bohras, Khojas, and Memons, all from Gujarat; Komatis from Andhra Pradesh, Chettiars and Muslim Labbais from Madras; and finally by Syrian Christians and Muslim Māpillas from Kerala. However, it was not always caste groups having trade as a hereditary occupation that took advantage of the new opportunities. The Pātidār of Gujarat are a peasant caste who took to trade and commerce only during the closing decades of the nineteenth century.[59] The Boad Distillers of Orissa provide another instance of similar change. In the Kondmals area of Orissa, until about 1870, the Konds and everyone else were able to make their own liquor:

> In 1870 the drink shops in the region to the south of the Kondmals were closed and the sellers of drink migrated in large numbers across the border from Ganjam into the Kondmals. Shortly after this the Government made it illegal for the Konds to distill their own liquor. Home-stills were closed and the Konds were compelled to patronize out-stills, which were run by men of Distiller castes, both those who had recently come in from Ganjam, and those from Boad, who had long been resident in the village.[60]

In their thirst for liquor, many Konds lost their land and became labourers in the service of the new landowners. The prosperity of the Boad Distillers continued till 1910 when the Government of Bengal, of which Orissa was then a part, decided to close down all drink shops in the Kondmals.

Before the Indian Mutiny of 1857, Rājpūts and Brahmins of Oudh dominated the Bengal army. But because of the role of these two groups in the Mutiny, the new Indian army excluded them and "brought in men from the Punjab, both Hindu and Muslim, the now reconciled Sikhs from the same quarter, Pathans from the frontier, and Gurkhas from Nepal."[61] However, Rājpūts from outside Oudh, and Marāthi Brahmins continued to be recruited. Jāts, Ahīrs, Dogras and Coorgs were some of the other groups showing a preference for careers in the army. The two World Wars, especially World War II, saw the entry into military service of sections of the population traditionally averse to it. The spread of education, increased spatial mobility, and unemployment were some of the factors responsible for this radical departure from traditional occupations. The Second World War witnessed the expansion of the Indian armed forces from 175,000 men in 1939 to about two million men in the course of a few years. According to Spear, "Though only a small proportion of the total went abroad, all were uprooted from their village homes, subjected to discipline and strange habits, and in many cases were taught trades and modern techniques. This in itself was a major jolt to a tradition-bound society. There were large openings for the middle classes in the officer cadres and in the enlarged bureaucracy which increased their sense of responsibility and self-respect."[62]

The fact that the traditional elites were able to extend their dominance to new, Western situations gave rise in some parts of the country to what has been called the "Backward Classes Movement". The lower castes wanted a share in the new opportunities, and they were also stirred by the new equalitarian winds blowing across India. The movement assumed a particularly vigorous form in peninsular India where the non-Brahmin castes succeeded in obtaining for themselves concessions and privileges, while at the same time they were able to have imposed on the Brahmins restrictions with regard to access to education and employment in the administration. The movement also occurred elsewhere in India, including Bengal, though there it did not assume the form that it did in the South. In Madras,[63] Bombay, [64] and Bengal[65] the leaders of the Backward Classes Movement stayed clear of the nationalist movement, and were avid in their support of the British rulers. The Backward Classes Movement everywhere went with a certain amount of anti-Brahminism; this found political and even cultural expression throughout South India, in Madras in particular. The Scheduled Castes (Harijan) Movement originated as a part of the Backward Classes Movement, though as the years went by it acquired distinctive overtones of its own.

Although the fact of overlap between traditional and new elites increased the cultural if not the structural distance between the higher and lower castes, it did indirectly give rise to the Backward Classes Movement which has as its aim the abolition of all distance between castes. It is understandable that the Movement has been strongest where the overlap was greatest; and it is arguable that the existence of a wide economic, cultural, and structural gulf between the higher and lower castes is a factor making for the speedier mobilization of the latter, once the door is opened to the new Western forces. It is also likely that the Bhakti movement's attack on the idea of inequality, which left a deep impression on the non-Brahmin castes of South India, was a factor in rousing them so quickly. A comparative study of the Backward Classes Movement, and of the social composition of the new elites in different parts of the country, would be necessary for a proper understanding of current regional variations in patterns of stratification.

I have earlier cited a few instances of discontinuity between traditional and modern elites. In all such cases there was a discrepancy between their traditional rank in the local caste hierarchy and their newly acquired secular position. This was usually resolved by the *nouveaux riches* Sanskritizing their way of life and claiming to be high castes. Bailey has shown how the Boad Distillers of Phulbani in Orissa rose up from their previous position as one of the "Low Hindu" castes, below the Barber, to the "High Hindu" category, disputing with Warriors for second place.[66] Sanskritization, then, restored the equilibrium, and traditionally it has been able to do this in the case of all castes except the Harijan. In the first place, there were very few opportunities for Harijans to acquire wealth or political power, and in those rare cases where they did acquire it, their being on the wrong side of the pollution line proved an almost insuperable obstacle to mobility. The position changed to some extent during the British period; the British law courts refused to give legal recognition to the disabilities traditionally imposed on Harijans, and this, when combined with new opportunities for education, trade and commerce, and spatial movement, laid the groundwork for social mobility. Given these preconditions, Sanskritization provided an established avenue to "passing". Thus Āgra Chamārs call themselves Jātab (corruption of Yādav), and it is not unknown for a Jātab to claim to be a Brahmin. In 1962 a Jātab claimed to be a Brahmin and married a Brahmin girl from Mount Abu in Rajasthan.[67] Similarly, André Beteille found a Pallan (Tamil Harijan) from another village passing for a Padaiyāchi in Sr̄ipuram, a village near Tiruvaiyār in Tanjore district. He was, however, discovered and beaten, after which he fled the village, leaving all his belongings behind him.[68]

In the case of Indian Muslims, however, a small body of politically powerful Muslims constituted a most important part of the pre-British aristocracy of India, while the bulk of them, converts from the low castes, remained poor and at the bottom of the hierarchy of Muslim castes. The aristocracy was resentful of the fact that they had been displaced by the British as rulers of India, and until the last quarter of the nineteenth century exhibited a strong resistance to Westernization. When the Muslims broke out of their self-imposed isolation and decided to swim with the new current, they found that the Hindus had drifted a long way down the stream. Of the founder of the movement toward Westernization among Muslims, Sir Sayyid

Ahmad Khan (1817–1898), the British historian Percival Spear has this to say:

> Thus the Sayyid sought to bring Islam in India into line with modern thought and progress. But there was no thought of union with the Hindus. They were still a heathen body tainted with idolatry and superstition. Toleration was matched with aloofness in his thought, co-existence with separateness. He preached cooperation with the British to avoid eclipse and absorption by the Hindus. When the Congress was founded in 1885, he advised Muslims to hold back on the ground that in an independent India the majority would rule, and the Hindus outnumbered the muslims by three to one.[69]

Sir Sayyid Ahmad Khan was the first Westernized Muslim to give expression to a separatist ideology, and this was further developed by the poet-philosopher Sir Muhammad Iqbal. In the hands of the astute M.A. Jinnah, it was translated into the political reality of Pakistan.

The Indian National Congress also included Muslims, some of whom were highly Westernized. But by and large it was the traditionalist Muslims such as the leaders of the Deoband School who supported the Indian nationalist movement.[70]

7

I have considered briefly the social background of the new elite groups, and shall now describe a few ideas and beliefs which formed part of their traditions. It is important to remember that the elite played a creative role in reinterpreting Indian thought, traditions, culture and history in response to European criticisms. Their role was far from restricted to borrowing things, ideas and institutions from the British; the borrowing was selective and the borrowed item subjected to elaboration and reinterpretation. A knowledge of the background and traditions of the elite groups explains to some extent this selectivity. Different elite groups looked up to their corresponding sections in British society in India—or rather, all sections of the population looked up to the British while some looked up to specific sections of it. While only a few Indian merchants in the big cities came into actual contact with their British counterparts, the entire Indian business community had its own myths and images about the ways, attitudes and ideas of British merchants.

The richness and heterogeneity of the religious, intellectual, moral, literary and artistic traditions of India have been widely commented upon by a host of scholars, and it is not necessary for me to add anything here. In the field of religion, for instance, every major religion of the world with the exception of Confucianism is represented in India.

Students of Indian culture and thought have remarked on the tolerance of Hinduism and its readiness to affirm the truth of all religions. Radhakrishnan has written, "No country and no religion have adopted this attitude of understanding and appreciation of other faiths so persistently and consistently as India and Hinduism and its offshoot of Buddhism."[71] The dominant trend was tolerance, though occasionally there were outbursts of bigotry and even persecution of people of other faiths. Thus there was a certain amount of intolerance between the Shaiva and Vaishnava sects in the South, and between them and the Jains. But in the main, "Hinduism is essentially tolerant, and would rather assimilate than rigidly exclude."[72] In fact, many educated Hindus find it difficult to comprehend how some people can believe their own religion to be true and all others false. They see evangelism as the expression of aggressive intolerance.

The caste system provided an institutional basis for tolerance. Living in a caste society means living in a pluralistic cultural universe: each caste has its own occupation, customs, ritual, traditions and ideas. Caste councils, especially the council of the locally dominant caste, are the guardians of such pluralism. Is cultural pluralism consistent with the fact that the castes of a region form a hierarchy, and that there is also mobility as well as argument about mutual rank? In the first place, the idea of hierarchy is favourable to, if not reinforced by, cultural differences between castes occupying different levels. Second, it is only the two ends of the hierarchy which are fixed, and in between there is much argument about mutual rank. When rank changes, the style of life becomes Sanskritized.

Again, the caste system made heresy-hunting unnecessary. A rebel sect or group in the course of time became a caste, which ensured its continuous existence though at the cost of sealing it hermetically from the rest of the society. To complete the irony, in some cases such a sect reflected in its microcosm the macrocosm of the caste system of the wider society. Witness, for instance, the Sikhs, Lingāyats and Jains. Occasionally, tribal groups such as the Kotas, Todas, Badagas and Kurumbas used the model of the caste system to regulate their mutual relations.[73]

The tolerance of Hinduism continued into the nineteenth and twentieth centuries. Not only did educated and Westernized Indians such as Rām Mohan Roy and Gandhi express their profound admiration for the personality and teachings of Jesus Christ, but the illiterate Brahmin Saint of Bengal, Rāmakrishna, in a unique effort at empathy tried to experience from the inside what it was to be a member of different religions.[74] The decision to make India a secular state is in tune with this tradition of tolerance, but the Indian concept of secularism is different, for instance, from the American. (For a stimulating discussion of the differences between the two views of secularism see Marc Galanter's 'East and West—a Review of Donald Eugene Smith", *India as a Secular State*, Princeton, 1963.[75])

The intellectual tradition inherited by the elite groups has been characterized by continuous self-criticism; this goes back to the later Vedic times. There was thus a strong reaction to the hyperdeveloped sacrificialism of the *Brāhmanas* (*circa* 900 B.C.) in Buddhism and Jainism, and also among some Brahmins.[76] The Indian philosophical tradition was rich in diversity, and public debates between members of different schools were an established institution. A teacher's greatest success was believed to be a student who defeated him in argument.

The Bhakti movement of medieval India embodied a revolt against the idea of inequality inherent in caste as well as against the intellectualism of the traditional paths to salvation (*moksha*). Thus Ramānanda, one of the medieval saints of northern India, attacked the idea of inequality and caste exclusiveness in food and drink. Of the influence of Vaishnavism on Hindus and society, Estlin Carpenter has written, "It sought to remove religion from the carefully guarded ceremonies of Brahminical ritual and throw open its hopes and privileges to men and women of every rank and caste, of every race and creed. It needed no priest, for the offering of love required no sacerdotal sanction, and the grace of god was in no man's keeping."[77]

The traditions of tolerance, syncretism and self-criticism manifested themselves early in British rule. Rām Mohan Roy, who may be rightly regarded as the prophet of modern India, was a severe critic of contemporary Hinduism, and took the lead in urging the British Government to wipe out *suttee* as well as to introduce schools for the imparting of modern knowledge in English. He actually opposed the establishment, in 1823, of the Sanskrit College in Calcutta; he did not want any public money to be spent on Sanskrit education, but on English education instead. He was himself, however, a product of the traditional educational system, and had studied Arabic and Persian before starting on Sanskrit, beginning the study of English only at the age of twenty-four. He was early influenced by Sufism, and later developed an admiration for Christianity. "He learnt Hebrew and Greek to pursue his researches in Christianity, and in 1820 wrote a book called *The Principles of Jesus: the Guide to Peace and Happiness*. In 1828 he established a theistic society called the Brahmo Samaj, and made a serious study of the Upanishads and the Vedanta Sutras which he found comparable to Sufism and Christianity."[78] Throughout his life Rām Mohan Roy fought the orthodox elements in Hindu society. He condemned many evil customs of the day as not sanctioned by the scriptures (*shāstras*), and he also appealed to the criterion of reason for which he found a source in the Upanishads.[79]

A Westernized intelligentsia had emerged among Indians by the sixties of the nineteenth century, and leaders of this class became the torchbearers of a new and modern India. The leaders included such great names as the Tagores, Vivekānanda, Rānade, Gokhale, Tilak, Patel, Gandhi, Jawaharlal Nehru and Radhakrishnan. The Westernized intelligentsia increased in strength and numbers, and the dawn of independence in 1947 invested them with the power to plan a peaceful revolution of Indian life.

8

I shall now refer to some of the dilemmas and conflicts of the new elite. The first, and a rather basic, characteristic of theirs was an ambivalence toward their own society as well as toward the ruling British. Their extreme self-criticism was expressed in their desire to alter or do away with several features and institutions of contemporary India. There were the egregious "evils" such as *suttee, thuggee,* human sacrifice, female infanticide, slavery, untouchability and religious prostitution. And then there were others, less conspicuous: polygyny, "child marriage", dowry, heavy expenditure at weddings and funerals, the segregation of women (*purdah*), and the traditional ban on divorce, widow marriage and sea voyage. Christian missionaries were quick to pounce on the evils of Hinduism, to denounce them and point out how immaculate Christianity was in contrast. According to O'Malley:

> For their part the missionary publications drew attention to the defects of Hinduism, the evils of the caste system, etc., and pointed out the truth of the Christian religion and the superiority of Western learning and science. Active missionary propaganda had now been in northern India for over a quarter of a century, and Lord Minto had noticed in 1807 that its effect was not to convert but to alienate the followers of both Hinduism and Islam owing to the crude methods it followed. ... Hindus were exhorted to abolish "the whole institution of caste, that is to say their whole system of civil polity, as well as their fondest and most rooted religious tenets"; and resentment was roused by invective launched against the revered order of Brahmins.[80]

This was, however, but one side of the coin. On the other side was the fact that beginning with the last quarter of the eighteenth century, the scholarly world witnessed the translation of Sanskrit literary, legal and philosophical works into English and German, and also the gradual unfolding of Indian history and prehistory through the work of archaeologists, numismatists and epigraphists.[81] The work of Western and Western-inspired scholars resulted in providing new and objective perspectives for Indian civilization: it was a civilization that went back in time to the third millennium B.C., and it was astonishingly versatile. Thus the new elite were given a sense of pride in their country, and its rich and ancient culture. This enabled them to stand up to the Western colossus, and was a continual source of strength in their longing to become a nation, independent, sovereign and equal to others. The discovery of the past was not, however, without its pitfalls and dangers. It produced a certain amount of paleocentrism in all educated Indians and, as is well-known, a great past can be either an energizer or an opiate. In the main, however, it acted as an energizer, and has provided modern India with a mystique for national identity as well as development. Simultaneously with the stimulation of national consciousness came regionalism, "communalism" and casteism; this posed—and continues to pose—serious problems for emergent India.

Related to the ambivalence toward their own society was the other ambivalence, that toward the British. The British were admired and envied for a variety of things: they had political and economic power, organization and discipline. They were the masters of the new knowledge, ideas and technology. They were, by and large, able and just administrators, honest merchants, brave warriors and intrepid hunters. (What also astonished all Hindus was that they ate meat at every meal, and all kinds of meat at that, including polluting pork and forbidden beef, consumed substantial quantities of liquor, and continuously smoked pipes or cheroots.) Even today one occasionally hears from elderly Indians compliments paid to the discipline, sense of dedication and fair-mindedness of the individual Britons with whom they had come into contact. While educated Indians dislike deeply the evangelizing aspect of missionary work, they readily acknowledge the good work done by the missionaries in providing education and medical relief to all sections of the population, and especially to Untouchables and women. Some Indian reform movements such as the Ārya Samāj, Sanātan Dharma Sabha and Khālsa of the Sikhs of the Punjab, the Rāmakrishna Mission of Bengal and the Servants of India Society and the Deccan Education Society of Poona—all emulated the missionaries by starting schools, colleges and hostels. The appreciation of missionary work often led Indians to be very critical of their own society. The continuous perception of the contrast between themselves and their rulers produced a feeling of inferiority among many educated Indians, a feeling which took a variety of expressions and postures from open self-debasement to bitter denunciation of everything Western. Xenophilia, paleocentrism and communism, and the extreme idealization of Indian life and culture coupled with crude caricaturing of Western life and culture, were among the varied reactions of educated Indians to the West, and the same individual often shifted from one posture to another.

The British, especially the less sensitive among them, were arrogant toward Indians and practised exclusiveness as rigorously as the highest of castes. According to Spear:

> A president of the Ethnological Society could argue that Indians were inferior as a race to Europeans. Lord Northbrook complained in the seventies of the general official opinion that no one but an Englishman could do anything.... India was commonly regarded as a conquered country and its people as a subject race. Here again a common evil provoked a common resistance; the Brahmin and the Shudra felt a common grievance and were drawn together for its redress in a way which would never have happened otherwise.[82]

The Christian attacks on Hinduism and India again were deeply resented, especially as the white missionaries enjoyed the tacit support of the British rulers. Racial as well as religious and intellectual arrogance and exclusiveness drove a deep wedge between the British and Indians, and it is generally recognized that the fears aroused by missionary conversions and attacks were a factor in the Indian Mutiny of 1857. The British tendency to treat all castes alike inspired the wrath of the higher Hindu castes and Muslim upper classes.[83]

The new elite had to be two-faced, one face turned toward their own society while the other was turned toward the West. They were spokesmen for the West as far as their people were concerned, and spokesmen for their people as far as the rulers were concerned. They became the indispensable intermediaries between the rulers and the non-Westernized masses, and they acted as a cushion softening the shocks which went periodically from one to the other.

The new elite had to face opposition from the leaders of orthodox opinion. The latter had the power to fine, and to excommunicate (*bahishkāra*), temporarily or permanently, the advocates of heterodoxy. Excommunication was a serious matter, as no member of the caste would have social intercourse, including marriage, with the excommunicated person and his family. Until the new elite increased substantially in numbers, they were subjected to harassment at the hands of the orthodox. D.D. Karve's *The New Brahmins*[84] gives some idea of the trials and tribulations undergone by this pioneer group of dedicated men, whose contributions to the cause of the modernization of Indian society have not been sufficiently appreciated by later generations.

In contending with the orthodox, the new elite had to use arguments which carried weight not only with them, but with the masses as a whole. Thus with the orthodox, the sacred literature of the Hindus, generally referred to as *shāstras*, had great authority, and a custom had to be observed, however obnoxious, because it had been sanctioned or approved by the *shāstra*. "*Shāstra*" is an omnibus term and refers to a number of works, not all of which are of the same degree of authority or always unanimous.[85] Furthermore, in the period before printing became popular, only a handful of learned pundits had access to the sacred literature, and in some cases the texts had been altered by later interpolations: "Later Orientalists like Wilson and Max Müller were to maintain that the one line in the Rig Veda which was held to enjoin *sati* was a deliberate distortion.... But it must be remembered that in 1808–30 the Pandits held the field and those whose opinion was sought by the government were little disposed to question the texts."[86]

Both the orthodox and the leaders of reform appealed to the *shāstras* in support of their views. Even the rationalist Rām Mohan Roy appealed to the *shāstras* in his fight against *suttee*.[87] Vidyāsāgar tried to prove that widowhood was not enjoined by the *shāstras*, and in Bombay, Mandlik sought the permission of pundits for several reforms including voyaging across the seas.[88] Rām Mohan went back to the Vedas in an effort to rid Hinduism of innumerable and evil accretions over the centuries, and Dayānand Saraswati was only following him when he denounced all post-Vedic accretions to Hinduism and founded, in 1875, the Ārya Samāj. It was only in the closing years of the nineteenth century that the leaders of reform began appealing to reason instead of *shāstras* in judging the desirability or otherwise of customs. And in the twentieth century Narayan Chandavarkar loved to call himself a "rational reformer unperturbed by the *shāstras*".[89] Perhaps this was hastened by the realization that caste was the crucial factor in determining customs, not the *shāstras*. Reason was henceforth to be the touchstone, and the new elite were to declare what was reasonable and what was not.

The very people who wanted radical changes in their society, and who were most articulate in denouncing its evils, spoke, when they were addressing the West, of the past glories of India, of the versatility and continuance of its civilization, of the many saints and thinkers India had produced through the ages, and the great and noble ideas they had expressed. This was not "double think", but only that different aspects of the same complex phenomenon were emphasized in different contexts to achieve certain definite ends. Thus Indian society had to be rid of its evils and put on a path that would enable it to develop and eventually compete with Western countries on equal terms. On the other hand, it should be made known to the West, and in particular, Britain, that India was a great country that had temporarily fallen on evil days and that wanted to be free at the earliest possible moment in order to be able to set its house in order. It is ironic that it was largely the work of British and European scholars that had brought to light the greatness, versatility and antiquity of Indian civilization. This discovery contributed to the self-respect of Indians and gave them confidence to face the West as equals, and to demand freedom and the right to develop. The greatness of India was also a familiar theme with Indian politicians addressing Indian crowds, here again it was used to rouse them to join the ranks of the fighters for Indian freedom. But in some Indians paleocentrism represented a flight from the harsh realities of the present.

Prior to the Indian Mutiny of 1857, the British rulers carried out some essential and overdue reforms, laid the foundations of the political, administrative and legal integration of India, and started schools and colleges. In 1857 the three universities of Calcutta, Bombay and Madras were started, and English was the language of teaching in high schools and colleges.

The Mutiny shook the rulers and forced them to an "agonizing reappraisal" of their policy toward India. It resulted in their turning away from innovation, in abandoning the reform of Indian institutions and customs however repugnant to them.[90] But just as the British hopes of the early modernization of India began to fade, the new class of the Westernized elite was beginning to emerge in some strength. The white man was unaware that his burden had already begun to shift onto brown shoulders, and that very soon he would start resisting the transfer of his burden. The new elite gradually grew in numbers, strength and influence, and its desire to introduce radical changes in its society became a passion, a passion with more than a touch of the religious in it. In the process of reforming society, the elite discovered that it needed political power to carry out quickly and successfully the task of modernizing India.

Following the Mutiny, the British decided to pursue a policy of non-interference in religious matters, but this was not easy in view of the pervasive character of Hindu and Islamic religions. They had to continue the work of administrative and political integration of India they had begun several decades earlier, even though this occasionally meant encroaching on religion. The three codes, Civil Procedure Code, Indian Penal Code and the Criminal Procedure Code, were enacted in 1859, 1860 and 1861 respectively, while the Indian Evidence Act came into force in 1872. The Indian Divorce Act was enacted in 1869, and the Special Marriage Act, enabling persons belonging to different castes to marry, in 1872. Several other acts were passed during this period, but codification may be said to have been practically completed by 1882. Legislation relating to land tenures, varying from region to region, was undertaken later. Finally, only Hindu and Muslim personal and family law were left uncodified, but the custom of having Brahmin Pandits and Muslim Kazis as advisors to judges was done away with in 1864.

Sir Charles Wood's dispatch of 1854 had emphasized the need to "extend European knowledge throughout all classes of the people," and this object was to be achieved "by means of the English language in the higher branches of instruction and by that of the vernacular languages to the great mass of the people."[91] In stressing the need to extend primary education through the medium of Indian languages, the government was showing a welcome appreciation of the need to spread education among the masses. Private enterprise in education, including foreign missionary enterprise, was encouraged through a system of grants-in-aid. An education department, headed by a British official, was instituted in each province in 1855.

9

Even to a superficial student of the nineteenth century it is clear that the urge to reform traditional Indian society preceded the urge for freedom. The first response on the part of the new elite was to agitate for the removal of the glaring social evils of contemporary India. The nationalist urge gained gradually in strength in the latter half of the nineteenth century, so much so that in the nineties the question was sharply posed as to whether reform should have priority over freedom or *vice versa*.

The new spirit of self-criticism and the desire to introduce radical changes in Indian society were visible quite early in the nineteenth century in Bengal, and Rām Mohan Roy's activities contributed much to this ferment. The missionary attacks on Hinduism roused both the orthodox and the reformers to close ranks and declaim against Christianity.

> Dr. Duff who arrived in India in that year [1830], noticed that the vernacular press began for the first time to make a vigorous assault on Christianity and bitter hostility towards it was the common characteristic of all the newspapers. A mushroom growth of ephemeral publications sprang up which relied largely on extracts from Paine's *Age of Reason* translated verbatim—*an interesting indication of the extent to which contemporary English literature was studied and used for political purposes.*[92] (Italics mine)

It may be recalled here that the first printing press for the Bengal region was set up in 1801 in Serampore near Calcutta by the Baptist missionaries Carey, Marshman and Ward, and that the first Indian language (Bengāli) journal was published by them in 1818.[93] Calcutta had, by 1830, and influential group of rationalists who were notorious for their total rejection of the indigenous society and who accepted in its place everything Western, including Christianity. It is only apt that they symbolized their acceptance of the West with a meal which included beef.[94] Raja Rām Mohan Roy was too deeply committed to his religion, culture and country to have any sympathy with the Occidentalists, and he founded in 1828 the Brahmo Samāj, a society for the reformation of Hinduism, which was to play an important role in the intellectual and social history of nineteenth century Bengal. The movement toward reform of Indian society continued to gain strength till the last quarter of the nineteenth century, when it found that suddenly a rival interest had begun to grip the minds of the new elite—nationalism. Indian nationalism was fed by the study of European history and English literature, and by the liberal strand—visible from very early in British rule—in British policy toward India. (Familiarity with English literature is visible as early as the 1830s. As far back as 1838, Trevelyan wrote, "Familiarly acquainted with us by means of our literature, the Indian youth almost cease to regard us as foreigners. They speak of our great men with the same enthusiasm as we do. Educated in the same way, interested in the same subjects, engaged in the same pursuits with ourselves, they become more English than Hindu....")[95]

In the latter half of the nineteenth century, the building of railways, the growth of the press and the spread of education all contributed to a sharp rise in nationalism. The failure to admit educated Indians to the higher ranks of the administration[96] and the army, and the practice of racial discrimination by the British, provided an additional impetus to the movement. The nationalist Sārvajanik Sabha was founded in Poona in 1870, and the Indian Association was founded by Sir Surendranath Banerjee in 1876. The latter was an organization of the new elite to create and rouse public opinion by direct appeals to the people. The Indian Association was the precursor of the Indian National Congress, founded in 1885: Its immediate goals were to make the legislatures representative and the civil service more Indian, and its long-term goals were to educate the people politically and secure a form of responsible government.

I shall not attempt here to trace the development of Indian nationalism through its various stages, and shall only point out the paradox that the new elite which started out early in the century with the aim of cleaning the Augean stables of contemporary India found itself overtaken by growing nationalism. Naturally enough, there was a debate, if not a struggle, between those who held that the reform of society should have priority over the demand for freedom and others who held the opposite view. The former section of the Congress were called the "moderates", and the latter, "extremists". The moderates were represented by M.G. Rānade and G.K. Gokhale while the extremists were led by B.G. Tilak. The difference between the two groups was found to be unbridgeable.

> The split came on the double issue over the attitude toward the British Government and the attitude toward social reform. Tilak coined the phrase "swaraj [self-rule] is our birthright"; he would tolerate no compromise with the foreigners, whom he would harry out of the land. In his own mind he drew the line at violence, but it is clear that this was a tactical decision [rather] than a moral conviction. Gokhale believed in reason, in liberal principles, in cooperation and in gradual reform, and he used his great powers of persuasion to advocate these views. They also differed about social reform, a burning question for all nationalists. Gokhale and the moderates wished to press on with this and welcomed government cooperation, for they believed that only through social regeneration could the new Indian nation become

> strong enough to take over the reins of power. Tilak, on the other hand, would have no interference from outside the Hindu body. In his view it should be independence first and social reform afterward.[97]

The conflict ended in a victory for the "extremists" when the Indian National Congress adopted, in 1906, as its goal the "system of self-government obtaining in the self-governing British colonies".[98] An open split between the "extremists" and "moderates" occurred during the following year, at the Surat session of the Congress, ending with the expulsion of the "extremists". However, when nearly thirteen years later Mahatma Gandhi assumed the leadership of the Indian National Congress, programs of social reform were woven into the freedom struggle. Gandhi stressed the need for the eradication of Untouchability, the uplift of women, communal harmony, revival of village industries, and in particular, *Khādi*, "basic" and adult education, propagation of Hindi and prohibition.[99] Louis Dumont observes:

> Gandhi's position between Tilak and Gokhale is highly characteristic; it looks likely that, as the reformists before him, Gandhi was conscious of the contradiction involved in a caste society demanding anything like "home rule", and it may be said that he blended the reformist and the extremist approach in so far as he insisted that India should show her capacity to reform herself even while asking to be left alone.... It is reasonable to suppose that Gandhi's objective was also double: to attain independence and to save Hinduism. In order to attain both ends it was necessary to show the beginning of reform, but reform was, in fact if not consciously, subordinated to independence.[100]

It is doubtful, however, whether anyone, even a Gandhi, could have persuaded the Indian people, after the end of World War I, that reform of their society was more important than Independence. That debate had been settled for good in 1906 at the Calcutta session of the Congress. Besides, the War had produced a marked rise in nationalism, and had roused the expectations of large numbers of Indians that its end would be marked by some form of responsible government for India.

The Westernization of India produced in Indians an urge to change their traditional society, but in the course of time it came to occupy a secondary place beside the even more powerful, in fact almost elemental, urge to freedom. In a country segmented along the lines of religion, caste, language and region, heightened national self-awareness necessarily implied heightened self-awareness at every level of the social structure from the highest to the lowest—the one could not be had without the other. The existence of a considerable degree of overlap between the old and new elites and the consequent exclusion of traditionally underprivileged groups from the new benefits—along with the presence of an alien and powerful ruler who not unnaturally took advantage of the deep divisions within the society—resulted in the division of the subcontinent into India and Pakistan. Independent India is forced, in the interests of her survival, to commit herself to a policy of quick elimination of traditional and hereditary inequalities, and in particular, of Untouchability. The impulse toward equality has resulted in a policy of protective discrimination—or discrimination in reverse—toward tribes, Harijans and backward castes to enable them to catch up with the advanced groups. Finally, in the case of sects and religions, self-awareness has resulted in the reinterpretation of traditions, "communalism",[101] and even revivalism. Revivalist movements such as the Ārya Samāj, the Sanātan Dharma Sabha, the Rāmakrishna Mission, the Sikh Khālsa and the Aligarh Movement, have founded educational institutions imparting modern knowledge, provided hostels and so on. This has produced in the course of time a body of men with western knowledge but who also emphasize the distinctness and superiority of their particular sect or religion. Between them and the nationalists there was an irreconcilable conflict, which has resulted not only in the creation of India and Pakistan, but has provided each country with certain built-in threats to its own survival and development.

NOTES

1. M.N. Srinivas, "A Note on Sanskritization and Westernization", in *Caste in Modern India*, pp. 42–62.
2. *Encyclopaedia Britannica*, vol. 22, 1962, p. 894A.
3. As a matter of actual fact, however, the British did not always insist on government schools being open to Harijan children. "Few, if any, of the *antyaja* [Harijan] are found in Government schools. This is to

be ascribed not only to the Brahmanical fear of contamination and the general caste prejudices of the people, but to the want of firmness on the part of the Government educational authorities as has been the case in some instances of the agents of the missionary bodies." (John Wilson, *Indian Caste*, vol. II, 1877, p. 45.) Professor Ghurye mentions that even as late as 1915 a press note of the Government of Bombay referred to the "familiar sight of Mahar and other depressed class boys in village schools where the boys are often not allowed to enter the schoolroom but are accommodated outside on the verandah." (*Caste and Class in India*, p. 166.)

4. See Benjamin Lindsay, "Law", in L.S.S. O'Malley (ed.), *Modern India and the West*, Oxford, 1941, pp. 107–137.
5. L.S.S. O'Malley, "The Impact of European Civilization", in L.S.S. O'Malley (ed.), *op. cit.*, p. 59.
6. P. Spear, *The Twilight of the Mughals*, Cambridge, England, 1951, p. 95.
7. See in this connection P. Spear, *India, a Modern History*, p. 286. Also Kingsley Davis, *The Population of India and Pakistan*, Princeton, N.J., 1951, pp. 38–41.
8. See D. Lerner, *The Passing of Traditional Society*, Glencoe, Ill., 1958, pp. 45–49.
9. *Ibid.*, p. 45.
10. *Ibid.*, p. 48.
11. *Ibid.*, p. 47.
12. *Ibid.*
13. *Ibid.*
14. R. Bellah, Epilogue to *Religion and Progress in Modern Asia*, edited by R.N. Bellah, Glencoe, Ill., 1965, pp. 195–196.
15. *Ibid.*, n. 23, p. 227.
16. Lynn White, Jr., *Medieval Technology and Social Change*, Oxford, 1962, pp. 129–130.
17. *Ibid.*, p. 131.
18. At festivals, however, dining leaves may be spread on the table, or the table given up for the floor.
19. Shanti Tangri, "Intellectuals and Society in Nineteenth Century India", *Comparative Studies in Society and History*, vol. III, no. 4, July, 1961, p. 376.
20. B.S. Cohn, "The British in Benares: A Nineteenth Century Colonial Society", in *Comparative Studies in Society and History*, vol. IV, no. 2, January, 1962, pp. 172–173. I have relied on Cohn's important paper for my view of British society in India at that time. See also R.E. Frykenberg's "British Society in Guntur During the Early Nineteenth Century", in *Comparative Studies in Society and History*, vol. 4, no. 2, 1962, pp. 200–208. Russell, writing in 1857, gave the following account of social distinctions among the British in

India: "The social distinctions are by no means lost sight of in India; on the contrary, they are perhaps more rigidly observed here than at home, and the smaller the society the broader are the lines of demarcation. Each man depends on his position in the public service, which is the aristocracy.... The women depend on the rank of their husbands. Mrs. A., the wife of a barrister, making £4000 or £5000 a year, is nobody compared with the wife of B. who is a deputy commissioner, or with Mrs. C., who is the better half of the station surgeon. Wealth can do nothing for a man or woman is securing them honour or precedency in their march to dinner.... A successful speculator, or a 'merchant prince' may force his way into good society in England ... but in India he must remain forever outside the sacred barrier, which keeps the non-official world from the high society of the services." Quoted in Hilton Brown, *The Sahibs*, London, 1948.

21. "The lower orders of British society are not represented at all in the civilians of the Company, and I have found no information that would lead me to suspect that the working class, or even small traders and merchants, provided sons for the service." Cohn, see *supra* note 20.
22. *Ibid.*, p. 199.
23. The official class in Madras also had similar ties. Frykenberg, see *supra* note 20, p. 207.
24. Cohn, *op. cit.*, pp. 173, 198.
25. "By the 1840s, however, the Company's officials themselves were heavily committed to mission work." Cohn, *op. cit.*, p. 196.
26. Cohn, *op. cit.*, p. 173.
27. Olive Douglas has narrated an incident which illustrates what I mean: "Coming home we saw a native cooking his dinner on a little charcoal fire, and as I passed he threw the contents of the pot away. Surprised, I asked why. 'Because,' I was told, 'your shadow fell on it and defiled it!'" (*Olivia in India*, London, 1913, quoted in Hilton Brown, *op. cit.*, p. 230.)
28. Frykenberg, see *supra* note 20, p. 205.
29. *Ibid.*, pp. 204–205.
30. *Ibid.*, p. 208.
31. Cohn, *op. cit.*, p. 190.
32. Kingsley Davis, *The Population of India and Pakistan*, pp. 115–117.
33. Tangri, see *supra* note 19, p. 287.
34. Peasants seem to have imported legal forms and concepts from British or British-inspired law courts to traditional village *panchayats*. See my "A Caste Dispute Among the Washermen of Mysore", *Eastern Anthropologist*, vol. VII, Nos. 3–4, March–August, 1954. The impact of British law on traditional *panchayats* needs to be

explored systematically if we wish to further our understanding of Westernization in an important area.

35. Tangri, *op. cit.*, p. 385.
36. Tangri, *op. cit.*, p. 384. Arrah and Chapra are both located in Bihar. They were formerly known as Shahabad and Saran respectively. In 1961 Arrah had a population of 76,766 and Chapra, 75,580.
37. The 1941 percentages were 71.09 for Hindus, 22.93 for Muslims, 1.58 for Christians, 0.27 for Jains and 1.33 for Sikhs. Figures are not available for Pārsis and Jews (Davis, *op. cit.*, p. 142.)
38. See for instance B. Shiva Rao, "Labor in India", *Annals of the American Academy of Political and Social Science*, vol. 233, 1944, p. 128. See also Randhakamal Mukherjee, *The Indian Working Class* (third edition), Bombay, 1951, p. 6.
39. M.D. Morris, "Caste and the Evolution of the Industrial Workforce in India", *Proceedings of the American Philosophical Society*, vol. 104, no. 2, April, 1960, p. 124.
40. *Ibid.*, p. 130.
41. R.D. Lambert, *Workers, Factories and Social Change in India*, Princeton, 1963, pp. 34–36.
42. See in this connection C.A. Myers, *Industrial Relations in India*, Bombay, 1960, p. 92, note 12. The Department of Sociology in the University of Delhi made a survey of the Okhla Industrial Estate near Delhi during 1961–1962, and it revealed that, out of a sample of 162 workers, 73 came from the high Hindu castes and the rest from the artisan castes. Sixteen of the Sikhs were from high castes and 13 from artisan castes, and the remaining 7 workers were Christians.
43. Lambert, *op. cit.*, pp. 161–162. Narayan Sheth who made an intensive study of an engineering factory in Baroda in 1957–1959 informs me that 26 per cent of the workers in it came from the high castes of Brahmin, Bania and Pātidār; 25 per cent from castes immediately below them; 14 per cent, artisan castes; 22 per cent, low castes (Bāria, Kolī, etc.); 7 per cent, Harijans; and 6 per cent, "others", including Muslims. Sheth thinks that the high percentage of the high castes among workers may have been due to the fact that the factory produced equipment like switch gear and electric motors which demanded skill from the workers. (Personal communication to the author.)
44. H.A. Gould, "Sanskritization and Westernization, a Dynamic View", *Economic Weekly*, vol. XIII, no. 25, June 24, 1961, p. 947.
45. *Ibid.*
46. See Dr. M.S.A. Rao, "Caste and the Indian Army", *Economic Weekly*, vol. XVI, no. 35, August 29, 1964, pp. 1439–1443. For the last forty years the Ahīr Kshatriya Mahāsabha of Uttar Pradesh has been publishing a monthly journal, *Yādav*.

47. See W. L. Rowe, "The New Chauhans: A Caste Mobility Movement in North India", in J. Silverberg (ed.), *Social Mobility in Caste in India*, special issue of *Comparative Studies in Society and History*. See *supra* chap. 1, note 27.
48. B.S. Cohn, "Changing Traditions of a Low Caste", in M. Singer (ed.), *Traditional India: Structure and Change*, pp. 209–211.
49. *Ibid.*
50. Morris, see *supra* note 39, p. 126.
51. E. Shils, *The Intellectual Between Tradition and Modernity: The Indian Situation*, The Hague, 1961, p. 20.
52. B.B. Misra, *The Indian Middle Classes*, Oxford, 1961, p. 54.
53. S. Harrison, *India: The Most Dangerous Decades*, Princeton, N.J., 1960, p. 55.
54. P. Tandon, *Punjabi Century, 1857–1947*, London, 1961, pp. 76–77.
55. The study of the elites in three different regions of India by historians confirms such continuity. The subsequent rise of what are called "counter-elites" in regions such as Madras and Uttar Pradesh also assumes continuity. See in this connection the following papers read at the meeting of the Association for Asian Studies in San Francisco, April 2-4, 1965: (1) J.H. Broomfield, "An Elite and Its Rivals: The Bengal Bhadralok at the Opening of the Twentieth Century"; (2) P.R. Brass, "Regionalism, Nationalism and Political Conflict in Uttar Pradesh"; and (3) E. Irschick, "The Brahmin and Non-Brahmin Struggle for Power in Madras". (Mimeographed)
56. P. Spear, *India, a Modern History*, Ann Arbor, Mich., 1961, p. 300.
57. *Ibid.* and Misra, *op. cit.*, pp. 53–54.
58. N.K. Bose, "Some Aspects of Caste in Bengal", in Milton Singer (ed.), *Traditional India: Structure and Change*, pp. 197–198.
59. D.F. Pocock, "The Movement of Castes", *Man*, vol. LV, May 1955, pp. 71–72.
60. F.G. Bailey, *Caste and the Economic Frontier*, Oxford, 1958, p. 186.
61. Spear, *op. cit.*, p. 278.
62. *Ibid.*, p. 397.
63. M.N. Srinivas, *Caste in Modern India*, Bombay, 1962, p. 24.
64. M. Patterson, "Caste and Political Leadership in Maharashtra", *Economic Weekly*, September 25, 1954, pp. 1065–1067.
65. N.K. Bose in Singer (ed.) see *supra* note 58, p. 200.
66. Bailey, *op. cit.*, p. 190.
67. Information given by Owen Lynch, Department of Anthropology, Columbia University.
68. A. Beteille, *Caste, Class and Power*, Berkeley and Los Angeles, 1966.
69. Spear, *op. cit.*, p. 409.
70. See Mrs. Aparna Basu's review of Z. H. Faruqi's *The Deoband School and the Demand for Pakistan* (Bombay, 1963), in *The Indian Economic*

and Social History Review, vol. 1, no. 3, January–March, 1964, pp. 101–103.

71. S. Radhakrishnan, *Eastern Religions and Western Thought*, New York, 1959, p. 313.
72. A.L. Basham, *The Wonder That Was India*, New York, 1959.
73. See D.G. Mandelbaum, "Culture Change Among the Nilgiri Tribes", *American Anthropologist*, vol. 43, January–March, 1941. The use of the caste model in tribal and other frontier areas needs to be studied. An understanding of this phenomenon will throw light on the spread of caste across the subcontinent in historical times.
74. Radhakrishnan, *op. cit.*, p. 312.
75. M. Galanter, *Comparative Studies in Society and History*, vol. VII, no. 2, January 1965, pp. 133–159.
76. Basham, *op. cit.*, pp. 240–241, 246.
77. J.E. Carpenter, *Theism in Mediaeval India*, London, 1926, p. 448. See also pp. 428 and 452.
78. Misra, see *supra* note 52, pp. 209–210.
79. Spear, see *supra* note 56, p. 293.
80. O'Malley, see *supra* note 5, p. 69.
81. Basham, *op. cit.*, pp. 4–8.
82. Spear, see *supra* note 56, pp. 306–307.
83. O'Malley, see *supra* note 5, p 78.
84. D. D. Karve, *The New Brahmins*, Berkeley and Los Angeles, 1963. S. Natarajan has remarked that "It is difficult in the light of existing conditions [today] to appreciate adequately the single-mindedness and high purpose which the social reformers brought to their work. That in itself is an index to the distance that the country has covered in a hundred years." (*A Century of Social Reform in India*, Bombay, 1959, p. 198.)
85. "*Sruti* is the highest authority; next in importance is *smriti*, or the tradition set up by human beings; and it is authoritative in so far as it is not repugnant to the Veda from which it derives its authority. Practices or customs (*ācāra*) are trustworthy if they are adopted by the cultured. Individual conscience is also authoritative." (S. Radhakrishnan, *Religion and Society*, London, 1947, p. 111.) The term "śruti" is used for Vedic literature which consists of the four Vedas and Brāhmanas, Āranyakas, Upanishads and Sūtras. Only the Vedas are revealed by God while the others are commentaries, and the former's authority is therefore superior to the latter's. Of the Vedas, the Atharva, containing as it does magical spells and so on, is inferior in authority to the others—it was not even recognized as a Veda till about 300 B.C. Yajur and Sāma Vedas are later than the first and highest Veda, Rig. Some of the material in Yajur and Sāma Vedas is a repetition of what is in the Rig Veda.

86. S. Natarajan, *A Century of Social Reform in India*, p. 34.
87. *Ibid.*, pp. 33–34.
88. O'Malley, see *supra* note 5, p. 67.
89. Natarajan, *op. cit.*, p. 117.
90. Spear, see *supra* note 56, p. 279.
91. J.R. Cunningham, "Education", in L.S.S. O'Malley (ed.), *Modern India and the West*, p. 153.
92. O'Malley, see *supra* note 5, p. 70.
93. Tangri, see *supra* note 19, p. 376.
94. Spear, see *supra* note 56, p. 292; see also N.K. Bose, "East and West in Bengal", *Man in India*, vol. 38, no. 3, July–September 1958, pp. 162–163.
95. C.E. Trevelyan, *On the Education of the People of India*, p. 190, quoted by O'Malley, see *supra* note 5, p. 92.
96. See Majumdar *et al.*, *An Advanced History of India*, pp. 888–898; and O'Malley, see *supra* note 5, pp. 88–92.
97. Spear, see *supra* note 56, p. 314. See also in this connection L. Dumont, "Nationalism and Communalism", *Contributions to Indian Sociology*, vol. VII, March, 1964, pp. 62–64.
98. Majumdar *et al.*, *op. cit.*, p. 981.
99. J.V. Bondurant, *Conquest of Violence*, Princeton, 1958, pp. 180–181.
100. L. Dumont, *op. cit.*, p. 63.
101. "Communalism in India is defined as 'that ideology which emphasizes as the social, political and economic unit the group of adherents of each religion, and emphasizes the distinction, even the antagonism, between such groups' (p. 185)." (L. Dumont, *op. cit.*, p. 39, quoting W.C. Smith, *The Muslim League*, Lahore, 1945.)

3

SOME EXPRESSIONS OF CASTE MOBILITY

1

THE FULL IMPLICATIONS of Westernization are indeed revolutionary for India, if what has already happened is any indication. That Westernization is indeed a fundamental process, and not something superficial and external, is made clear by the fact that it is the Indian elite who have taken upon themselves the great task of modernizing their society. Indeed, it is my contention that no alien body, however powerful and competent, could have introduced the changes which the indigenous elite have, in the brief period since India became independent.

The foundations for these changes were laid by the establishment of British rule over India, and the consequences, direct and indirect, which flowed from it. In the first place, the new technology brought by the British made possible the effective administrative and political integration of the entire subcontinent. The building of a network of roads, the creation of a modern country-wide bureaucracy and the steps taken toward establishing a uniform legal system were all indispensable to administrative and political integration. These, together with the ending of local wars everywhere, the stamping out of *thuggee*, the abolition of slavery, the introduction of tenurial reforms, the opening up of plantations for such crops as tea, coffee, cotton, tobacco and indigo, and the development of towns and cities laid the basis for the eventual economic development of the country. The establishment of schools and colleges for imparting modern education, and the institution of law courts, both being in theory open to all irrespective of caste or religion, were striking departures from similar, pre-British institutions. The study of Western literature, political thought, history and law made the Indian elite sensitive to such new values as the equality of all men (and women) before the law, and civil rights. European missionary attacks on Hinduism, Untouchability and caste, and missionary-run schools, orphanages and hospitals all played their part in the social reforms which have been introduced in the last 140 years in India, and in creating an ideological and moral climate favourable to Westernization.

I am aware that in the above passage I have not only oversimplified facts but somewhat idealized them; but my aim here is only to provide a background to the discussion of social mobility in the caste system and not to attempt a critical evaluation of British rule.

The new opportunities—educational, economic, political—were *in theory* caste-free; that is, they were open to all, and no one was banned from having access to them by reason of birth in a particular caste or sect or religion. Actually, however, as I pointed out earlier, they were ordinarily more accessible to the high castes with a tradition of learning, employment in the government, and urban residence. In addition there were, in each region, a few castes which, although not regarded as high, became relatively wealthy by reason of their ability to exploit certain special opportunities that came their way during British rule. Examples of such success are provided by the Teli or Oilman castes of Eastern India, the Distillers in Orissa and elsewhere, the Noniyas (salt-makers) of Uttar Pradesh, the Koḷīs of coastal Gujarat and the Khārwas of Saurāshtra. (Bailey mentions how a Ganjam Harijan became wealthy by local standards by engaging himself in trade in hides and skins, for which modern communications had provided a much wider market than would have been available traditionally. The handling of hides and skins is traditionally done by the Untouchable castes, and here is a good example of caste providing a monopoly.[1])

When a low caste became wealthy, it usually followed this up by Sanskritizing its style of life and ritual and claiming to be a high caste. Noniyas, Ahīrs, Distillers and many others took this beaten track to high status. (As I have said elsewhere, similar mobility was extremely difficult for Untouchable castes who had become wealthy by local standards.[2]) Sanskritization was able to resolve the inconsistency between newly acquired wealth and low ritual rank. In the Indian context, it made "passing" possible.

I would like to mention yet another consequence, perhaps much more important from a long-range point of view, of the occasional upward mobility of a low caste. It had what economists call a "demonstration effect" on all low castes in the region, bringing home to them in a poignant way that they could move out of their own unenviable position. They could, as it were, get their own back on those who had looked down on them. It was as though they suddenly woke up to the fact that they were no longer inhabiting a prison.

What were the effects of the more common phenomenon of the high castes' obtaining the new education and, through it, prestigious and well-paid positions including jobs in the administration? In the first place, it increased the cultural, social and economic distance between them and the lower castes. Second, it provided the higher with a new area for emphasizing their distinction from the lower: the lower castes may Sanskritize their style of life—this was not too difficult in view of there being no legal ban on Sanskritization under the British—but Westernization requires money, time and effort, and contact with influential people.

As far as the lower castes were concerned, Westernization became doubly desirable—it subsumed not only things valuable in themselves but something which the high castes had and they did not. To catch up with the high castes, mere Sanskritization was not enough. Thus they became more determined to obtain Western education and the fruits that only it could yield. High-caste dominance in education and in the new occupations thus provided the *raison d'être* for the Backward Classes Movement.[3] It is no accident that the Movement was strongest in peninsular India where only one caste (in the *varna* sense), the Brahmins, enjoyed a preponderance in higher education, the professions and government employment. It is also an area where a wide social and cultural gulf obtained between the Brahmins and others.

The desire for social mobility was articulated through caste groups. The increase in horizontal solidarity which occurred with improvement in communications enabled allied *jātis* living over a wide region to be drawn into the mobility process. Caste associations came into existence in different parts of the country, and each association had as its aim the improvement of the social and economic standing of its caste. Many published journals devoted to caste welfare, collected funds for endowing scholarships and building hostels for students from their respective castes, and undertook programs of reform of caste customs. These reforms were generally aimed at Sanskritizing the style of life and ritual, and occasionally at reducing the expenditure on weddings and funerals.

Mobility aspirations became interwoven with pre-existing rivalries between local castes; this had the effect of further intensifying the rivalries. In this context, the urge to be a step ahead of one's structural neighbours must be distinguished from a general movement toward equality. While a caste struggled for a higher position for itself in the local hierarchy it resented the efforts of others, in particular lower castes, to move up. Its attitude may be summed up as, "I am equal to those who think of themselves as my betters, I am better than those who regard themselves as my equals, and how dare my inferiors claim equality with me?" G. Berreman's account of the situation in the Himalayan village of Sirkanda is probably true of large areas of India: "In Sirkanda those low caste people who spoke most piously against high-caste abuses were likely to be equally abusive to their caste inferiors. However, no low caste was encountered whose members did not seriously question its place in the hierarchy."[4]

But implicit in the general struggle of castes for upward movement is the idea of equality. It is true that the peasant who says he is as good as the Brahmin resents the Harijan's claim that he is as good as the peasant and the Brahmin, but in the long run both the higher castes have to accept it. Currently, clashes between high castes and assertive Harijans are reported from different parts of the country, but this is part of the process of translating rights given in the Constitution to Harijans into reality at the village level. As more and more Harijans become educated and seek the enforcement of the constitutional rights, local clashes are likely to increase rather than decrease.

In the course of taking advantage of the new opportunities and improving their position, caste groups are undergoing change in their very nature; this has recently been the subject of some discussion.[5] I shall consider this later. But I would like to refer briefly to the common assumption in all these writings that the traditional system was a closed one and that in it no mobility was possible. I cannot subscribe to that view; in chapter 1, I have tried to show that mobility was possible, though not easy, in the traditional system, and that it did actually occur occasionally. One of the most potent sources of mobility lay in the system's political fluidity. Any caste that achieved political power at the local level could advance a claim to be Kshatriyas. Second, the king in traditional India had the power to promote as well as to demote castes, and he occasionally exercised this power to bestow a favour on a caste or punish it. It is presumed that the king consulted Brahmins learned in the law before he promoted or demoted a caste, but this meant only that the power exercised had to be subject to some conditions. Third, the availability, in pre-British India, of land which, with some effort, could be brought under the plough enabled families that were dissatisfied with local conditions to move out into new areas. Burton Stein thinks that the fear of such movement on the part of discontented peasants acted as a check on the arbitrariness of rulers. He contrasts the mobility characteristic of the medieval, open agrarian system with mobility in modern times which occurs within a narrow, localized ranking system, and argues that the divisions characteristic of the great peasant castes of India have arisen from the former.[6]

Sanskritization, as mentioned earlier, enabled low castes which had acquired wealth or political power to shed their low ritual status and be included among the high castes. We may recall, however, that while the traditional system allowed individual castes to move up or down, the system itself remained unaltered. In other words, there was only positional change, not structural change.

Traditional or pre-British India may be regarded as on the whole a religious society, whereas modern India has experienced steadily increasing secularization since her conquest by Britain. Religious values were both pervasive and dominant, and the king had the final responsibility to enforce caste distinctions as well as to arbitrate in disputes regarding caste matters. In traditional India Sanskritization was not only of great importance for the ambitious caste but was difficult of achievement, as there were both religious and legal sanctions against taking over the ritual and style of life of the twice-born castes. The British refusal to enforce the ban on Sanskritization made it accessible in theory to everyone, though everywhere the locally dominant castes often used the sanctions at their disposal—boycott and physical violence—to prevent lower castes from rising. But with the increase in spatial mobility and urbanization, and with more and more castes participating in the new educational and employment opportunities, fear of boycott and physical violence by the dominant caste diminished if it did not disappear. Sanskritization came to be seen by the lower castes as an adjunct to other and more important things, such as education, prestigious employment and political power. They also saw that by itself it was of extremely limited value in raising the position of a caste. This is illustrated clearly in the Backward Classes Movement, which I shall consider presently.

2

An indication of the widespread desire for mobility among the backward castes comes from an unusual source, namely, the census operations. The first time a nation-wide census was undertaken was during the years 1867–1871, and on this occasion two Tamil peasant castes, Vellālas and Padaiyāchis, wanted to be recorded as belonging to a higher *varna* than that popularly conceded to them; the Vellālas protested against being included among Shūdras and wanted to be called Vaishyas, while the Padaiyāchis wanted to be called "Vanniya Kula Kshatriyas". Twenty years later a book was written, *Vanniyakula Vilakkam*, in support of the Padaiyāchi claim.[7] This tendency on the part of castes to take advantage of the census operations for achieving mobility became widespread with the census of 1901, when Sir Herbert Risley, the Census Commissioner, decided to provide in the census an accurate record of the ranking of *jātis* in the local hierarchy as well as the *varna* affiliation of each. The results could have been predicted by anyone who had a knowledge of the dynamics of caste system at the local level. In Ghurye's words:

> Various ambitious castes quickly perceived the chances of raising their status. They invited conferences of their members, and formed councils to take steps to see that their status was recorded in the way they thought was honourable to them. Others that could not but resent this "stealthy" procedure to advance, equally eagerly began to controvert their claims. Thus a campaign of mutual recrimination was set on foot. "The leaders of all but the highest castes frankly looked upon the Census as an opportunity for pressing and

> perhaps obtaining some recognition of social claims which were denied by persons of castes higher than their own."[8]

It might be said that the historical role which Indian rulers had played as the final arbiters of the ranking of castes within their jurisdiction, including the ability to promote as well as demote castes, was now transferred by the people to the new rulers; and the ranks accorded to castes in census reports became the equivalent of traditional copper-plate grants declaring the status, rank and privileges of a particular caste or castes.

The tendency on the part of castes to claim to be recorded in the census as a high caste increased as the years went by, and more and more people became aware of the existence of a new and government-sponsored channel of caste mobility. O'Malley has recorded that at the time of the 1911 census operations:

> There was a general idea in Bengal that the *object of the census is not to show the number of persons belonging to each caste, but to fix the relative position of different castes and to deal with questions of social superiority.* The feeling on the subject is largely the result of castes having been classified in the last census report in order of social precedence. This warrant of precedence gave rise to a considerable agitation when the census operations were instituted in 1911. *Hundreds of petitions were received from different castes—their weight alone amounts to one and a half maunds*[9]*—requesting that they might be known by a new name, be placed higher up in the order of precedence, be recognized as Kshatriya and Vaishya, etc.* Many castes were aggrieved at the position assigned them, and complained that it lowered them in public estimation."[10] (Italics mine)

Over the years this tendency became so pronounced that at the 1941 census the British Census Commissioner eliminated the column about caste.[11]

The method of making a claim was more or less stereotyped. The occupation, style of life, or name of the caste group would be mentioned in support of the claim. The similarity of caste name to the historical name of a respectable caste or tribe would be pointed out, the myth regarding the origin of the caste would be described, and its linkage with an epic hero, or divine or semi-divine figure, would be stressed. Thus the Hunters (Bedas) of Mysore would claim kinship with Vālmīki, the putative author of the epic Rāmāyana about whom there is a legend that he was a hunter; and similarly the Shepherds (Kurubas) link their caste history with the name of the great Sanskrit poet and playwright, Kālidāsa, who is believed to have been a shepherd by caste. Reference would also be made to the sacred literature of the Hindus and a few Sanskrit quotations thrown in to add strength to the claim. In Uttar Pradesh the ambitious claimants were able to find obliging Brahmin pandits who provided *vyavasthas* or rulings to the effect that the caste in question was indeed a high one. The ruling was usually followed by citation of 'evidence' of the kind I have already mentioned.

In the beginning the demand for being recorded in the census as a high caste emanated from leaders of the caste groups concerned. This resulted in some cases in a certain amount of confusion, since different sections of a single caste claimed to be different *varnas* in different places, and the same caste changed its claim from census to census (see Table 1). The chances of the occurrence of such discrepancies diminished, though were not entirely obviated, with the formation of caste *sabhas* or associations. Such *sabhas* were not unknown previously, but the census operations of 1901 made them more popular. There were numerous caste *sabhas* in several areas including Madras Presidency in 1911, and by the time of the next census—which, incidentally, came after the passing of the Government of India Act of 1919—they were an all-India phenomenon.[12] The caste *sabhas* articulated as well as organized the new urge to mobility. They represented to the census authorities the demand of individual castes to belong to a particular *varna* and not to a lower one. The Superintendent of the 1931 United Provinces Census, for instance, received 175 claims (13 from outside the United Provinces), of which 34 were made through caste *sabhas*. (See Table 2 for an analysis of the claims received at the 1931 census from a few North Indian areas.) Second, the *sabhas* altered the style of life of their castes in the direction of Sanskritization. This often involved the giving up of the forbidden meat (chicken, pork and carrion beef) and liquor, and the donning of the sacred thread; and in Uttar Pradesh and Bihar, the shortening of the mourning period to correspond with that of the twice-born castes. In the case of very "low" castes it also involved the nonperformance of a traditional and degrading duty such as *corvée* or other free labour, or carrying palanquins, or beating the tom-tom on ceremonial occasions. The reactions of the dominant high castes to such efforts at reform on the part

TABLE 1
Status Claims of Some Castes at Census

Caste	*Occupation*	*1911 Census*	*1921 Census*	*1931 Census*
Kamār	Blacksmith	—	Kshatriya	Brahmin
Sonār	Goldsmith	Kshatriya-Rājpūt	Kshatriya-Rājpūt	Brahmin-Vaishya
Sutradār	Carpenter	Vaishya	Vaishya	Brahmin
Nāī	Barber	—	Thākur	Brahmin
Nāpit	Barber	Kshatriya	Baidya	Brahmin
Rawani Kahār	Water/palanquin carrier	—	Vaishya	Kshatriya
Mochi	Cobbler	—	Baidya Rishi	Kshatriya
Chamār	Tanner	—	Baidya Rishi	Kshatriya
Bhatt	Musician	Brahma Bhatt	Brahma Bhatt	Brahmabhatt-Brahmin
Chandāl	—	Nāmashūdra*	Nāmashūdra-Brahmin	Nāmashūdra-Brahmin
Chāsi Khaibarta	Fisherman	Mahisya	Mahisya	Mahisya Kshatriya
Khatri	Trader	—	Kshatriya	Vaishya
Teli	Oil miller	Rāthore-Teli	Not available	Rāthore-Vaishya

* They were allowed this name in 1911.

TABLE 2

Caste Claims Advanced During the 1931 Census

	No. of castes	*New status claimed*													*More than one claim*[2]	*Total claims*[3]
		Brahmin			*Kshatriya*			*Vaishya*			*New name*			*Muslim*		
		S[1]	U	T	S	U	T	S	U	T	S	U	T			
United Provinces	63	13	1	1	25	11	1	6	3	—	8	5	—	7	15	81
Bengal & Sikkim	44	6	1	—	13	6	1	3	2	1	12	6	—	—	6	51
Bihar & Orissa	17	7	—	—	4	3	1	—	—	—	2	—	1	1	2	19
Central Provinces & Berar	24	5	—	—	7	6	2	—	—	—	—	2	1	1	—	24
Total	148[4]	31	2	1	49	26	5	9	5	1	22	13	2	9	23	175

1. S (Shūdra), U (Untouchable) and T (Tribal) refer to traditional positions in the particular province.
2. Wherever a caste claimed more than one status, all the claims were settled.
3. There were 34 claims to Brahmin status, 80 claims to Kshatriya status, 15 claims to Vaishya status and 37 claims were new names. Among Muslims, 9 groups took new names.
4. 148 castes made 175 claims, 23 of them making more than one claim., a few making three.

Source: 1931 Census Report, Part I:
A.C. Turner, United Provinces of Agra and Oudh, Vol. XVII, pp. 529–532.
A.E. Porter, Bengal and Sikkim, Vol. V, pp. 427—428.
W.G. Lacy, Bihar and Orissa, Vol. VII, p. 263.
W.H. Shoobert, Central Provinces and Berar, Vol. XII, p. 354.

of their traditional inferiors varied from indifference, on the one hand, to the use of violence in order to enforce performance of duties, and keep the parvenus in their place. Thus the Rājpūts and Bhumihār Brahmins of North Bihar used violence against the Ahīrs (Cowherds) who claimed to be Kshatriyas and donned the sacred thread.[13]

> In Cuttack and Balasore, for example, the Gauras were striving to get themselves recognized as Yaduvanshi Kshatriya. They not only assumed the sacred thread but refused to work as palanquin-bearers. Their attempt to discard their traditional occupation was resisted by other communities. The Khandaits and Karans who were generally the most influential and well-to-do among the local inhabitants led the opposition and the rivalry ripened into actual riots at several places. Similar situations arose at several other places.[14]

Heightened self-awareness among castes and the formation of caste *sabhas* resulted in increasing the "horizontal stretch" of castes. A classical example of horizontal stretch is provided by the Ahīrs, who founded the Gopi Jatiya Sabha in 1912, and which included, in a few years' time, cowherding *jātis* from all over North India from the Punjab to Bengal. The Sabha published a monthly journal, *Ahīr Samāchār* (Ahīr News), from Mainpuri in the United Provinces. An annual conference attracted several thousand Ahīrs from different parts of North India. This started interdining among different cowherding *jātis*.[15]

In short, the attempt to use the census to freeze the rank of castes had the opposite effect of stimulating mobility, and also increased intercaste rivalry. It is small wonder, then, that nationalist Indians began to regard the recording of caste at the census as yet another manifestation of a sinister design on the part of the imperialist British to keep alive if not exacerbate the numerous divisions already present in Indian society. Their suspicions were further strengthened by the attempt to distinguish Untouchables from other Hindus in the 1911 census operations.[16] Moreover, while the earlier census reports recorded caste divisions not only among Hindus but also among Muslims and Christians, the later reports recorded only the former; this confirmed the nationalists in their worst suspicions.[17]

The thirties were marked by a sharp rise in nationalism. Indian nationalists were opposed not only to the recording of caste in the census but to the fact that areas inhabited predominantly by the tribes were excluded from popular control in the Government of India Act of 1935.[18]

3

I shall now discuss briefly the Backward Classes Movement. Signs of the awakening of the backward classes are to be found in every part of the country, and one of the urgent tasks before sociologists studying India is to obtain well-documented accounts of this movement, so important a part of modern India's social, ideological and political history. While the movement was—and still is to some extent—very prominent in South India, and the Tamil country its heart and soul, it showed itself elsewhere too, sometimes disguised under other movements. For instance, even in Bengal, where caste consciousness is alleged to be weak, the Yogis and Nāmashūdras evinced a keen desire to improve their status about the beginning of this century.[19] In its later phase—around 1911—the Arya Samāj movement of North India seems to have made a strong appeal to "low" castes in some districts of the Punjab and Uttar Pradesh. The Samāj founded the *Shuddhi* movement to prevent low castes from being converted to other religions and to reclaim those who had been already. In the Punjab, a separate society was formed to raise the status of Untouchables through the *Shuddhi* movement.[20]

Recent village studies confirm that the Arya Samāj did have an appeal to Harijan castes in Western Uttar Pradesh. In Bihar and Orissa, it had a strong appeal for low castes such as Kūrmis, Goalas and Musahārs.[21] Sikhism also provided a channel of mobility for several low castes:

> The proselytizing activities of the Akāli movement induced a large number of persons, particularly sweepers, to return as Sikhs instead of Hindus. The members of the lower castes, artisan and occupational groups, obviously considered that they gained in status as soon as they ceased to be Hindus and became Sikhs.... A Māli, for instance, whose numerical strength showed great variations in 1931, gained in prestige by becoming a Sikh, Māli being a distinctly inferior caste. Similarly, the Jāt in Jullunder and Hoshiārpur, if a Hindu, was

> looked down upon by his Hindu Rājpūt neighbours, and so became a Sikh. On the other hand, in the south-east of the Province a Hindu Jāt took pride in his caste and even looked down upon a Brahmin who in that area was not a priestly caste but cultivators. Similar influences were operative in castes such as Tarkhāna, Lohār, Nāi, Sonār, etc.[22]

The Pātidārs, the great landed caste of Gujarat, have been moving up in caste and class hierarchy in the last two hundred fifty years or so, and in particular since the closing years of the nineteenth century. In the years since 1947, the "low" but populous Koḷī-Bāriā castes have shown much dynamism, and are seeking mobility through the acquisition of political power. This is accompanied by much hostility toward their traditional masters, the Pātidārs.

In India south of the river Godāvari—with the exception of Hyderabad and parts of Kerala—the term "Backward" included until the 1950s, all castes except the Brahmin; in fact anti-Brahminism provided a rallying point for a highly heterogeneous group which included a wide variety of castes from different linguistic areas, even Muslims, Christians and Pārsis. The ideological center of this movement was Madras City though there were other, secondary centers such as Madura, Kalladakurichi, Chidambaram, Bāngalore, Kolhāpur and Poona. The composite character of the former Madras Presidency enabled the seeds of the new ideology to spread to the whole of South India. Old Madras included, besides the Tamil and Telugu areas, parts of Malayālam- and Kannada-speaking areas. Ideas could therefore travel quickly from Madras to other parts of South India. The cultural and intellectual predominance of Madras in the life of South India in the pre-Independence period had the effect of causing educated groups everywhere in the South to look to Madras for leadership, just as Western India looked to Bombay. The non-Brahmin movement of Maharāshtra was largely, though not entirely, autonomous, the leaders in the two areas keeping in touch with each other.[23]

While Brahmin dominance in certain areas is general to peninsular India, it is particularly striking in Tamilnād. Like other Brahmins in peninsular India, Tamil Brahmins have a tradition of scholarship, but what distinguished the latter was the striking lead they had obtained over everyone else, including non-

Tamil Brahmins, in Madras Presidency, with regard to English education.[24] Beteille has stated that in Madras "between 1892 and 1904, out of 16 successful candidates for the I.C.S., 15 were Brahmins; in 1913, 93 out of 128 permanent district *munsifs*[25] were Brahmins; and in 1914, 452 out of the 650 registered graduates of the University were Brahmins."[26] In 1918 the Brahmins in the Presidency numbered 1.5 million out of a total of 42 millions, but 70 per cent of arts graduates, 74 per cent of law graduates, 71 per cent of engineering graduates, and 74 per cent of graduates in teaching were Brahmins. Out of 390 higher appointments in the Education Department 310 were held by Brahmins, in the Judicial Department, 116 out of 171, and in the Revenue Department, 394 out of 679.[27] It is wrong, however, to conclude from all this that non-Brahmin castes were all economically or politically weak. Not only did they greatly outnumber the Brahmins but many were landowning members of rurally powerful dominant castes. According to Irschick, all *zamindārs* in the Presidency were non-Brahmins,[28] and Beteille has pointed out that even in a district such as Tanjore, having the highest concentration of Brahmin landowners, the three biggest landowners, prior to the imposition of ceilings, were non-Brahmins.[29] The dominant peasant castes wielded considerable political and economic power at the village and *tehsil* levels. In urban areas, non-Brahmins controlled trade in food-grains, cloth, groceries and precious metals. Irschick has pointed out that in 1911 while Brahmins owned 35 factories, the non-Brahmin castes, Balija Nāidus, Kāpus, Komatis, Vellālas and Nātukotti Chettis together owned 91 factories.[30] It is only in the context of English education and the fruits that it yielded that the Brahmins enjoyed an overwhelming advantage over all the others. Brahmin dominance extended also to the nationalist movement, though nationalism was a later arrival in Madras than in Bengal or Bombay. *The Non-Brahmin Manifesto* (December 1916) pointed out, for instance, that only one out of fifteen members elected to the All-India Congress Committee from Madras Presidency was a non-Brahmin.[31] However, there were several non-Brahmin leaders in the Madras Congress, and after the Justice Party was formed in 1916 they came together to found the Madras Presidency Association which, while supporting the nationalist demand for home rule, asked for communal representation to safeguard non-Brahmin interests.[32]

The opposition to Brahmin dominance did not come from the

low and oppressed castes but from the leaders of the powerful, rural dominant castes such as the Kammas and Reddis of the Telugu country, the Vellālas of the Tamil country and the Nāyars of Kerala. According to Irschick, "It is important to note that these non-Brahmins, whether from the 'up-country' Telugu areas or from the 'home' Tamil areas were high caste groups, immediately below the Brahmin in caste status, with a position of social prestige among non-Brahmin ranks and with a relatively high English literacy rate."[33] They could not be said to be the representatives of the Harijans and other low castes. In fact, at the village level they were, along with the Brahmin, the exploiters of Harijan labour.

The Backward Classes Movement from its earliest days developed a mythology of its own. Contemporary speculations identifying the Brahmins with Aryans, and Tamil with the original Dravidian language, were eagerly seized on by the leaders of the non-Brahmin castes to manufacture an elaborate theory of Brahmin Machiavellianism throughout the centuries. The Brahmin invader had brought the evil institution of caste into India, and had used his great prestige and power to strengthen his hold on the society by making laws in his own favour, and worse, by shackling people's minds with the ideas of *varna*, *āshrama* (stages in an individual's life), *dharma* (moral law) and *moksha* (salvation). (The sacred writings of the Hindus, and in particular of the law-giver Manu, are even today quoted by reformist speakers to point out the injustices of the caste system and the iniquities perpetrated by Brahmins. It is tacitly assumed that Manu's writings provide an accurate description of extant social conditions everywhere in India.) Pristine Dravidian society, which created the glorious literature of Tamil, was caste-free till the Brahmin came, established his hegemony over everybody and suppressed Dravidian culture. According to Irschick:

> For the Tamil non-Brahmins the rewards of exploiting their Dravidian origin were immense. By the second decade of the twentieth century the cultural hypothesis that Tamil culture predated Aryan Sanskritic culture was widely known. The cultural content of this hypothesis was also endowed with a social and political significance for by it the Aryan Brahmins could be shown as invaders and as usurpers, who had introduced the caste system into a society that previously had been classless in order to enslave those whom they had

> conquered. To condemn the Brahmins as strangers in the Tamil land was a handy weapon for the non-Brahmins to beat the Brahmins with, but the popularizing of the myth of their Dravidian origin also gave to Tamil non-Brahmin caste Hindus both an identity which was independent of Aryan Brahminism and a sense of cultural self-confidence which was to play an important role in the creation of this new elite.[34]

For centuries the Brahmins had systematically exploited the others; this had enabled them to obtain their great lead in education and the new employment opportunities, and leadership of the nationalist movement. If the historically suppressed sections of Indian society were to obtain their share of the new opportunities, they would have to be granted some concessions and privileges, at least for a period. This would necessitate discriminating against Brahmins, but it would be infinitesimal compared to what the non-Brahmins had suffered for centuries. In other words, present-day Brahmins should pay for their ancestors' sins. This was roughly the theory of "social justice", providing the rationale for a policy of preferential treatment of non-Brahmins and discrimination against Brahmins. The policy was put into effect in Madras Presidency in the early nineteen-twenties and saw its heyday in the thirties and forties.

The other important strand in the ideology of the non-Brahmin movement is "swayam maryādé" or self-respect. Although explicitly formulated by E. V. Ramaswamy Naicker in 1925, its seeds go back to the Satya Shodak Samāj, founded in 1873 by Jyoti Rao Phūle, a leader from the Māli (gardener) caste of Poona in Maharāshtra in peninsular India. The *samāj* aimed at stressing the worth of the human individual irrespective of caste. Phūle was against the employment of Brahmin priests for conducting weddings, and to this end he greatly simplified marriage ritual.[35]

Ramaswamy Naicker, an ex-Congressman, broke with the Congress "because of what he considered to be a series of attacks on him and on all non-Brahmins within the Madras Congress Organization and formed his own group which he called the Self-Respect Movement."[36] The movement was pronouncedly anti-Brahmin, and encouraged non-Brahmins not to call upon Brahmin priests to perform weddings and other rituals. Its followers were required to use the Tamil language for political and other purposes and to regard themselves as Dravidians and members of a sovereign, independent state.[37] The movement was anti-Brahmin, anti-North, anti-Hindi, anti-Sanskrit and finally, anti-God. It included an attempt to rid Tamil of long-established Sanskrit words, and to introduce the singing of exclusively Tamil songs at public concerts (classical South Indian music includes songs in Tamil, Telugu, Kannada and Sanskrit). Ramaswamy Naicker founded the Dravida Kazhagam (Dravidian Federation) in 1945, and in 1949 a new organization, the Dravida Munnetra Kazhagam (Dravidian Progressive Federation) was born, the immediate reason being a split between Naicker and his gifted young lieutenant, C. Annadurai, over the former's marriage, when in his seventies, to a girl decades younger. Under Naicker's leadership the Dravida Kazhagam continued to pursue anti-Brahminism in the social and cultural fields; this occasionally expressed itself in assaults on individual Brahmin priests, destroying images of Hindu deities—in particular, the elephant-headed Ganesha[38]—trying to burn copies of the epic Rāmāyana, regarded by the DK and the DMK as an expression of Aryan racialism, and tarring Hindi writing in railroad stations and elsewhere. The DMK, like its parent DK, is an advocate of Tamil separatism, and is also anti-North and anti-Hindi. It is rationalist in ideology, and has been an advocate of the economic development of the south, and of social and economic equalitarianism.[39] It is no longer anti-Brahmin; at the 1962 elections the Swatantra Party in Madras, which has the support of many Brahmin landowners, occasionally entered into electoral pacts with the DMK to defeat the Congress. The DMK has penetrated the prosperous Tamil film industry, whose members, including the founder Annadurai, are authors of film scripts having as their themes opposition to caste and Brahmins, and regional patriotism. Its recent advocacy of the continuance of English as the all-India link language has won for it support not only among all castes in Tamilnād but in all other southern states.

4

It is significant that while all the ingredients for a Backward Classes Movement were present by about the beginning of this century, it was the prospect of the transfer of political power from British to Indian hands that enabled it to develop. The

Morley-Minto Reforms of 199 had enlarged somewhat the powers of Provincial councils and, as observed earlier, had conceded separate electorates to Muslims, Sikhs in the Punjab, Indian Christians, Anglo-Indians and Europeans. The first decade of the twentieth century saw a sharp increase in nationalism[40] as well as caste-consciousness all over India. During the war years there was not only a striking growth of nationalist sentiment, but also an expectation that at the end of the war there would be a transfer of more power to Indian hands. The leaders of the non-Brahmin movement were afraid this might be seized on by the Brahmins, and that they might be left high and dry. They wanted to make sure they would also benefit, and to this end they regarded communal representation as absolutely essential. Otherwise there would be a Brahmin oligarchy which would use its power to oppress everyone else. Some leaders of the movement in Madras openly gave expression to such a sentiment.[41] The Maharajah of Kolhāpur, the Marātha leader of the movement in Bombay, however, took a more nationalist stand, saying that he was for "home rule", but that communal (that is, caste-based) representation was necessary for at least ten years in order to teach the non-Brahmin castes their rights.[42] The Maharajah's position corresponded to that of the non-Brahmin leaders in the Madras Presidency Association. But the Justices openly looked to the British to protect them from the more immediate if not more sinister foe, the Brahmin.[43] It is indeed significant that an identical view was expressed in distant Bengal in the *Patāka*, a journal of the Nāmashūdra caste: "The British government itself has now come to the aid of the uneducated; they have ever been the help of the poor, and the hope of the downtrodden castes."[44] N.K. Bose notes that the Nāmashūdras had abstained from the anti-partition agitation of Bengal in 1905, and that at the height of the *Swadeshi* movement in 1907, "a deputation of representative Nāmashūdra citizens waited upon the Lieutenant Governor and prayed for the perpetuation of British rule."[45] It needed the inspiring leadership of Gandhi and the Civil Disobedience Movements of the twenties and thirties to cut across caste and regional differences and bring the Indian masses into the nationalist stream.

During the decade 1910–1920 a section of the British in India made the Brahmin out to be their archenemy. There was, first, the publication in 1910 of Valentine Chirol's *Indian Unrest*, the main thesis of which was that Brahminism and Western education constituted a serious threat to the continuance of British rule in India. The second was the publication, in 1918, of the Rowlatt Report (*Report of the Committee Appointed to Investigate Revolutionary Conspiracies in India*) which "showed conclusively that revolutionary conspiracy in Bombay was 'purely Brahmin and mostly Chitpavan' and that elsewhere in India the Brahmins had played a large part in fomenting and carrying out revolutionary crime."[46] Finally, there was the association of Brahmins, especially Madras Brahmins, with Mrs. Besant's Home Rule Movement (1916–1917) and the playing up of this fact by the Justice Party in Madras to promote their interests.

One of the chief beneficiaries of the identification of the Brahmin with nationalism was the Justice Party, which was able to obtain communal representation for non-Brahmins in the face of serious opposition. Thanks to communal representation and to the Congress boycott of the elections, the Justice Party captured the polls at the elections, held under the Government of India Act, 1919, and the leaders of the party became ministers in charge of transferred subjects. They remained in power until 1926, when the Swaraj Party swept them out of office. But they continued to be a force in the politics of the Presidency until the Congress won a resounding victory at the polls in the elections of 1937 held under the Government of India Act of 1935. The position taken by the Justice Party revealed such a complete preoccupation with the problem of improving the social position and increasing the power of the non-Brahmin castes that it was not only unresponsive to nationalist sentiment but saw in home rule only the prospect of Brahmin oligarchy. It also had a clear conception that Western education, government jobs and political power were the crucial means to mobility. As a Party statement put it:

> We claim our social, moral and political rights, and our share of government appointments, not because we think that government appointments will transform the non-Brahmin communities into the most prosperous of mankind, but because they carry with them political power, of which as lords of the soil and inheritors of noble traditions, they must have their legitimate share.[47]

From the point of view of public life, education and administration, the most far-reaching accomplishment of the Justice Party was the introduction everywhere in South India of the principle of giving preference to backward castes in the matter of government jobs, and admission to engineering, medical and science courses. A system of caste quotas was established; this often resulted in better qualified Brahmins being rejected in favour of less qualified non-Brahmins. The principle of "protective discrimination" or "discrimination in reverse" became so firmly established that since 1920, in Madras Presidency, out of every twelve posts five had to go to non-Brahmin Hindus, two to Brahmins, two to Muslims, two to Anglo-Indians or Christians, and one to the Depressed Classes (Harijans).[48] With regard to admission to medical and other colleges, out of every fourteen seats six were allotted to non-Brahmin Hindus, two to Backward Hindus, two to Harijans, two to Brahmins, one to an Anglo-Indian or Indian Christian, and one to a Muslim. Such a distribution of seats among the communities according to a fixed ratio continued for three decades and was declared unconstitutional only in 1951 by the Supreme Court in the case of the State of Madras *v.* Sm. Champakam Dorairajan. This decision resulted in a constitutional amendment [article 15 (4)] which enabled the state to make any special provision for the advancement of any socially and educationally backward classes of citizens or for the Scheduled Castes and Tribes. "It is important to note that the amendment does not validate the distribution of seats on communal lines (as was done in the Madras G.O.), but only validates reservation of seats for these weaker sections of the population."[49]

In the adjoining and former princely state of Mysore, from 1921 to 1959 Brahmins could compete for only three out of every ten posts, and in 1959 the Government of Mysore passed an order reserving 75 per cent of jobs in government, and seats in medical and engineering colleges, to the Backward Classes (57 per cent) and Scheduled Castes and Tribes (18 per cent). Only 25 per cent was open to general competition. The Mysore High Court declared, in 1960, that this policy violated article 15(4) of the Constitution.[50]

The Mysore Government appointed in January 1960 a committee under the chairmanship of Dr. R. Nagan Gowda to lay down criteria for the classification of backward classes. The Committee took "caste" as the unit for consideration, and the backwardness, or otherwise, of a caste was to be determined by its representation in government service and the number of high school students per thousand of its population.[51] On the basis of these criteria, the

Lingāyats were classified as a "Forward" caste while their chief rivals for power at the state level, the Okkaligas, were classified as "Backward". This was first mentioned in the Committee's interim report; the Lingāyats promptly mounted a strong attack on the decision, but the Committee remained unimpressed. They reiterated their earlier decision in the final report.[52] Eventually, however, the Mysore Government yielded to pressure and restored to Lingāyats the coveted "Backward" status.[53]

The extent to which the two dominant castes of Lingāyats and Okkaligas had developed a vested interest in backwardness is seen in the persistent adherence of the Mysore Government to caste quotas in spite of strong judicial disapproval. Thus, two years after the unfavourable verdict of the Mysore High Court:

> On July 31, 1962, the Mysore Government issued an order providing for reservation of 68% of seats in medical and engineering colleges for backward classes and Scheduled Castes and Tribes. The order listed 81 "backward classes" and 135 "more backward classes". In striking down the order two months later the Supreme Court declared that it was "a fraud on the Constitution". The judgment held that the classification of backward classes on the sole basis of caste was not permitted by article 15(4). Furthermore, the reservation was clearly excessive, as it reduced the field of general competition to a mere 32% of the seats. The special provision, in other words, had so weakened the fundamental rule (equality of opportunity) as to rob it of most of its significance.[54]

The principle of caste quotas is also in vogue in Andhra and Kerala. Until as recently as May 1961, 55 per cent of government jobs in Andhra were being reserved for the Backward Classes (including Scheduled Classes and Tribes), and such reservation was also operative in promotions to higher levels.[55] In Kerala, until 1958, 40 per cent of jobs were being reserved for Backward communities, and 10 per cent for Scheduled Castes and Tribes.[56] In the field of education 35 per cent of seats were reserved for the Backward communities.[57]

I have said earlier that the non-Brahmin movement was started by the wealthy and somewhat Westernized leaders belonging to peasant or higher castes and that there was a marked cleavage, economic and social, between them and the Scheduled and allied castes. Anti-Brahminism, however, provided a rallying point though it was not always enough to hold together the heterogeneous elements forming the non-Brahmin category. Sometime after caste quotas had been fixed, a few castes such as the Padaiyāchis or Vanniya Kula Kshatriyas felt that they deserved more than they had been given. The Padaiyāchis are a dominant caste in Madras, constituting about ten per cent of the State's population and dominating the two districts of North and South Arcot. They demanded that one out of every five non-Brahmin posts be reserved for them.[58] The "Depressed Classes" were also dissatisfied. The number of castes constituting the "Depressed Classes" was brought down in 1935 from 140 to 86, presumably by removing from the list those who did not really belong to that category but who had been enjoying the benefits.[59]

Although the Justice Party was pushed out of political life after its crushing defeat in the 1937 elections, this did not mean the end of the non-Brahmin movement. Irschick mentions that it "was forced in 1927 to pass a resolution allowing its members to join the Congress in an attempt to flood that organization in Madras with non-Brahmins."[60] With Independence and adult suffrage, the dominant peasant castes became so powerful that all political parties had to come to terms with them. They were well represented in State legislatures and cabinets, and the introduction of *panchāyati rāj* conferred power on them at the village, *tehsil* and district levels. Political power enhances the status of the individual and his group; anyone who has talked in recent years to Lingāyats, Okkaligas, Pātidārs, or Kallars in rural areas can testify to this. And political power can be translated into economic term—not only for oneself but for one's relations, clients and castefolk—and can determine the future of young men and women by obtaining for them right careers and well-paid and prestigious jobs. This is where caste quotas are of crucial significance.

Usually, there is more than one dominant caste in a state, and conflicts between them for political power are only to be expected. The Kammas and Reddis of Andhra and the Lingāyats and Okkaligas of Mysore, provide well-known examples of such conflict. From the point of view of the non-dominant castes, however, the dominant castes have monopolized most of the benefits available in the new system. The non-dominant castes naturally feel frustrated and bitter. Today, in Mysore, men from non-dominant castes style themselves as "minor" castes, and complain about the "ruthless manner" in which the Lingāyats and Okkaligas are collaring jobs and the licences and permits necessary for every type of entrepreneurial activity. That this is a widespread feeling is borne out by the Nagan Gowda Committee's recommendation that the Backward classes be divided into "backward" and "more backward" (excluding Scheduled Castes and Tribes) to ensure a fair deal for the latter.[61] This feeling is not confined to Mysore but occurs also in Kerala and Madras.

The formation of linguistic states on November 1, 1956, resulted in greatly reducing, in each state, the political power of castes speaking minority languages. Thus today in Mysore, for political purposes, an Okkaliga means a member of this Kannada-speaking, dominant caste, and no longer includes the Telugu-speaking Reddi. This is ironic, for the non-Brahmin movement in Mysore, in its early phase, as in Madras, drew its leadership largely from Telugu, Tamil, Malayālam speakers, and not only from Hindu castes, but also from Muslims and Christians.

The situation with regard to the "Backward Classes" in the 1950s can now be summarized: There was a widespread desire among non-Brahmin castes to be categorized as "Backward" in Western contexts, while the dominant castes had developed a vested interest in "Backwardness". It was the best hope of securing education, especially technological and medical education, of prestigious and well-paid employment, and of mobility in class as well as caste systems. The minority castes felt that the dominant castes were helping themselves to all the benefits, and at their expense; and the State governments had either devised, or were considering devising, new procedures to safeguard the interests of "truly backward" castes. The conflict would have been much sharper but for the special measures in the Constitution protecting the interests of Scheduled Castes. Without these, social conflict between the Scheduled Castes and others, quite marked at the village level, would have been further exacerbated by the struggle for political power and for various privileges.

It is only fair to mention that the fifties also marked the beginning of a different approach to the problem of backwardness, and this approach issued from both the Central and State levels. The Backward Classes Commission, appointed by the Government of India to determine the criteria by which sections of the population, other than the Scheduled Castes and Tribes, could be treated as socially and educationally backward, submitted its report in 1955, and a majority of its members were of the view that caste determined the extent of an individual's backwardness. They listed 2399 castes as backward, and recommended that these be made eligible for benefits similar to those enjoyed by the Scheduled Castes and Tribes. But the Chairman of the Commission, Kaka Kalelkar, in his letter forwarding the report to the President of India,

> repudiated the fundamental conclusions of his commission. He wrote that, almost at the end of the Committee's labours, he realized that the remedies suggested were worse than the evils they sought to combat. ... He decided that the whole line of investigation pursued by the Commission was "repugnant to the spirit of democracy", since in democracy it is the individual, not the family or the caste, which is the unit. He recommended that the state regard as backward and entitled to special educational and economic aid all persons whose total family income is less than 800 rupees per year, regardless of their caste or community. Kalelkar opposed reservation of posts for the backward classes in the government services, which was recommended by the Commission.[62]

The Government of India expressed its disapproval of the recommendations of the Commission, and five years later, on the 14th of August, 1961, the Home Ministry wrote to the State governments asking them to do away with the caste criterion and adopt instead income.

At the State level, Madras took the lead in 1955 by expressing its intention to implement gradually a policy of exempting all poor children from payment of fees in elementary and secondary schools. It was able to achieve its objective fully by February, 1961. In 1959 Bombay decided to exempt all poor children in primary and secondary schools from payment of fees, and other states such as Andhra Pradesh and Mysore followed shortly after.[63]

5

I see the Backward Classes Movement of South India as fundamentally a movement to achieve mobility on the part of groups which had lagged behind the Brahmins in Westernization. Education, employment in the government, and participation in the new political processes were essential for such mobility, and education was an indispensable means for securing the other two. It was inevitably a secular movement. The idea of equality was inherent in it. It led to widespread rivalry between castes which were eager to move up, and to the Self-Respect Movement, and it had to make an assault on the Brahmin's cultural and social dominance and exclusiveness. In the process of participating in the modern political and other processes subsumed under Westernization, the caste system underwent certain significant changes which I shall briefly consider here.

The point that comes first to mind in this connection is the freeing of caste from its traditional, local and vertical matrix. Within the local matrix the emphasis was on the interdependence of castes or local sections of castes, which in fact meant the dependence of several households of clients from the servicing and artisan castes on each patron household from the dominant, landowning castes. The coming into existence of new opportunities, educational, economic and political, brought about an increase in horizontal solidarity. I shall not concern myself here with how this happened but only with its significance for mobility. A caste dispersed over a wide area increasingly tended to ignore differences between its sections (Leach's "Caste Grades").[64] When I call them "different sections of a caste" I am only noting how educated members of the caste regard them. Indeed, I suspect that in the case of the big peasant castes, different members would differ in their estimate of who belonged to their caste and who did not. For instance, in a caste such as the Okkaligas of Mysore-Mandya districts, an elderly, rural and illiterate member may not regard the Nonaba, Hallikāra, Hālu and Morasu divisions as Okkaligas at all. As far as he is concerned, his effective social space would be Okkaligas living in an area within a radius of about twenty-five miles. But an Okkaliga lawyer or doctor would regard all the divisions as Okkaligas, and he might give his daughter in marriage to the son of an urbanized and educated Okkaliga from distant Shimoga in the west. Clearly, a class element is involved here, but that horizontal integration is taking place is beyond dispute, and a critical factor in such integration is the increased politicization of Indian society.

Previous students of caste such as Risley have drawn attention to the "fissiparous nature of caste".[65] In traditional India, fission seems to have been the dominant process, whereas today the trend has been reversed and *fusion* has replaced *fission*. And as Beteille has pointed out, fusion does not take place arbitrarily but takes into account traditional alignments. He also comments that such fusion "is not infrequently associated with a widening of cleavages, particularly in the political sphere, between the larger segments."[66]

I have called this "horizontal integration", but the term "horizontal" is not quite accurate as the units involved do not really regard themselves as equal, and each has a feeling that it is superior to the others. It would be more accurate to say that structurally neighbouring units become part of a single large entity. In most cases the larger entity is still in the process of emerging, and the Westernized elite from the various units are bringing these different units together.

In the absence of empirical investigation it is not possible to say whether the increase in horizontal solidarity has occurred equally with all castes or has been greater in some than in others. It is certainly occurring among the high castes, including the dominant peasant castes. The Scheduled Castes have come together for political purposes, but it is not known how far this has been followed up by the widening of the social and cultural fields. The artisan and servicing castes are usually numerically weak and are nowhere prominent in state politics. It is not unlikely that they have been least influenced by the modern tendency toward increasing horizontal solidarity. The subject of the referents of caste has recently been discussed by F.G. Bailey and Beteille.[67] Beteille has stated:

> The fact that caste is a segmentary system means (and has always meant) that people view themselves as belonging to units of different orders in different contexts. A Smārtha sees himself as a Smārtha in relation to a Srī Vaishnava, and as a Brahmin in relation to a non-Brahmin. There is no reason to believe that this is a new phenomenon. What is new is the focus which has been given by party politics to wider entities partly at the expense of narrower ones.[68]

It is true that political forces—much wider, however, than party politics—have played a part in stimulating horizontal solidarity, but they are not the only ones. Urbanization, increased spatial mobility, Westernized style of life, and modern ideology have also played their part. With specific reference to endogamy, so crucial to the identification of a caste, the institution of dowry has forced people to look for bridegrooms beyond the traditional unit. The huge sums demanded as dowry, and in many cases, the institution itself, are a product of increased monetization, and Western education and the job opportunities which it has opened the door to. The "matrimonial" advertisements in Indian newspapers show how urban, Westernized Indians are willing to overlook traditional barriers in their anxious search for a suitable spouse.

The castes of modern India perform several functions such as providing hostels, cooperative housing and banks, and they act as interest groups in the political arena. They offer a sharp contrast to the role caste groups played in the traditional context of village and region. The interdependence characteristic of castes in the local, village economy and society—and it is well to remember that behind this interdependence lay the coercive power of the dominant caste and the chief—has given way to competition for power between rival groups. Kathleen Gough regards such activity as one among many symptoms of caste disintegration, and to Leach it is behaviour in "defiance of caste principles."[69] Bailey considers the emergent entities "'castes' in a loose way [though] they are not operating in a caste system."[70] Nur Yalman[71] and Beteille[72] also regard these entities as castes, and Beteille stresses the continuity between the different levels of the segmentary system that is caste.

If the traditional village community or chiefdom is regarded as the norm, then the new alliances being forged between "caste grades" or cognate *jātis*, and the keen competition for political power and economic benefits, seem to constitute a new phenomenon, even though they continue to perform certain traditional functions such as defining the endogamous field. These changes in caste could not, however, have come into existence without one hundred fifty years of Westernization, and when I say Westernization I refer to the entire gamut of forces included in the term. The emergence of the big and powerful castes, the great occupational heterogeneity within each of them, the keen competition between castes for political and economic power, the spread of equalitarian ideology, and increasing political and social mobilization—all suggest that changes of a fundamental kind are occurring. It cannot be described as a simple movement from a closed to an open system of social stratification. For one thing, as we have seen earlier, the traditional system was not entirely closed, and mobility was possible for both groups and individuals. For another, though the scope for individual and familial mobility has increased strikingly since Independence, caste continues to be relevant in subtle and indirect ways, in such mobility.

NOTES

1. F.G. Bailey, *Caste and the Economic Frontier*, pp. 159, 163.
2. M.N. Srinivas, *Caste in Modern India*, p. 59.
3. See section II of the Reading List for books and articles on the Backward Classes Movement.
4. G.D. Berreman, "Caste in India and the United States", *American Journal of Sociology*, vol. LXVI, no. 2, September 1960, p. 125.
5. F.G. Bailey, "Closed Social Stratification", *European Journal of Sociology*, vol. IV, 1963, pp. 107–124; and A. Beteille, "Closed and Open Social Stratification in India" (to be published).
6. B. Stein, "Social Mobility in Medieval South Indian Hindu Sects", in J. Silverberg (ed.), *Social Mobility in Caste in India*, special issue of *Comparative Studies in Society and History*. See *supra* chap. 1, note 27.
7. Edgar Thurston, *Castes and Tribes of Southern India*, vol. VII, p. 366, and vol. VI, p. 1.
8. See G.S. Ghurye, *Caste and Class in India*, pp. 169–170.
9. A *maund* is a traditonal Indian weight varying from area to area. The standard *maund* is equal to 100 lb (troy) or 82 2/7 lb (avoirdupois).
10. *Bengal, Bihar, Orissa and Sikkim Census Report*, 1911, p. 440.
11. Donald E. Smith, *India as a Secular State*, Princeton, 1963, p. 304.
12. *Madras Census*, 1911, p. 178; *Census of India Report for 1921*, pp. 231–232.
13. *Census of India Report for 1921*, pp. 231–232.
14. *Bihar and Orissa Census Report*, 1931, pp. 267–268.
15. *Census of India Report for 1921*, pp. 231–232.
16. S. Natarajan, *A Century of Social Reform*, p. 119.
17. *Ibid.*, p. 118.
18. See, for instance, J.H. Hutton, "Primitive Tribes", in L.S.S. O'Malley (ed.), *Modern India and the West*, Oxford, 1941, pp. 443–444; and G.S. Ghurye, *The Aborigines, So-Called and Their Future*, Poona, 1943, pp. 111–154.
19. N.K. Bose, "Some Aspects of Caste in Bengal", in Milton Singer (ed.) *op. cit.*, pp. 199–201.
20. *Census Report for the Punjab*, 1911, p. 149 and *Census Report for India*, 1911, pp. 123–124.

21. Pauline M. Mahar, "Changing Religious Practices of an Untouchable Caste", *Economic Development and Cultural Change*, vol. VIII, no. 3, April, 1960, pp. 279–287.
22. *Punjab Census Report*, 1931, pp. 293–294.
23. M.N. Srinivas, *Caste in Modern India*, p. 25 n.
24. In 1911, 35.75 per cent of Tamil Brahmin males were literate in an Indian language while 11.07 per cent were literate in English. Next to them were Telugu Brahmins with 33.93 and 7.34 per cent respectively. Of the non-Brahmin castes, the Nāyars led the others with 20.16 and 1.43 per cent respectively, followed in order by the Tamil Vellāla with 12.09 and 1.04, the Telugu Balija Nāidu with 10.33 and 1.29, the Kamma with 6.12 and 0.1, and Kāpu with 4.46 and 0.11 per cent. (From E. Irschick, *Politics and Social Conflict in South India—the Non-Brahmin Movement and Tamil Separatism*, p. 12.)
25. A *munsif* is a subordinate civil judge.
26. A. Beteille, "Caste and Politics in Tamilnad" (to be published).
27. E. Irschick, *Politics and Social Conflict in South India—the Non-Brahmin Movement and Tamil Separatism*, p. 113.
28. *Ibid.*, p. 13.
29. Beteille, see *supra* note 26.
30. Irschick, *op. cit.*, p. 14.
31. G.V. Subba Rao, *Life and Times of K.V. Reddi Naidu*, Rajahmundry, 1957, p. 19.
32. Irschick, *op. cit.*, p. 14.
33. Irschick, "The Brahmin Non-Brahmin Struggle for Power in Madras", p. 1. (Mimeographed.)
34. *Ibid.*, p. 3.
35. Ghurye, see *supra* note 8, p. 178.
36. Irschick, "The Integration of South India into the National Movement", pp. 12–13. (Mimeographed.)
37. R. Jayaraman in his review of T.M. Parthasarathy's *History of D.M.K., 1916–1962* (Madras, 1963), *Economic Weekly*, September 26, 1964, pp. 1555–1556.
38. Ramaswamy Naicker, it is interesting to note, was influenced by the American agnostic Robert Ingersoll. "Ingersoll's attack on the Bible and Christianity inspired similar arguments against the Puranas and Hinduism." (*India as a Secular State*, p. 157.)
39. Srinivas, see *supra* note 23, p. 22.
40. Sir Percival Griffiths, *The British Impact on India*, London, 1952, pp. 295–296.
41. Irschick, see *supra* note 27, pp. 55–56.
42. Ghurye, see *supra* note 8, p. 179.
43. Irschick, see *supra* note 27, p. 55.
44. Bose, see *supra* note 19, p. 200.

45. *Ibid.*
46. Irschick, see *supra* note 27, pp. 118–120.
47. Irschick, "The Brahmin Non-Brahmin Struggle for Power in Madras", p. 4.
48. G.O. no. 1129 dated December 15, 1928 (Public Service Department).
49. Smith, see *supra* note 11, p. 122.
50. *S.H. Partha and others v. State of Mysore and others, Mysore Law Journal*, 1960, p. 159 (quoted in Donald E. Smith, *op. cit.*, p. 318).
51. These criteria were adopted even though statistics regarding the strength of castes are not beyond doubt, and it is not easy to say whether a subcaste is part of a large caste such as Lingāyat or Okkaliga.
52. *Mysore Backward Classes Committee: Final Report*, Bāngalore, p. 20.
53. Srinivas, see *supra* note 23, p. 2.
54. *The Hindu*, September 30, 1962 (quoted in Donald E. Smith, *op. cit.*, p. 320).
55. Smith, *op. cit.*, p. 318.
56. Srinivas, see *supra* note 23, p. 3 n.
57. Srinivas, "Pursuit of Equality", *Times*, London, January 26, 1962 (*The Times Survey of India*).
58. G.O. no. 247 dated February 4, 1939.
59. G.O. no. 1949 dated December 6, 1938 (Public Service Department).
60. E. Irschick, "The Integration of South India into the National Movement", p. 13. A similar phenomenon occurred in Maharashtrian politics. See M. Patterson, "Caste and Politics in Maharashtra", p. 1066.
61. *Mysore Backward Classes Committee: Final Report*, p. 20.
62. Smith, *op. cit.*, p. 317.
63. *Ibid.*, p. 321.
64. E.R. Leach, "Introduction: What Should We Mean by Caste", in *Aspects of Caste in South India, Ceylon and North-West Pakistan*, Cambridge, 1960, p. 7.
65. Quoted by Hutton, *Caste in India*, Oxford, 1963, p. 51.
66. A. Beteille, "A Note on the Referents of Caste", *European Journal of Sociology*, vol. V, 1964, p. 134.
67. F.G. Bailey, "Closed Social Stratification", *European Journal of Sociology*, vol. IV, 1963, p. 123; and Beteille, see *supra* note 66.
68. Beteille, see *supra* note 66, p. 133.
69. Leach, see *supra* note 64, p. 7.
70. Bailey, see *supra* note 67, p. 123.
71. N. Yalman, "The Flexibility of Caste Principles in a Kandyan Community", in *supra* note 69, pp. 87, 106.
72. Beteille, see *supra* note 66, p. 133.

4

SECULARIZATION

1

BRITISH rule brought with it a process of secularization of Indian social life and culture, a tendency that gradually became stronger with the development of communications, growth of towns and cities, increased spatial mobility, and the spread of education. The two World Wars, and Mahatma Gandhi's civil disobedience campaigns, both of which socially and politically mobilized the masses, also contributed to increased secularization. And with Independence there began a deepening as well as a broadening of the secularization process as witnessed in such measures as the declaration of India as a secular state, the Constitutional recognition of the equality of all citizens before the law, the introduction of universal adult suffrage, and the undertaking of a program of planned development.

We have seen earlier that Sanskritization is also spreading, and it may seem paradoxical that both it and secularization are simultaneously gaining ground in modern India. Of the two, secularization is the more general process, affecting all Indians, while Sanskritization affects only Hindus and tribal groups. Broadly, it would be true to say that secularization is more marked among the urban and educated groups, and Sanskritization among the lower Hindu castes and tribes. It is necessary, however, to reiterate that one of the results of a century of Westernization—secularization is subsumed under Westernization—is a reinterpreted Hinduism in which Sanskritic elements are predominant.

The term "secularization" implies that what was previously regarded as religious is now ceasing to be such, and it also implies a process of differentiation which results in the various aspects of society, economic, political, legal and moral, becoming increasingly *discrete* in relation to each other. The distinction between Church and State, and the Indian concept of a secular state, both assume the existence of such differentiation.

Another essential element in secularization is rationalism, a "comprehensive expression applied to various theoretical and practical tendencies which aim to interpret the universe purely in terms of thought, or which aim to regulate individual and social life in accordance with the principles of reason and to eliminate as far as possible or to relegate to the background everything irrational."[1] Rationalism involves, among other things, the replacement of traditional beliefs and ideas by modern knowledge.

It would probably be safe to assume that Hindus were more affected by the secularization process than any other religious group in India as, first, the concepts of pollution and purity which are central as well as pervasive in Hinduism were greatly weakened as a result of the operation of a variety of factors already mentioned. Moreover, the fact that Hinduism lacks a central and nation-wide organization with a single head, and that it is largely dependent for its perpetuation on such social institutions as caste, joint family and village community—institutions which are changing in important respects—renders it peculiarly vulnerable to the forces of secularization. Different sections among Hindus are affected in different degrees by it, and generally speaking, the new elite are probably much more affected by it than everyone else. In my discussion of secularization I shall be referring principally to the new elite in Mysore, though it is probable that my remarks also apply with some variations to the elite in other parts of the country. I shall consider first the effects of secularization on ideas regarding pollution and purity, then the changes in the lives and position of priestly Brahmins and finally, the implications for Hinduism of changes in caste, village community and joint family.

No student of Hindu religious behaviour can afford to ignore the concepts of pollution and purity.[2] Terms exist for pollution and purity in every Indian language, and each of these terms has a certain amount of semantic stretch enabling it to move from one meaning to another as the context requires. Thus pollution may refer to uncleanliness, defilement, impurity short of defilement and indirectly even to sinfulness, while purity refers to cleanliness, spiritual merit and indirectly to holiness.

The structural distance between various castes is defined in terms of pollution and purity. A higher caste is always "pure" in relation to a lower caste, and in order to retain its higher status it should abstain from certain forms of contact with the lower. It may not ordinarily eat food cooked by them, or marry or have sex relations with them. Where one of the castes is very high and the other very low, there is a ban on touching or even getting very close to one another. A breach of rules renders the higher caste member impure, and purity can only be restored by the performance of a purification rite and, frequently, also by undergoing such punishment as the caste council decides upon. Sometimes, however, the offence is so serious—as, for instance, when a Brahmin or other high-caste woman has sex relations with an Untouchable man—that the former is permanently excommunicated from her caste. The concepts of pollution and purity are important not only in a static but also in a dynamic context: traditionally, when a caste group or its section wanted to move up it would Sanskritize its style of life and stop accepting cooked food from those castes with which it had previously inter-dined.

Corresponding to the caste hierarchy are hierarchies in food, occupation and styles of life. The highest castes are vegetarians as well as teetotalers, while the lowest eat meat (including domestic pork and beef) and consume indigenous liquor. Consumption of the meat of such a village scavenger as the pig pollutes the eaters, while the ban on beef comes from the high place given to the cow in the sacred texts of Hinduism. Among occupations, those involving manual work are rated lower than those which do not. Manual occupations may involve the handling of dirty or polluting (for example, human waste matter) objects, or engaging in butchery which is regarded as sinful. At the lowest level of the caste system are occupations that are sinful or polluting or both.

Not only caste but also kinship is bound up with pollution ideas. Thus, birth as well as death results in pollution for specific periods for members of the kinship group, death pollution being more rigorous than birth pollution. Within the kinship group, the mourning period is longer for the closest relatives, such as widow, widower and sons, and the taboos are also more elaborate. The onset of puberty for a girl was traditionally marked by confining her to a room for several days, at the end of which time there was a purificatory bath and ritual. A woman was considered polluting during her monthly periods. Traditionally, women kept away from all activity and contact with other members of the household for three days during their periods. All bodily waste matter, with the exception of sweat, was regarded not only as dirty but as polluting. This is one of the reasons why a bath was a condition precedent to prayer; and while praying or performing ritual, the subject had to exercise sphincter and bladder control. Restraint on sex was also imposed on religious occasions, including pilgrimages to such shrines as the Mādeshwara temple in Kollegal tāluk in Mysore district and the famous temple to Shāsta in southern Kerala.

The daily routine was also permeated with ideas of pollution and purity. A person's normal condition was one of mild impurity, and he exchanged this for short periods of purity or serious impurity. He had to be ritually pure not only while praying but also while eating (see in this connection pp. 53–54). In order to be pure, he had to have a bath, change into ritually pure clothes, and avoid contact even with other members of his family who were not in a similar condition. During certain festivals and the *shrāddha* (annual ceremony for dead father or mother) the subject had to abstain from even a drink of water till the ritual was over.

Traditionally, a man did not shave himself. He was shaved by a member of the barber caste, and the barber's touch as well as shaved hair were both polluting. After he was shaved, he was not allowed to touch the bathroom vessels, but someone poured water over him while he sat on the bathroom floor. Only when he had been thoroughly drenched, and had gargled his mouth with water, was he allowed to touch the vessels. The place where the tonsure had been performed was purified with cowdung. There was some resistance initially to the use of the safety razor among the high castes, as its use involved pollution. The institution of the daily shave also violated the ban on shaving on certain days of the week, and other inauspicious days. The safety razor enabled a man to shave when and where he liked. I remember that once during my field work in Rāmpura I shaved after I had had my morning bath and the Peasant headman mildly reproved me for it. (His granddaughter, then about ten, was critical of my indifference to pollution.) In his own house, the safety razor had been tabooed, and when his graduate son came on an occasional visit from Mysore, he was allowed to use the razor only in an adjoining building used for guests.

Women, especially widows, and elderly men are generally more particular about observing the rules of pollution than others. The upper castes are more particular than the lower Brahmins are the most particular among the former, and among Brahmins priests outdo the laity. Indeed, Brahminical preoccupation with purity-pollution ideas and ritualism is the subject of much joking if not criticism. Traditional Brahminical life requires not only leisure but also an absence of spatial mobility. Travel subjects orthodox Brahmins to great hardship and privation.

Just as notions of uncleanliness and even sinfulness lie close to pollution, so do cleanliness, spiritual merit and holiness lie close to purity. While all baths purify the bather, bathing in a sacred river cleanses him, in addition, of sin (*pāpa*), and earns him *punya* or spiritual merit. A daily bath in a sacred river (*punya snāna*), worshipping in a temple, listening to the narration of religious stories (*harikathā kālakshepa*), singing devotional songs in company with other devotees (*bhajan*), keeping the company of religious persons (*satsanga*), frequent fasting (*upavāsa*), prayer and meditation (*prārthana, dhyāna*)—these constitute the essence of a religious life as distinguished from a life devoted to secular concerns.

The notion of pollution and purity has both weakened and become less pervasive in the last few decades as a result of the forces already mentioned. It may be noted here that the popularity of travel and teashops is not confined to city folk but extends to villagers as well. When I began my field work in Rāmpura in 1948 villagers were surprised to find me walking to neighbouring villages. Why did I walk when there were buses? When I revisited the village in 1952 I found bus travel had greatly increased in popularity, and the headman himself had invested money in buses.

Urban life sets up its own pressures, and a man's daily routine, his place of residence, the times of his meals, are influenced more by his job than by caste and religion. This is all the more true when the city he lives in is a highly industrialized one such as Bangalore or Bhadrāvati, and not like Mysore, which derived its importance from being the traditional capital of the state until

November 1, 1956, when it became part of a larger Kannada-speaking state. Even more influential is the fact that immigrants from the villages to cities are freed to some extent from caste and kin pressures, and must instead conform to the norms of work-mates and neighbourhood groups. I am not arguing that urban living leads to a total abandonment of the traditional way of life; in fact, it is a commonplace of observation that behaviour varies according to context, and people are not always worried by inconsistencies in it. A Nāyar informant told Kathleen Gough, "When I put on my shirt to go to the office, I take off my caste, and when I come home and take off my shirt, I put on my caste."[3] On a long-term basis, however, such contextual variation usually paves the way for the eventual overall secularization of behaviour. Thus, for instance, in Mysore in the early 1930s priestly (*vaidika*) Brahmins did not patronize coffee shops, even coffee shops where the cooks were Brahmins. Elderly lay (*loukika*) Brahmins also did not like to visit them; on those infrequent occasions when they did, they sat in an inner room specially reserved for Brahmins and ate off leaves instead of pollution-carrying aluminium and brass plates. Now very few coffee shops have rooms reserved for Brahmins—in fact, such reservation would be against the law. The most popular coffee shops in the city have a cosmopolitan clientele, and few customers bother about the caste of cooks and waiters. Even women occasionally visit them, and there are "family" cubicles where they can eat in privacy.

The more educated customers show concern about cleanliness in coffee shops and not about caste. Many of them prefer Western-style "coffee houses" as they appear to be cleaner, quieter and serve novel items. Often these "coffee houses" serve both vegetarian and non-vegetarian foods, and Brahmin youths are found experimenting with omelettes and other forbidden foods.

As a result of the spread of education among all sections of the population, traditional ideas of purity are giving way to the rules of hygiene. Purity and cleanliness are often at loggerheads; I have heard many an educated Brahmin expressing his disgust at the dirt and unhygienic character of "pure" clothes worn by the orthodox. Brahmin cooks are often found wearing or using for handling hot vessels, dirty clothes which have been rinsed but not cleaned with soap or sterilized. The unsanitary conditions prevailing in pilgrim centers is a frequent subject of conversation among educated Hindus, who are more conscious of the drains flowing into the Ganges than of the river's holiness. This is not, however, the only tendency; educated Hindus are also found rationalizing traditional behaviour. Purity, according to them, is nothing more than hygiene, and it was brought within the field of religious behaviour only to make people more particular about it.

Any consideration of changed attitudes toward pollution must note the great popularity of education among Brahmin women in Mysore.[4] In the old days, women were extremely particular about pollution, and the kitchen was the heart of the pollution system. The modern educated housewife, on the other hand, is much less particular about pollution and more conscious of hygiene and nutrition. Many observe rules of pollution only when they are living with their parents or in-laws. They become lax about the rules when they form separate households; a punctilious observance of pollution rules is not easy when there is only one adult woman in the house, unlike in a traditional joint family. Even in the latter, pollution rules are observed more strictly when there are old women who are widows and whose lives are centered in the kitchen and in the domestic altar (usually located in or near the kitchen).

Another and a potent source of criticism of orthodox Hinduism's obsession with pollution and ritualism lay in the nineteenth century movement to reinterpret traditional religion. It was essentially a puritanical movement in which an attempt was made to distinguish the "essence" of Hinduism from its historical accretions. Ritualism and pollution rules were interpreted as extrinsic to true religion, and as even wrong, while devotion and simplicity were of the essence. There was support for such a view in the Bhagavad Gita and in the lives of the saints.

2

Another area which has been affected by the secularization process is life-cycle ritual. There has been an abbreviation of the rituals performed at various life-cycle crises, while at the same time their purely social aspects have assumed greater importance than before. Ceremonies such as name-giving (*nāmakarana*), the first tonsure (*chaula*) and the annual ritual of changing the sacred thread (*upākarma*) are beginning to be dropped.[5] For girls, the attainment of puberty is no longer marked by the elaborate ritual that characterized it a few decades ago. The shaving of a Brahmin widow's head, as part of the funeral rite for her dead husband, has also largely disappeared, and among the educated, widow marriage is no longer strongly disapproved.

Rituals are not only omitted or abbreviated but are also telescoped with others, though this seems to be rarer than the other two phenomena. Thus the wedding ritual may be combined with the donning of the sacred thread at the beginning of the ceremony, and with the consummation ritual (*garbhādana*) at the end. In fact, only funeral ritual and the annual *shrāddha* continue to be performed with the same strictness as before, though even here changes seem to have occurred with respect to the kin groups participating in the ritual. The scattering of agnates over a wide area is one of the factors responsible for this change.

The manner in which the wedding ritual has been abbreviated is interesting. Formerly, a full-blown Brahmin wedding would last between five and seven days. Now, however, much of the non-Sanskritic and folk ritual, traditionally the exclusive preserve of women, is being dropped. There is even an increasing tendency to compress Sanskritic ritual into a few hours on a single day. The crucial religious rituals such as *kanyādāna* (gift of the virgin) and *saptapadi* (seven steps) are witnessed only by the concerned kindred, while the main body of guests attends the secularly important wedding reception. At the latter the bridal couple sit on a settee at the back of a hall, both in their best clothes, the groom generally sporting a woollen suit, usually a gift from his father-in-law. The guests are introduced to the couple after which they sit for a while listening to the music and then depart, taking with them a paper bag containing a coconut and a few betel leaves and areca nuts. The reception is a costly affair as both the price of coconuts and the fees of musicians are high during the wedding season. But the number of guests, their social importance, the professional standing of the musician hired for the occasion, the number of cars parked on the street outside the wedding house, the lights and decorations, and the presents received by the bridal couple are all indicators of the status and influence of the two affinal groups in the local society. Invitations are extended to ministers and other prominent politicians, to high officials and various local worthies to develop, strengthen and exhibit links with these important people. The wedding reception is a recent institution—the word "reception" has passed into Kannada—and its great popularity is one of the many pointers to the increased secularization of Brahminical life and culture.

Another evidence of increased secularization is the enormous importance assumed by the institution of dowry in the last few decades. Dowry is paid not only among Mysore and other South Indian Brahmins, but also among a number of high-caste groups all over India. The huge sums demanded as dowry prompted the Indian Parliament, in 1961, to pass the Dowry Prohibition Act (Act 28 of 1961). So far the Act has not had much success in combating the institution.

The interesting feature of dowry among Mysore Brahmins—and this is probably true of several other groups as well—is that engineers, doctors and candidates successful in the prestigious Indian Administrative Service seem to command much bigger payments than others.

The amount of time spent on daily ritual has been steadily decreasing for Brahmin men as well as for women. Ingalls has stated, "The head of the family might spend five hours or more of the day in ritual performances, in the *samdhya* or crepuscular ceremony, in the bathing, the offerings, the fire ceremony, the Vedic recitations. The Brahmin's wife or some other female members of his family would devote an hour of the day to the worship of the household idols."[6] In order to be able to spend five hours every day in performing ritual, a man had to have an independent source of income or have priesthood as his occupation. Traditionally, Hindu kings at their coronation made gifts of land and houses to pious Brahmins, as well as on other occasions such as birth, marriage and death in the royal family. Such acts conferred religious merit on the royal house. However, as Brahmins in Mysore became more urbanized and as Western education spread among them, they found it increasingly difficult to lead a life devoted to ritual, prayer, fasting and the punctilious observance of pollution rules. Milton Singer has recorded a similar process among Brahmins in Madras:

> That is to say, they found in their new preoccupations less time for the cultivation of Sanskrit learning and the performance of the scripturally prescribed ritual observances, the two activities for which as Brahmins they have had an ancient and professional responsibility. They have not, however, completely abandoned these activities and to some

extent they have developed compensatory activities which have kept them from becoming completely de-Sanskritized and cut off from traditional culture.[7]

The sharp rise in the age of marriage of Brahmin girls enabled them to take advantage of opportunities for higher education, and this resulted in a breach in the crucial locus of ritual and purity—the kitchen.[8] Traditionally, a young Brahmin girl worked in and around the kitchen with her mother until her marriage was consummated and she joined her affines. All that was required of her was knowledge of cooking and other domestic chores, the rituals that girls were expected to perform, knowledge of caste and pollution rules, and respect for and obedience to her parents-in-law and husband and other elders in the household. Education changed the outlook of girls and gave them new ideas and aspirations. It certainly made them less particular about pollution rules and ritual, though as long as they lived with their affines they could not completely ignore them.

Very few urban Brahmin parents would now deny that education is a necessity for girls, though they would certainly differ as to how much education is desirable. Aileen Ross, who recently made a field study of the urban family in Bangalore, sums up the position as follows:

> On the whole this study shows that most young Hindu girls of the middle and upper classes are still educated with a view to marriage rather than to careers. However, a number of parents were anxious to have their daughters attend universities. Perhaps one of the main reasons for this new trend is that, with the change from child to adult marriage, the leisure time of girls must now be filled in up to nineteen or even twenty-five years. And college is one way of "keeping them busy" until marriage. Another reason mentioned by interviewees was that the difficulty of finding suitable mates for daughters sometimes forces parents to prolong their education further than they had first intended.[9]

Many girls, then, enter careers apparently not because they want them, but because there is nothing else to be done until their parents find them husbands. But it is a fact that a large number of women are employed today in the cities as teachers, clerks, doctors, nurses, welfare workers, and from the point of view of the traditional society, this is indeed revolutionary. It is only to be expected that women's education will bring about radical changes in domestic social life and culture. Ross concludes from her study of educated women in Bangalore that "women of the household will gradually cease to be the strong backbone of family tradition and caste customs."[10] This does not, however, mean that there is a complete breakaway from tradition; while hours may not be spent in ritual, there is usually a domestic altar where lamps are lit and prayers said. Freedom from pollution does not go so far that educated Brahmin women eat in the homes of all other castes, let alone Harijans. While the endogamous circle has widened and subcaste barriers are crossed—for example, a Mandya Srī Vaishnava Brahmin may ignore all subdivisions among Srī Vaishnava Brahmins—marriages between Brahmins and other castes such as Okkaligas or Lingāyats are few and far between. While the Brahmin dietary may be enlarged to include the traditionally banned eggs, meat-eating is still rare.

The religious beliefs and practices of educated Hindus are only now beginning to be studied. Apart from the intrinsic importance of the subject, no study of the processes of Westernization can afford to neglect changes in religion.

Secularization, even politicization, is an important tendency in urban religion, though not the only one. For instance, the famous Dasara or Navarātri festival which was bound up with the royal family of Mysore, and celebrated with great pomp and pageantry, has changed its character with the merger of the former princely state into new and enlarged Mysore. The rise to power of the dominant Lingāyat caste in state politics, and increased regionalism, have both found expression in the festival commemorating the birth of Basava, founder of the Lingāyat sect, becoming more popular since the early fifties. The festival lasts several days, and is celebrated in all the big towns and cities that have Lingāyat concentrations. *Deepavāli* (festival of lights), *Sankrānti* (harvest and cattle festival), *Ugādi* (New Year) and *Rāma Navami* (birthday of Rāma) are common to most Hindu groups in the state, while others such as *Gokulāshtami* and *Shivarātri* (Night of Shiva) have a predominantly sectarian character. The *Rāma Navami* has become, throughout South India except Kerala, an important "cultural" occasion, concerts of classical South Indian music being held in all cities during the nine days of the festival period. The popularity of South Indian classical music has increased greatly in the last two or three decades, and music lovers, whether religious or not, look forward eagerly to the *Rāma Navami*. The concerts are well attended, and open to all who can afford the price of admission. But while there is no doubt that the festival has undergone some secularization, classical South Indian music is essentially devotional, and the great composers whose songs are sung at the concerts were all very devout men. As Singer has rightly observed, "There is no sharp dividing line between religion and culture and the traditional culture media not only continue to survive in the city but have also been incorporated in novel ways to an emerging popular and classical culture."[11]

In recent years, temples have shown considerable activity, and have organized *harikathas* (the narration of religious stories by experts in the art) during *Dasara, Rāma Navami* and other occasions. The *harikathas* continue for several days, sometimes even for several weeks, and attract large audiences who spill over from the temple yard to the roadside, listening to the story and song. Sound amplifiers are regarded as essential at these narrations.

Pious individuals with a flair for entrepreneurial activity organize Vedic sacrifices (*yajnya*) which involve a large investment of money, time and energy, and which go on for several days. The sacrifice may, for example, be to end a drought or for the "welfare of mankind" (*lōka kalyāṇa*). Another popular activity is to undertake to write the name of *Rāma* or some other deity a billion times, and then celebrate the occasion with a big sacrifice.[12] Hundreds of volunteers are enrolled for writing the name, huge sums of money are collected, elaborate arrangements are made for the accommodation of devotees who wish to witness the celebration, and attempts are made to involve important people including ministers and members of the state legislatures in this activity. Local newspapers give much space to describing the final phase of the celebration, the number of people who had gathered, the arrangements made for their comfort, the ritual and, of course, the speeches.

Pilgrimages are very popular and enable large numbers to satisfy their religious aspirations as well as to see the country tourist buses cater to both these needs, as they include shrines as well as objects of tourist interest in each tour. The social and religious horizons of the people have widened considerably; the peasants of Rāmpura village now regularly visit the famous Tirupati temple in Andhra Pradesh, whereas before World War II they only visited shrines which were nearby. The richer peasants in Rāmpura have visited the big pilgrimage centers in South India, such as Rāmeshwaram, Madurai and Shrīrangam. The urban-educated manage to visit at least once the great pilgrimage centers of Banaras, Allahābād and Hardwār in the far north. A well-known South Indian travel agency runs special pilgrim trains for their benefit.

Educated pilgrims are not indifferent to good accommodation, nor to food at the centers they visit. They also do a certain amount of sightseeing and shopping on the side. Sometimes this is given as evidence that the religious motive has become extremely weak, if not totally absent in modern pilgrimages, and that these only provide a good excuse for travel and "patriotic sightseeing". This assumes among other things that the only motive in traditional pilgrimages was the religious one—which, indeed, is questionable. For traditional pilgrimage centers were also shopping centers, and orthodox women who returned from pilgrimages waxed eloquent about the sights they had seen, the abundance or scarcity of vegetables and fruit, and the local price of milk and *ghee*.

The Brahmins of Mysore—like other Dravidian-speaking Brahmins in South India—are all traditionally followers of one or another of the three well-known sects: Smārthas (pure Monists), Srī Vaishnavas (qualified Monists) and Mādhvas (Dualists). Each sect has a few monasteries (*mathas*, each presided over by a head (*mathādhipathi* or *swāmi*), and traditionally the monastic head exercised control over the conduct of his flock. Members had to be initiated into the sect by the monastic head, and when the latter visited their town or village they showed the respect due him by performing the "pāda puja" (worshipping his feet and drinking the water used in the worship). The monastic head was the final authority in all religious matters, including caste disputes, and a follower could appeal to him against a decision of the caste council excommunicating or otherwise punishing him. This power of the monastic head has fallen into disuse. Even the purificatory ritual (*prāyaschitta*) which a returnee from a trip abroad used to undergo has lapsed, owing to the popularity of foreign travel and the increased secularization of Brahmins. But while the power of the monastic heads has eroded greatly, they still command the respect and loyalty of their followers. In recent years contact between monastic heads and the laity seems to have increased. The state governments passed land reform and other legislation which hit the monasteries hard economically, and which have made inroads into their religious autonomy; this has resulted in the monastic heads making greater efforts than before to cultivate their followers.[13] Many educated people now turn to heads of their sects for spiritual and other guidance.

New cults, built around saints, either alive or recently deceased, have come into existence in recent years. Saibāba, a saint of modern India whose tomb is in Shirdi in Maharāshtra, has a large following in South India, and there are Saibāba prayer groups in several South Indian cities. Shirdi is a favourite place for pilgrimage. The shrine of Ramana Maharishi at Tiruvannāmalai in Madras state is also visited, though his cult is not as popular as the Saibāba cult. Among the living *gurus* or teachers, Swāmi Chinmayānanda is very popular and his lectures attract large audiences. The Rāmakrishna Mission also provides a focus for the religious interests of many people. The rise of new cults and the functions they fulfil are subjects that need to be studied systematically.

Singer has commented that "The effect of mass media ... has not so much secularized the sacred traditional culture as it has democratized it."[14] School textbooks contain incidents from the Hindu epics and Purānas, the lives of regional saints, and extracts from old poets whose themes are almost always religious or moral. Journals and books contain much religious matter, and the popular children's story magazine *Chandamāma* exploits the inexhaustible mine of the epics, Bhāgavata, the Purānas and others, for stories for children.[15] The All-India Radio broadcasts devotional music every morning and, occasionally, *harikathas*.[16] It also marks the big festivals by special programs which again draw on the traditional culture of the Hindus. The themes of many films are drawn from the epics, although "social themes" and romantic stories are not unimportant. The Dravida Munnetra Kazhagam (Dravidian Progressive Federation) writers' use of films to conduct propaganda against caste and traditional religion is not without its effects. Tamil films are popular in Mysore, it being common for them to run for several weeks in the big towns and cities. Occasionally the themes are drawn from regional history and the lives of regional saints. But whatever the theme—mythological, historical or social—every film is long, has songs and dances, and comic and romantic interludes. Democratization, whether through films or the All-India Radio or in popular books and journals, brings about radical changes in the content of traditional culture.[17] The highbrow and the purist would call it vulgarization, but what is interesting to note is that it involves an appeal on the one hand to particularistic loyalties such as region, language, sect and caste, and on the other to the universal attraction of sex, dance and song.

3

I discussed earlier how the orthodox elements in Hindu society were put continuously on the defensive ever since the early years of the nineteenth century when European missionaries began attacking Hinduism for its many ills and shortcomings. While the new Hindu elite deeply resented such attacks, they were themselves sufficiently Westernized to be able to take a critical view of their religion. Thus began a long era of reform of Hindu society and religion, and of reinterpretation of the latter. The path of the reformers was far from smooth; in fact, they were martyrs to the cause of modernization of Hindu and Indian society and culture. They and their families had to endure the criticism of kinsfolk, castefolk and others whose opinions they were sensitive to. Some were even thrown out of caste. As already noted, the revolutionary changes that have occurred in Hinduism in the last one hundred fifty years—to which the reformers contributed so significantly—make it very difficult for Hindus today to understand the difficulties faced by their forbears.

The orthodox elements among the Hindus, the foremost among them being priestly Brahmins (*vaidikas*), steadily lost prestige in the face of growing secularization and Westernization of Hindu life and culture. They were for a long time out of sympathy with, if not entirely critical of, the attempts to reform Hindu religion and society. Those among the *vaidikas* who had a reputation for Sanskrit learning continued to command the respect of the people, but with the institution of Sanskrit teaching in modern schools and colleges they began to lose their valued monopoly over the language. Sanskrit learning became open, in theory at least, to everyone irrespective of caste and religion. The development of the disciplines of comparative philosophy, archaeology, numismatics and history provided a broad chronological framework for Sanskrit literature, and freed it from much myth and legend. Those Pandits who did not take note of these new developments began to be regarded as intellectual anachronisms. And the last few decades have seen the rising prestige of technology, engineering, medicine and the sciences generally, while the other subjects, the humanities in particular, have lost much of their prestige. Students with the highest grades seek admission to courses in the prestigious subjects. Initially, parents were motivated by the economic security and high income available to doctors and engineers, but now prestige—the student's as well as the family's—seems to be equally important.

The Brahmin priests fought a continuous rearguard action against secularization of the life of lay (*loukika*) Brahmins. The Brahmins in Mysore state are among the most urbanized and educated of the local Hindus.[18] Thanks to their early and great lead in education, they secured a large share of the high administrative posts, and dominated the professions. As their style of life gradually underwent change, a conflict arose between them and the priests. Many wore Western clothes, they met people from many castes and religions in the course of their work, and they did not perform the various daily rituals as scrupulously as before. Many had their heads cropped, and this went against the Vedic rule which required them to keep the *shikhā* (a long tuft of hair at the top of the skull)[19] just as the habit of the daily shave violated certain other rules. These deviations—along with the tendency to drop the painting of caste marks on the forehead, and to sit down to meals in secular clothes—drew the wrath of the priests. Even more serious were violations of the rules regarding food and drink, and the marrying of girls after they had attained puberty. The people who did these things had power and prestige, but more humble folk imitated them in course of time. The priests lacked the courage—except during the early years of British rule—to throw their powerful patrons out of the caste, and as secularization spread among Brahmins, the priests had no alternative but to bow to the inevitable. Meanwhile, the style of life of the priests themselves became Westernized to some extent. Many even acquired a nodding acquaintance with English and were proud of displaying it.

Regrettably, there have been no studies of occupational changes among different generations of priestly families. But evidence already available shows that in both Bangalore and Mysore cities intergenerational occupational changes have been highest among Brahmins. Noel Gist, who studied intercaste differences in Mysore and Bangalore cities in 1951–1952, has reported that intergenerational occupational differences were highest among Brahmins as compared with other caste categories. In Mysore city, for instance, 82.7 per cent of household heads had occupations different from those of their fathers, and 76.8 per cent of their own sons had departed from paternal occupations. For the non-Brahmin group, the percentages of deviation were 55.7 and 49.4 respectively, while for the Scheduled Castes they were 44.8 and 56.8.[20] Gist's sample does not distinguish between priestly and lay Brahmins, but there is no reason to assume that the former were exempt from processes which affected the latter. From my own experience, I can recall many of my contemporaries in Mysore who came from priestly and orthodox families, but who chose secular careers.

In a word, then, the gradual erosion of priestly authority and prestige, and the secularization of priests, have brought about a situation in which priests lack the confidence to take any initiative in religious or social reform. They do not have the intellectual equipment or the social position to undertake a reinterpretation of Hinduism that would suit modern circumstances. Since the beginning of the nineteenth century, such reinterpretation has come from the Westernized Hindu elite. The fact that this elite has been anti-ritualistic, as well as inclined to frown upon popular sacrifices, beliefs and practices, has stripped Hinduism of a great deal of its content.

The situation depicted above highlights the fact that, unlike the Biblical religions, Hinduism is without a universal organization and a hierarchy of officials whose function it is to interpret it in the context of changing circumstances. While it is true that some Hindu sects—such as the Smārthas, Srī Vaishnavas and Mādhvas, the Lingāyats and several others—have elaborate organizations headed by pontiffs, these pontiffs have authority only within their sects or divisions within sects, and not for Hinduism as a whole.

4

Another characteristic of Hinduism has been its extraordinary reliance on, if not inseparability from, the social structure. The three main elements of the social structure are caste, village community and family system. In Hindu India the political head, the king, was also the head of the social system, including caste. The relation of Hinduism to the state changed with the Muslim conquest of large parts of India. Some Muslim rulers were tolerant of Hinduism, while others who were not sought to convert infidels to the true faith and imposed *jiziya* or poll tax on non-Muslims. The British in their turn observed, on the whole, a policy of neutrality toward all religions, though the Church of England in India was supported from Indian revenues, and European missionaries enjoyed a favoured position thanks to the religious, cultural and racial links between them and the British rulers. It was only in the "native states" ruled by Hindu princes—such as Nepal, Travancore, Cochin, Mysore, Baroda, Jaipur and Kashmir—that royalty discharged some of the functions traditionally expected of it with regard to caste and appointment of monastic heads. The Hindu kingdom of Nepal was, and is, far more traditional in character than Hindu kingdoms elsewhere in the subcontinent, and today Nepal is the only Hindu kingdom in the world: "Until recently, the penal code of Nepal was based on the Shastras, and social, religious and criminal offences were dealt with by identical procedures. Brahmins were immune from capital punishment, and the crime of killing a cow could bring the death penalty."[21]

If we are to understand future trends, the absence of a central organization for Hinduism, as well as lack of support from the political authority for maintenance of Hindu religion and social structure, must be viewed along with the radical changes occurring in the three institutions of caste, village community and family system. I have already dealt with the changes occurring in caste and shall not repeat them here. I shall merely point out that as a result of increased secularization and mobility and the spread of an equalitarian ideology, the caste system is no longer perpetuating values traditionally considered to be an essential part of Hinduism.

The changes that have occurred in the Indian village community have resulted in its more effective integration with the wider economic, political, educational and religious systems. The vast improvement in rural communications that has taken place in the last few decades, especially since World War II, the introduction of universal adult franchise and self-government at various levels from the national to the village, the abolition of Untouchability, the increased popularity of education among rural folk, and the Community Development Program—all these are changing the aspirations and attitudes of villagers. The desire for education and for a "decent life" is widespread and vast numbers of people are no longer content to live as their ancestors lived. Villages in India today are very far indeed from the harmonious and cooperative little republics that some imagine them to be; it would be more accurate to describe them as arenas of conflict between high castes and Untouchables, landlords and tenants, "conservatives" and "progressives" and finally, between rival factions. Everywhere social life is freer than before, as pollution ideas have lost some of their force. Secularization and politicization are on the increase and villagers ask for wells, roads, schools, hospitals and electricity.[22]

It is easy, however, to exaggerate the increase in the secularization of village life. It is true that the unit of endogamy has widened somewhat, but this is more true of the higher castes than of others. The widening is, moreover, along traditional lines; a crude way describing the situation would be that while barriers between sub-sub-subcastes or sub-subcastes are beginning to break down, marriages spanning wide structural or cultural gaps are rare. That is, Peasants are not marrying Shepherds or Smiths or Potters, but different Peasant subcastes speaking the same language are coming together. (However, alliances involving structural and cultural leaps occur occasionally among the new elite in the big cities.) Inter-dining among castes is slightly more liberal than before, but only slightly. All the "touchable" castes will unite against Harijans who want to exercise their constitutional right of entering temples and drawing water from village wells.

The processes which have affected caste and the village community have also affected the family system. This has happened at all levels and in every section of the society, but more particularly among the Westernized elite, that is, the upper castes living in the larger towns and cities. The traditional system of joint families assumed the existence of a sufficient quantity of arable land and a lack of spatial mobility and diversity of occupations.[23] The idea of selling land in the open market, which became popular during British rule, also contributed to the mobility of people. The development of communications, the growth of urbanization and industrialization, and the prestige of a regular cash income from employment in an office, factory or the administration, dispersed kin groups from their natal villages and towns. Yet it would be a gross oversimplification to suggest that the Indian family system has changed or is changing from the joint to the nuclear type. The process is extremely complicated, and there are not enough studies of changes in family patterns in different regions and sections of the society. Enumeration of the size of households or even their kinship composition is not enough, as an urban household may be perfectly nuclear in composition while kinship duties, obligations and privileges overflow it in many important ways. Many an urban household is only the "satellite" of a dominant kin group living in a village or town several hundred miles away. The Indian family system, like caste, is resilient, and has shown great adaptability to modern forces. It is still true, however, that significant changes have taken place in the family system of the Hindus, and these processes are not clearly discernible among the new elite groups. It is among them that there is great spatial mobility, and members who establish separate households in the large cities certainly live in a cultural and social environment significantly different from that obtaining in a traditional joint family in a small town or village. The urban household often lacks those elders who not only are tradition-bound but also have knowledge of the complex rituals to be performed at festivals and other occasions. Their mere presence exercises a moral influence in favour of tradition—as was vouched for by my Andhra Brahmin Communist informant, who said that he changed into pure clothes at meals "because of his grandmother". The education of women has produced a situation in which young girls do not have the time to learn rituals from their mothers or grandmothers, and the small households in big cities frequently lack the old women who have the knowhow and the leisure. The educated wife has less of the traditional culture to pass on to her children, even should she want to.[24] Still more significant is the fact that elite households have become articulators of the values of a highly competitive educational and employment system. Getting children admitted to good schools, supervising their curricular and extracurricular activities, and worrying about their future careers absorb the energies of parents.[25]

These changes in family system occurring among the new elite groups are, however, somewhat offset by other forces. In large cities such as Bombay, Delhi, Calcutta and Madras, voluntary associations tend to be formed on the basis of language, sect and caste, and these make up in some ways for the loss of a traditional social and cultural environment. In a city such as Delhi, for instance, practically every linguistic group of India has voluntary cultural or other organizations which try to recreate for the speakers of each language their home environment. Concerts are held, plays are staged, *harikathas* are organized, regional festivals are celebrated, and regional politicians and other celebrities are welcomed. There is also a certain amount of residential clustering on the basis of language, and this is achieved even in housing projects built by the Government of India and which ostensibly do not recognize regional claims in allotting flats and houses! A homesick South Indian or Bengāli likes to rent an apartment in an area where other South Indians or Bengālis live, and soon there come into existence shops selling the spices, pickles, vegetables, household utensils and cloth he was used to in his home area. The social network of an educated, white-collar South Indian or Bengāli who is living away from his linguistic area does include many people who speak a different language, but those who speak his language will perhaps preponderate in it. To obtain a seat in a school or college or a job for a relative or fellow townsman, he may have to approach a Hindi or Punjābi speaker, but he does this usually through intermediaries who speak his own language.[26]

Nevertheless, the traditional environment that is recreated in a big city differs significantly from the environment that has been left behind. It is a freer, more cosmopolitan and streamlined version, and it lacks the rich detail, complexities, rigidities, nuances and obligatoriness of the traditional environment. Besides, it caters more to the parental generation of immigrants than to the offspring generation. The latter do not think of their parents' natal region as "home", and many of them dislike visiting it even for brief periods. Their participation in the local culture and institutions is far greater than their parents . Occasionally, marriages cutting across the linguistic and caste barriers occur between them and local folk.

The processes of secularization and politicization have also affected monasteries and monastic heads. I have in mind not monastic or other organizations which came into existence during British rule (for example, Rāmakrishna Mission, Arya

Samāj and Sanātan Dharma Samāj) but traditional and pre-British monasteries such as those of the Smārthas, Srī Vaishnavas, Mādhvas and Lingāyats. Gradually the feeling has grown among educated Hindus that the wealth and prestige of these organizations should be used for promoting education and the social welfare of the people; this is one of the reasons why acts passed by state legislatures giving the government considerable powers over the administration of temples and monasteries have not evoked more opposition. The Lingāyats, a highly organized sect, have shown much sensitivity to this new demand, and Lingāyat monasteries operate their own hostels, schools and colleges. Land legislation has everywhere abolished concession tenures such as *zamindāri, jāgīrdāri, inām* and *jodi.* Those who enjoyed such tenures have been paid compensation and the land has been sold to former tenants and lessees. (Lands which were under the "personal cultivation" of *zamindārs* were exempt from such legislation and, as could be expected, many of them took advantage of legal and even extralegal, loopholes to retrieve as much land as they could.) In many states, land held by temples was also affected by this legislation:

> In Orissa, the High Court upheld the compulsory acquisition by the state, with the payment of compensation, of lands which had been dedicated to a Hindu deity (Chintamoni *v.* State of Orissa, A.I.R., 1958, Orissa, p. 18). In Mysore, the Religious and Charitable Inams Act of 1955 empowered the government to resume lands which had been assigned by the maharaja to religious institutions; as compensation the state now makes an annual payment to the institutions. A number of state legislatures are presently in the process of fixing ceilings on land holdings. Uttar Pradesh, Madhya Pradesh, Orissa, Assam and West Bengal have agreed to exempt temple lands from these ceilings. In some of the other states, especially in South India where some of the wealthiest temples are found, a maximum has been fixed for temple land holdings, although higher than that for individual landowners.[27]

Those educated Hindus who did feel such legislation to be unfair criticized the government sharply and monastic heads saw in them a valuable ally against an ever-encroaching state. The reduced resources of monasteries caused some of the heads to turn to their followers for money. They began to undertake tours to raise funds and cultivate the laity and these activities were reported in the press, vernacular as well as English. The monastic heads not only continue to enjoy the esteem of the people but are cultivated by many politicians and they in turn appreciate the usefulness of having friends in political parties and legislatures. Studies of the changing role of monastic heads and other religious figures in modern Indian life would be a valuable contribution to the literature on secularization.

The process of secularization began with British rule and has become increasingly wider and deeper with the passage of years. But it is neither the only process during this period nor has it been always a pure and unmixed one. For instance, nationalism, a secular phenomenon, became enmeshed with Hinduism at one stage. Hinduism has assumed a political form in the Rāshtriya Swayamsevak Sangh (RSS) and the Jan Sangh. The move to abolish Untouchability owed as much to a realization of the inhumanity of the institution as to an appreciation of the political loss that would result from the conversion of Harijans to another religion. The term "communalism", which is an Indian contribution to the English language, testifies to this tendency of religion to become mixed up with politics.

Sanskritization is not only spreading to new sections and areas, it is also increasing among groups which are considered to be already Sanskritized in their style of life. The spread of Sanskritization is aided by mass media and by such secular processes as the increased popularity of education and greater mobility, spatial as well as social. The idea of the equality of all men before the law, and the abolition of Untouchability, are throwing open a culture which was the monopoly of small traditional elites to the entire body of Hindus.[28] The effects of some acts of legislation, such as the introduction of prohibition of the consumption of alcoholic drinks in many states, and the banning of the sacrifice of birds and animals in Hindu temples, are such as to make the government an unwitting but powerful agent of Sanskritization.

5

The significant changes occurring in the triad of institutions—

caste, family system and village community—have resulted in Hinduism becoming, to some extent, "free floating". But this again is only a part of the story. New agencies have emerged to provide a structure for reinterpreted Hinduism. These agencies are still somewhat fluid and emergent. They are, on the one hand, such new institutions as the Rāmakrishna Mission and Arya Samāj and, on the other, old sects and monasteries which are trying to adjust themselves to the new circumstances, and in that process are undergoing change.

Other traditional institutions such as *bhajans* (groups of people who meet periodically for singing hymns and worshipping a deity or saint), *harikathas* and the cults of saints are also contributing to the evolution of a new structure. Milton Singer has described in detail how the Rādhākrishna *bhajans* function in Madras today, and he thinks that their popularity has increased in recent years.[29] *Bhajans* are an all-India phenomenon, and were developed as an institution by the saints who sought salvation (*moksha*) through the pursuit of the *bhakti mārga* or the path of devotion.[30] *Bhajans* are popular in both rural and urban areas and among all classes of Hindus. The relative freedom of *bhajans* from ritual,[31] their great aesthetic and emotional appeal and their ability to cut across caste distinctions, are some of the reasons for their popularity with urban and educated Hindus.

Although *bhajan* groups are sometimes organized around the worship of a saint, the cult of saints is not always associated with *bhajans*, and devotees may worship saints individually in the privacy of their homes. An occasional pilgrimage to the saint's *āshram* (hermitage) if he is alive, or to his tomb if he is dead, is also customary. The cult of saints is an old institution which has continued to modern times. Sects have occasionally emerged from such cults. Allegiance to a sect may be hereditary, entire lineages and subcastes being thus marked off from others, or it may be purely voluntary as in the case of modern saints. Where allegiance is voluntary it usually ignores caste, region and even religion. Saibāba, for instance, is a Muslim saint worshipped by a large number of Hindus, many of whom are educated. Pictures of the saint are kept and worshipped, and the writings by or about the saint are read and discussed. Most Hindus are articulate about their religious observances and beliefs and theological discussions are freely entered into by people who meet for the first time in trains, on buses or in hotel lobbies.

Organizations which profess to propagate Indian culture and thought also propagate Hinduism. The classical literature and thought of India are all Hindu, Buddhist and Jain, and books which popularize classical thought cannot help spreading a body of ideas shared by these three faiths. It is difficult indeed to draw a sharp line between the cultural and the religious in a country such as India, which has a long and recorded history, and where religion has been pervasive.[32] Indian music, painting, sculpture and dance draw greatly on Hindu religion, iconography and mythology. An interesting development in the twentieth century is the emergence of Indian dance and ballet divorced from the traditional contexts of temple and festival, as purely aesthetic forms.

The government, too, is playing an important role in modernizing Hinduism through legislation and other means. It is doing this in spite of the fact that the Constitution declares India to be a secular state. I have already referred to the outlawing of Untouchability. Changes have also been introduced in Hindu personal and family law: bigamy is punishable by law; divorce and intercaste and widow marriage are permitted; and widows and daughters have been given shares in ancestral immovable property. The administration of Hindu temples and monasteries is being radically altered by legislation undertaken by the states.[33] The first of such attempts was embodied in the Madras Religious Endowments Act of 1927, and under it the government appointed a Board of Commissioners headed by a president to supervise the administration of Hindu endowments. This gave way in 1951 to the Madras Hindu Religious and Charitable Endowments Act, under which was created a new department of government headed by a Commissioner. "The task of supervising temples and *mathas* thus passed from a regulatory commission to an executive department directly under a cabinet minister."[34] This Act, which conferred great powers on the Commissioner, was challenged in the courts and the Supreme Court declared some of its provisions invalid. A new act was passed in 1959 with a view to meeting the objections of the court, and while it curtails some of the powers of the Commissioner vis-à-vis *mathas* and denominational temples, "the whole system of control over temples belonging to the general Hindu public, with vast powers vested in the Commissioner, has remained intact. As has been mentioned, these temples constitute the great majority of the Hindu religious institutions."[35]

Other states such as Mysore, Bombay, Bihar and Orissa have also passed legislation, though not so far-reaching as in Madras, controlling the administration of Hindu religious endowments. In 1960 the Government of India appointed a Hindu Religious Endowments Commission, under the chairmanship of Sir C.P. Ramaswamy Aiyer, to examine the administration of Hindu religious endowments and suggest measures for its improvement. The Commission's report, submitted in 1962, urged the speedy enactment of legislation providing for governmental supervision of temples in states which did not already have such legislation, namely, Assam, West Bengal, Uttar Pradesh and Punjab, and the setting up of institutes to provide priests with instruction in Sanskrit, scriptures and ritual, and of theological colleges for the study of religion along with the humanities. Moreover, the Commission recommended that the Government of India give consideration to enacting uniform legislation regulating endowments for all communities. (Bombay state already has such legislation in the Bombay Public Trusts Acts of 1950.)

Legislation undertaken by several states, ostensibly to ensure that endowment funds are not misspent, has resulted in establishment of government departments which determine how Hindu temples and monasteries are to be run and how their money is spent.[36]

> Thus funds from the famous temple at Tirupathi (regulated by special legislation) have been used to establish a university, schools, orphanages, hospitals, etc. Throughout South India, Tirupathi has become the symbol and the model of the new Hinduism which transforms the offerings of individualistic piety and devotion to God into social institutions, dedicated to the service of man. Hinduism is being infused with a modern outlook and a new sense of social responsibility. This is a religious reformation of a fundamental nature. But as the agency of this reform is to a large extent the state, it should not be surprising if devout Hindus object to the liberties being taken with their religion.[37]

Thus the state has become an important means of reinterpretation of Hinduism in the middle decades of the twentieth century, and this in spite of India's proclaimed policy of being a secular state. The state, though most important, is not the only organization performing this function, as I have pointed out earlier. Political parties such as the Hindu Mahāsabha and the Jan Sangh, and "cultural" organizations such as the militant Rāshtriya Swayamsevak Sangh, become agencies for the perpetuation and reinterpretation of Hinduism. In a word, Hinduism is becoming increasingly, though very slowly, dissociated from its traditional social structure of caste, kinship and village community, and is becoming associated with the state, political parties and organizations promoting Indian culture. Traditional institutions such as monasteries and temples, cults of saints, *bhajan* groups, and pilgrimages have shown resilience and adaptability to new circumstances. Mass media such as the films, radio, books and newspapers are playing their part in carrying Hinduism to all sections of the Hindu population, and in the very process of such popularization are reinterpreting the religion.[38]

NOTES

1. *Encyclopedia of the Social Sciences*, vol. XIII, p. 113.
2. For a discussion of the concepts of pollution-purity, see Chapter IV of my *Religion and Society Among the Coorgs of South India*; and L. Dumont and D.F. Pocock (eds.), *Contributions to Indian Sociology*, vol. III, Paris, 1959.
3. Personal communication to the author.
4. In a study undertaken in 1963–1964 of girl students in two colleges in Mysore city, it was found that in the pre-university and B.Sc. classes, 803 out of a total of 1423 in one, and 113 out of 128 in the other, were Brahmins. The former is an exclusively girls' college run by the Government of Mysore, while the latter is a coeducational college run by a private body. I owe these figures to the courtesy of Miss. M.N. Chitra, Department of Sociology, Delhi University.
5. It would be interesting to find out what percentage of Mysore Brahmins between the ages of 15 and 40 wear the sacred thread and try to correlate the results with other social indices such as education, occupation, income and spatial mobility. Thirty years ago practically everyone in that age group would have been found wearing it, and some even performing the daily ritual of *sandhya*.
6. D. Ingalls, "The Brahmin Tradition", in Milton Singer (ed.), *Traditional India: Structure and Change*, p. 6.
7. M. Singer, "The Great Tradition in a Metropolitan Center: Madras", in Milton Singer (ed.), *Traditional India: Structure and Change*, p. 176.
8. See, in connection with the education of women and its effects on

family life, Aileen D. Ross, *The Hindu Family in Its Urban Setting*, Toronto, 1961, pp. 208–231.

9. *Ibid.*, p. 229.
10. *Ibid.*, p. 232.
11. Singer, see *supra* note 7, p. 173.
12. This is perhaps derived from "the cult of *nāma-siddhānta*, recital of God's name as the most potent means of salvation ... developed by saint-authors of the eighteenth century, like Srīdhara Venkatesa and Bodhendra." (V. Raghavan, "Methods of Popular Religious Instruction in South India", in Milton Singer (ed.), *op. cit.*, p. 136.) T.B. Naik in his essay, "Religion of the Anāvils of Surat", in the same book, mentions the existence of the cult of *nāma-siddhānta* in Gujarat also: "Blank notebooks are sold too, each page of which is full of small squares; in each square a god's name has to be written. There are books for 51,000 names, 125,000 names and so on, sold on a non-profit basis by an organization called the Rāmnām Bank (the bank specializing in Rāma's name), c/o Pandit Sevāshram, Mani Nagar, Ahmedabad" (p. 186).
13. Singer, see *supra* note 7. p. 176, and D.E. Smith, *India as a Secular State*, pp. 245–259.
14. *Ibid.*, p. 173.
15. I am excluding from consideration the publications of monasteries and other religious organizations such as the Rāmakrishna Mission. The Lingāyat monasteries are very active in publishing as in other fields. According to William McCormack, Lingāyats publish six magazines and there are about two hundred pamphlets and twenty-five scholarly publications. See his article, "The Forms of Communication in Vīraśaiva Religion", in Milton Singer (ed.), *op. cit.*, pp. 126–127.
16. "Dharwar radio station began broadcasting in 1949, and though hardly a sectarian institution, the station does present many programs of religious interest to Vīraśaivas. The birthday of Basava was celebrated by special program in 1957, which occupied most of the evening broadcast time. Villagers with access to radio sets try not to miss the *bhajan* programs, which are labelled simply 'For Villagers' in the station program guides. *Vacanas* [aphoristic preachings in Kannada of Lingāyat saints] sung in the style of classical music are the most common of the sectarian broadcasts. The Dharwar and Bangalore stations have many *vacana* records and *vacana* programs occur on the average once in two days from each of the two Kannada broadcasting stations. Radio dramas are occasionally produced which narrate the lives of Vīraśaiva saints, as for example, Akkamahādevi." (*Ibid.*, p. 128.)
17. See in this connection McKim Marriott's "Changing Channels of

Cultural Transmission", in V.F. Ray (ed.), *Intermediate Societies, Social Mobility and Communication*, 1959, pp. 66–74.

18. See N. Gist, "Caste Differentials in South India", in *American Sociological Review*, vol. 19, No. 2, 1954, p. 134.
19. "The devout Hindu also wears on his head the little lock of hair, the *śikhā*, sometimes knotted, sometimes merely a tuft of hair slightly longer than the rest, which the Tantric devotee regards as the orifice of the spirit, the point at which the spirit entered at initiation (before initiation one is as good as dead) and leaves at death. The *śikhā* is the repository of the spirit because all spiritual energy lies there. An old Vedic text runs, 'Void is he if he is not covered and is clean shaved; for him the *śikhā* is the cover (protection).' The *śikha* is regarded as the symbol of a Hindu's resolve to face life unmoved." (S. Bhattacharyya, "Religious Practices of the Hindus", in Kenneth Morgan (ed.), *Religion of the Hindus*, New York, 1953, p. 165.
20. Gist, *op. cit.*, pp. 128–129. A similar situation obtains in Bengal: "In the case of castes like Brahmin or Vaidya, the departure from traditional occupation has been very high indeed; while there has been a corresponding concentration, not in agriculture or industries, but in 'higher professions,' like medicine, law, office work of various kinds, or landowning or land management." (N.K. Bose, "Some Aspects of Caste in Bengal", in Milton Singer (ed.) *Traditional India: Structure and Change*, p. 198.)
21. Smith, *op. cit.*, p. 299.
22. But it is obvious that India has a long way to go. See in this connection R. Bendix, *Nation-Building and Citizenship*, New York, 1964, pp. 248–263.
23. F.G. Bailey, *Caste and the Economic Frontier*, Bombay, 1958, pp. 9–10 and 91–93.
24. Aileen Ross found that in Bangalore city in South India, "the type of family structure, however, had a decided relation to the rate of change. The majority of the 141 interviewees, for example, who said that they no longer followed the family customs they had learned as children came from nuclear families, whereas about one-third of those coming from joint families said that they still followed the traditional family customs wholly or in part. Interviewees who had been brought up in orthodox homes or in closely knit joint families, also felt that they had changed less from the customs learned as children than those who had grown up in 'progressive' homes.... Age, marital status and number of generations in city were other important variables which seemed to effect family change." (*The Hindu Family in Its Urban Setting*, Toronto, 1962, p. 281.)
25. *Ibid.*, p. 225.
26. This happens at all levels, including those who are barely literate.

When I was teaching at the M.S. University, Baroda, a Marāthi-speaking peon in the University who knew me well requested me to recommend his cousin for a job in a big pharmaceuticals firm in Baroda. I told him that I did not know anyone there. He then reminded me that the works manager of the firm came from my part of the country! The systematic study of the role of kin, caste and local networks, and of *the links between these networks* in the urbanization process, is an important area of research.

27. Smith, *op. cit.*, p. 244 (n. 13).
28. J.N. Farquhar comments on the paradox of the Sanātan Dharma Sabha selling cheap editions of the Vedas to all Hindus, irrespective of caste: "Yet this most orthodox movement, backed by the heads of all the greatest Hindu sects, sells copies of any part of the Vedas to any one who cares to buy them, and encourages their study, no matter what a man's caste may be." (*Modern Religious Movements in India*, New York, 1915, p. 322.)
29. M. Singer, "The Rādhakrishan Bhajans of Madras City", in *History of Religions*, vol. 2. No. 2, 1963, p. 184, and see *supra* note 7, p. 149.
30. See V. Raghavan, *supra* note 12, pp. 136–137.
31. Some *bhajans* do, however, involve performing elaborate ritual. See Singer, "The Rādhakrishna Bhajans of Madras City", pp. 194–196.
32. For a discussion of the relation between Indian culture and Hinduism in the context of independent India's policy of a secular state, see Smith, *op. cit.*, pp. 374 ff.
33. *Ibid.*, pp. 245 ff.
34. *Ibid.*, p. 245.
35. *Ibid.*, p. 250.
36. *Ibid.*, pp. 245–257.
37. *Ibid.*, p. 254.
38. See Marriott, *supra* note 17.

5

SOME THOUGHTS ON THE STUDY OF ONE'S OWN SOCIETY

1

IN THE PRECEDING CHAPTERS I have tried to analyze some aspects of social change in modern India. I shall now consider briefly some methodological issues which stem out of the study of one's own society, particularly when that society is undergoing rapid transformation. In order to do this I shall have to refer to myself and my work, and embarrassing as this is I hope that the exercise will clarify for me, and perhaps for others also, certain problems which anyone engaged in the study of his own society has to face. It may also induce some of my colleagues to make a similar effort, so that the net result might be greater objectivity in the work we are engaged in, work which an increasing number of scholars from the developing countries are likely in the near future to be engaged in.

One of the things that strikes me as I look back on the reception accorded my work outside my country is the repeated reference to my being an Indian sociologist engaged in the study of my own society. One view was that it gave me a great advantage; according to another, my description as well as interpretation was better when I forgot that I was a social anthropologist; and a third view raised the methodological question, "*Just how far can any sociologist understand his own society*?" Radcliffe-Brown took the first view when he wrote in the Foreword to my book on the Coorgs, "This book by a trained anthropologist, who is himself an Indian, and who has therefore an understanding of Indian ways of thought which it is difficult for a European to attain even over many years, gives us a scientifically valuable and objective account of the religious behaviour of a particular Indian community."[1]

The *Times Literary Supplement* reviewer took the second view: "... is a Brahmin as well as an anthropologist and he looks at the Coorgs from both angles. Perhaps he is at his best when he ceases to feel that he must write in the language of social anthropology and allows his other self, the cultured Indian townsman, to describe and interpret the life of some of the peasantry of his country."[2]

The third view is forcefully expressed in a review by E.R. Leach of my *Caste in Modern India*:

> "For Professor Srinivas there are aspects of Hinduism in general and Brahminism in particular which he *knows* from the inside but which even the most erudite European can never learn. But is this an advantage or a disadvantage from the viewpoint of sociological analysis?
>
> One of Professor Srinivas' most notable contributions to Indian sociology has been his development of the concept of "sanskritization", the basic theme of which is that there is a long term tendency for caste groups which are low in the social hierarchy to imitate the style of life of high caste Brahmins, thus introducing a certain fluidity into the total hierarchy of castes. That such fluidity exists has been clearly demonstrated, but that it should be seen as arising from an emulation of the Brahmins seems to me odd—a specifically "Brahminocentric" point of view! If Professor Srinivas had been of Shudra origin, would this have coloured his interpretation?[3]

My Indian colleagues from outside South India have pointed out to me that my preoccupation with pollution-purity, ritual, Sanskritization, caste and the Backward Classes Movement arises from my being a South Indian. They are of the view that the cultural and social distance between the Brahmin and the others is greater in the South, and that pollution ideas have received greater elaboration there, and finally, that the Backward Classes Movement is characteristic only of the South. One North Indian colleague is emphatic that he could not have located Sanskritization in Bengal while he could not have missed it in Tamilnād. According to him, the Sanskritization of the spoken language is conspicuous in the Dravidian-speaking areas as it results in the juxtaposition of words and speech forms from two different language families. In areas where one or the other of the Indo-Aryan languages prevails, increased Sanskritization does not produce a similar anomaly.

Sanskritization as a term appears for the first time in my Coorg book, but the seeds of the idea probably go back to my master's degree thesis, *Marriage and Family in Mysore*, published in 1942 (and now, fortunately, out of print).[4] It was based primarily on a study of earlier published work on Mysore. Even such a callow researcher as I was at that time could not help noticing that non-Brahmin institutions were "liberal" while those of the Brahmins were not, and generally, that the lower the ritual position of the caste the more liberal were its institutions. More importantly, the upward movement of a caste was marked by, among other things, the banning of divorce and widow marriage: "We may even go so far as to say that the farther removed a caste is from the Sanskritic influence the less respect does it pay to these ideals. But imitation of the higher castes has set in, and soon Kannada society as a whole (with the exception of the highest castes among whom the old ideals are cracking up) will be swinging in the direction of these ideals."[5]

When I was doing fieldwork among the Coorgs of South India I was essentially interested in the reconstruction of their traditional culture, and this resulted in my being myopic toward the changes which Coorg society was undergoing. It was only in Oxford, and at the suggestion of Radcliffe-Brown, that I looked at my material on Coorg ritual from a "structural-functional" point of view. I could then not help concluding that Coorg religion was a variant of Hinduism, the latter consisting of several levels which I labelled "local", "regional", "peninsular" and "All-India". All-India Hinduism was synonymous with Sanskritic Hinduism. Coorg customs had undergone a process of Sanskritization over the centuries, the two most important agents of the process being Lingāyats and Brahmins. An awareness of the influence of Lingāyatism on the life style of the Coorgs was an important factor in my preferring "Sanskritization" to the narrower "Brahminization". Thus, I find myself stating in the Coorg book,

It is not always the Brahmin priest who is the agent of

> Sanskritic Hinduism. In every part of the Kannada country and in Coorg, the Lingāyat sect, consisting exclusively of non-Brahmins, have exercised in the past a Sanskritizing influence. Lingāyat ritual is Sanskritic (though not Vedic), and the Lingāyat Rajas of Coorg have been responsible for the Sanskritization of the customs, manners and rites of the Coorgs. Customs like marking the forehead every morning with three stripes of sacred ashes (*vibhūti*), celebrating the festival of Shivarātri and erecting tombstones, surmounted by the figure of the Nandi Bull, over the graves of important persons, reveal Lingāyat influence.[6]

Leach's assertion that I see Sanskritization "as arising from an emulation of the Brahmins" is, therefore, not correct.

My being a Brahmin did, however, influence in several other ways my observation and understanding of the Coorgs. Throughout the Coorg book there are comparisons, occasionally explicit but most of the time implicit, between Coorgs and Mysore Brahmins. To quote an example of explicit comparison: "Not only widows but remarried widows, are excluded from auspicious rituals but such exclusion is not as thorough among Coorgs as it is, for instance, among Brahmins."[7] Comparison, however, seems inevitable in the process of understanding of another society or even a different section or period of one's own. All new social experience is referred to a pre-existing base of known and understood framework of social institutions, values and ideas.

My model of Sanskritization was derived, as I have stated earlier, from both the Brahmins and Lingāyats. I did miss the Kshatriya and Vaishya models—as Pocock and Singer have pointed out—not because of "Brahminocentrism" but because the Mysore region lacks Kshatriya and Vaishya castes whose style of Life is markedly different from that of the Brahmin or Lingāyat. The Arasus (Kannada-speaking Kshatriyas) have themselves been influenced by Brahmins and Lingāyats and the Komatis (Telugu-speaking Vaishyas) by Brahmins. Both are, by tradition, vegetarians and teetotalers, and call on the Brahmin priest to minister to them at various *rites de passage*.

I am now surprised to find that when analyzing my Coorg material I missed the significance of Westernization. This certainly was not due to my being a Brahmin, but to concentration on the traditional aspects of Coorg society to the total neglect of social change. In a sense, the style of life of Coorgs in the 1940s was far more Westernized than that of Mysore Brahmins. But it was only in 1954 when, at the suggestion of Milton Singer, I started writing the essay, "A Note on Sanskritization and Westernization", that the importance of Westernization and its linkage with Sanskritization suddenly became clear to me. I found that Mysore Brahmins were rapidly Westernizing themselves just as castes ritually lower to them were moving in the direction of Sanskritization. (A similar process has been reported by Gould for some villages in Uttar Pradesh.[8]) This, however, is only one aspect of the process, and there are other and counteracting processes. Westernization is becoming broader, deeper and more powerful as the years go by, and this will necessitate a continuous examination of the dynamic relationship between it and Sanskritization.

Dumont and Pocock have suggested that I transplanted the notion of "dominance" from the African to the Indian field.[9] I used the term "dominant caste" for the first time in my essay, "Social System of a Mysore Village", and it is probable that I was unconsciously influenced by references to dominant clan and dominant lineage in contemporary anthropological literature on Africa. But in a sense the Coorg book is also about a dominant caste, and it was but a step from it to a formulation of the idea of the dominant caste. Moreover, when I was engaged in fieldwork in Rāmpura in 1948, the dominance of the local Okkaligas made a powerful impression on me. The few Brahmins who were resident there were completely, even pathetically, dependent on the powerful Okkaliga landowners. (In some villages in this area Brahmins had previously enjoyed dominance, but their gradual movement since the 1920s into the cities in search of education and employment, had been followed by their selling land to Okkaligas and others.) From my talks with elders in Rāmpura and neighbouring villages I got the impression that even as recently as the World War I years, leaders of the locally dominant castes had enjoyed considerable power and autonomy at the village level thanks to poor communications, and to the absence of any effective involvement on the part of the State in village affairs. This impression was confirmed when I read N. Rama Rao's *Kelavu Nenapugaḷu*, a masterly book of reminiscences of the days when he was an *Amildār* (official in charge of a *tāluk*) in this region.[10] The government officials, as far as people living in any village were concerned, were occasional and unwelcome visitors, and villagers normally went about their work untroubled by them. The leaders of the dominant castes resembled chieftains, and evoked fear and respect from ordinary folk. Each leader was the head of a faction composed of kinfolk, castefolk, and clients from other castes, and relations between leaders of rival factions were distinctly unfriendly.

The dominant caste could be a local source of Sanskritization or a barrier to its spread. Studies of locally dominant castes are, therefore, essential to an understanding of regional cultural differences. More important, a realization of the power, influence and prestige of dominant castes enables the sociologist to view in a new light the ideas and sentiments expressed in the sacred literature of the Hindus. A Brahmin who went to a peasant-dominated village and behaved like a "deity on earth" would indeed get short shrift. Manu would be a bad guide for fieldworkers; urban and upper caste sociologists in India need to keep this constantly in mind.

Finally, my stressing of the importance of the Backward Classes Movement and of the role of caste in politics and administration, are very probably the result of my being a South Indian and a Brahmin at that. The principle of caste quotas for appointment to posts in the administration and for admissions to scientific and technological courses, produced much bitterness among Mysore Brahmins. Some of these were my friends and relatives and I could not help being sensitive to their distress as well as to the steady deterioration in efficiency and the fouling of interpersonal relations in academic circles and the administration—both results of a policy of caste quotas. As one with a strong attachment to Mysore, I could not but be affected by the manner in which conflict between castes prevented concentration on the all-important task of developing the economic resources of the State for the benefit of all sections of its population. I must add, however, that in spite of the Backward Classes Movement, members from different castes were frequently bound together by strong ties of friendship. Sometimes such friendships occurred between entire families, continuing from one generation to the next. I was fortunate in that my natal family had close friends from different castes, sects and religions, and this was a factor in my being able to view the Movement with some detachment. I could also not help noticing how the caste-centered comments of the Brahmins often annoyed sensitive non-Brahmins.

The character of the Backward Classes Movement changed with the transfer of power to the people. The numerical strength of caste groups became critical in a political democracy based on universal adult suffrage and dominance based on economic power and education alone was not enough. Dominant castes tried everywhere to increase their strength by ignoring subdivisions among them previously regarded as important. Sometimes, however, the numerical strength of the caste varied according to the context; for instance, subdivisions were ignored in political contexts while for marriage they continued to be relevant. An extreme example of this is to be found in the Gujarat Kshatriya Sabha, which is made up of Rājpūts as well as Koḷīs who form distinct castes, the Koḷīs being regarded as decidedly inferior to the Rājpūts.

2

Leach has asked whether, from the point of sociological analysis, it is an advantage or a disadvantage for a sociologist to be studying his own society. Whatever the disadvantage, it has certainly not been so great as to prevent the emergence of the discipline of sociology. Marx, Weber, Mannheim and several other sociologists have been continuously preoccupied with the study of their own societies.

It is evident, however, that a sociologist engaged in the study of his own society enjoys advantages as well as disadvantages, and pedagogically it is very important to ensure that the disadvantages are minimized while the advantages are retained. This problem is urgent as an increasing number of sociologists from developing countries are likely to be studying, in the near future, aspects of their own society.

The sociologist who is engaged in the study of his own society is likely to be influenced by his social position, not only in his observations but also in the problems he selects for study. But this need not always be a source of error—it might even be a source of insight. Insights, however, have to be subjected to rigorous testing before they can become valid generalizations. The moral, then, is that an idea is not necessarily wrong because its originator occupies a particular position in the society. Its validity or invalidity has to be independently established. In the words of Bernard Shaw, "The test of sanity is not the normality of the method but the reasonableness of the discovery."[11]

The examination of one's ideas and interests, and relating them to one's social background and intellectual history are, however, necessary in order to make one's work more objective. For the very awareness of subjectivity—and the areas and forms in which it is most likely to occur—is a step toward achieving greater objectivity. But that alone is not enough. It has to be supplemented by several other measures. One obvious measure would be to have the problem—any one problem—studied by sociologists with different backgrounds and indeed, from different countries. International cooperation among professionals is indispensable for achieving greater objectivity in sociology.

Since subjectivity is inescapable as well as serious, a continuous effort must be made to reduce it. This is best done by recognizing its existence and by exposing the student, from the very beginning of his academic career, to the culture and institutions of alien societies. It is in this context that the traditional but irrational distinction between sociology and social anthropology is so disastrous. A true science of society must include the study of all societies in space as well as time—primitive, modern and historical. This is forcibly brought home to the sociologist of Indian society; not only has India a long, recorded history, but Harijans (about 66 millions in 1965) and tribal folk (about 30 millions in 1965) have always been a part of Indian culture and society. Interaction between the various segments and levels of Indian society has been continuous. Over a period of time tribal groups have succeeded in establishing claims to Kshatriyahood, and elements of tribal ritual and social life have found their way into higher Hinduism. Pollution ideas have been elaborated in tribal groups as well as in the high castes. Vested interests continue, however, to regard sociology and social anthropology as separate disciplines.

3

In order to be able to observe any society, the observer needs a measure of detachment from his own, and for detachment to be effective, it must be as much a matter of the emotions as of the intellect. Fieldwork, as I shall explain later, is one of the surest ways of attaining such detachment. It is true that some of the greatest names in the history of sociology did not themselves engage in field research, but the discipline which they worked devotedly to found has grown since their days and field research has contributed significantly to this growth. Anyway, my concern here is with the training of ordinary students and geniuses can be safely left to themselves.

Fieldwork in an alien society constitutes an excellent preparation for the observation of one's own society, but it is very expensive and developing countries will not be able to afford it. Under the circumstances it is best if the young sociologist begins fieldwork in a section of the society different from that to which he belongs. It is well to remember that a classic of descriptive sociology, W. F. Whyte's *Street Corner Society*, was the author's first study and was carried out in a community not far from his university. An urban Indian sociologist coming from a middle-class family would likewise find a village a few miles away or even a slum in his own city a startlingly new social world. One of the consequences of a sharp stratification system is an indifference among the upper groups toward the culture and life of the lower; and in a large country such as India there is in addition considerable regional diversity. Both these factors compensate to some extent for the non-availability of resources enabling Indian sociologists to carry out their first field study in an alien society.

I have so far spoken of fieldwork as though it was of one, homogeneous kind; the fact remains that this is not so. There are different kinds of fieldwork, from the intensive study of a small community or group by a single investigator, to a large, country-wide survey employing a large number of investigators doing the actual interviewing of respondents. And there are various gradations in between. In what follows I have in mind primarily intensive fieldwork using the method of "participant observation", but I expect that all fieldwork which involves the sociologist's coming into some form of close contact with people having institutions, ideas and values different from his own will be productive of detachment, though not in the same degree as intensive fieldwork.

I shall not try to define intensive fieldwork; instead I refer readers who wish to know what it is to Evans-Pritchard's *Social Anthropology*,[12] and to the appendix on fieldwork in Whyte's *Street Corner Society*.[13] Successful fieldwork involves not only the sociologist's painstaking collection of a vast amount of the minutiae of ethnography, but also his exercising his powers of empathy to understand what it is to be a member of the community that is being studied. In this respect, the sociologist is like a novelist who must of necessity get under the skin of the different characters he is writing about. Some institutions of the community or group he is studying may appear strange and others even outrageous. But he should make an effort to overcome his hesitance, if not revulsion, and try to see them as does an ordinary member of the host community. Needless to say, this involves not only his intellect but his emotions as well.

In the process of putting himself in the shoes of the members of another community, the sociologist becomes to some extent detached from his own. Whyte sums up a typical process when he says:

> I began as a non-participating observer. As I became accepted into the community, I found myself becoming almost a non-observing participant. I got the feel of life in Corneville, but that meant that I got to take for granted the same things that my Corneville friends took for granted. I was immersed in it, but I could as yet make little sense out of it. I had a feeling that I was doing something important, but I had yet to explain to myself what it was.[14]

The transition from a non-participating observer to a participating observer cannot happen without the sociologist's exercising all his powers of empathy. As Stark has said,

> the problem of penetrating through the outer shell of an alien society is only partly an intellectual problem; it is partly also a moral one: it is an intellectual effort in so far as it presupposes the collection and comprehension of a good deal of factual material; but it is a moral effort—*un effort de sympathie,* as Bergson, with singular felicity, expressed it—in so far as we can make nothing of that factual material, in so far as it will remain dead in our hands, unless we summon up sufficient willingness to think the thoughts and feel the feelings of the people whose life is involved in these facts.[15]

Generally, after finishing fieldwork, the sociologist goes back to his university to write up the results of his study. Physical distance from the field, as well as the necessity of describing and analyzing his experiences in terms that will be intelligible to his colleagues all over the world, forces him to emerge from his previous role of participant-observer and become an impersonal analyst. This is not an easy task, as any fieldworker can testify. For the first few days or even weeks after his return he will tend to be bewildered by the adjustments he is called upon to make. The seminars and lectures, the informal discussions outside the classroom and lecture hall, and most of all the very process of writing about his experience for an impersonal and professional audience, gradually produce for him a measure of distance from the field he has left behind.

The field study of an alien society, or of a different segment of his own society, prepares the sociologist for the more sophisticated task of studying his own society or that segment of it to which he belongs. Though he still remains a member of his society, he is able to look at it to some extent as an outsider. His position is again similar to that of a novelist who manages to observe his fellow man as well as participate in the life around him. Unlike the novelist, however, the sociologist is primarily interested in a theoretical explanation of human social behaviour and in generalizations rather than the development of concrete particularizations.

I have spoken earlier of the diversity of Indian society and culture, but diversity is only one aspect of the matter. The Indian subcontinent is, in a broad sense, one culture area, and over the centuries ideas, institutions and artifacts have frequently moved from one part of the country to another, undergoing modifications at every step. Thus, as one moves across the country, seemingly familiar things are seen to reveal unsuspected unfamiliarities just as seemingly unfamiliar things reveal familiarities. The unity as well as the diversity of India has to be borne in mind continuously, for otherwise there is likelihood that a village or tribe will be regarded as an isolate. A knowledge of regional history and culture, if not of Indian history and culture, would be a necessary preparation for undertaking a community study. But this can easily be carried too far, and in another sense one's knowledge of the regional or overall culture can never be adequate. Actually, the study of a village or a small town or a caste provides a strategic point of entry for the study of Indian society and culture as a whole. It forces the young scholar to keep his mind steadfastly on the existential reality as contrasted with the book-view of society. It also poses the all-important question, "What is the relation between the sacred literature and the existing institutions during various—that is, any particular—periods of Indian history?" A satisfactory answer to this can only be provided after years of painstaking research into regional history and culture.

While intensive field studies have a very important place in the study of Indian society,[16] it is obvious that they must be supplemented by several other kinds of studies using a variety of techniques. Macro-studies involving the cooperation of several workers, as well as interdisciplinary studies, are essential. But it is best—from the point of view of the researcher's career—that an intensive field study precede rather than follow a macro-study, as it trains the sociologist to look at a fact or event in its total matrix, and to perceive subtle and remote relationships which are frequently missed out in broad surveys of a limited set of facts or relationships.

The study of one's own society while it is changing rapidly—as all developing societies are indeed doing—poses a challenge that calls for the mobilization of all the intellectual and moral resources of the sociologist. The changes might seriously threaten his own social position and sense of security and the difficulty of retaining a measure of detachment under these circumstances can be imagined. Many of my colleagues in India, for instance, come from urban but landowning middle-class families and they have been adversely affected by recent land reform legislation, inflation and the prospect of a change from the use of English to regional languages in the administration and universities. They also see that the political changes which have occurred since Independence have brought to power in many areas leaders of the dominant, peasant castes, whom their fathers used to look down upon only a generation ago. Political dominance at the regional and State levels yields economic and other rewards to the dominant castes, and along with this there has been a steady decline in the power and influence wielded by the urban middle class. Under the circumstances, it is understandable if some Indian sociologists from the middle class become hostile to all change, while others move to another type of subjectivity in which they become the enthusiastic exponents of a radicalist ideology which holds the upper castes and the urban middle class responsible for all the ills of modern India.

Developing countries are today arenas for conflict between the old and the new. The old order is no longer able to meet the new forces, nor the new wants and aspirations of the people, but neither is it moribund—in fact, it is still very much alive. The conflict produces much unseemly argument, discord, confusion, and on occasion, even bloodshed. Under the circumstances, it is tempting for the sociologist to look to the good old peaceful days in sheer nostalgia. But a moment's reflection should convince him that the old order was not conflict-free and that it perpetrated inhuman cruelties on vast sections of the population. A theoretical approach that regards conflict as abnormal, or that invests equilibrium with a special value in the name of science, can be a handicap in studying developing societies. But that is precisely what has happened under functionalism. Leach has pointed out the consequences of preoccupation with equilibrium and solidarity:

> English social anthropologists have tended to borrow their primary concepts from Durkheim rather than from either Pareto or Max Weber. Consequently they are greatly prejudiced in favour of societies which show symptoms of "functional integration", "social solidarity", "cultural uniformity", "structural equilibrium". Such societies, which might well be regarded as moribund by historians or political scientists, are commonly looked upon by social anthropologists as healthy and ideally fortunate. Societies which display symptoms of faction and internal conflict leading to rapid change are on the other hand suspected of "anomie" and pathological decay.[17]

Conflict ought to be seen as inhering in social life everywhere. The institutional devices which every society has provided for the solution of conflict may work with greater or less efficiency. Or the devices may work efficiently in some areas and not in others. There may be more conflict in some societies than in others, and in the same society there may be more conflict in some periods than in the others. Conflict may be uniform over almost the entire range of institutions, or more frequent in some than in the others. It may be much greater over some objects and events than over others. But conflict as such is an inescapable part of social existence and should be of serious concern to the sociologist.

It is necessary to distinguish between forms of conflict that can be resolved by existing institutional mechanisms and more fundamental conflicts that threaten the entire social order. The social order may change gradually over a period of time, or suddenly and with violence. The suddenness of the change may, however, be more apparent than real, the dynamic forces having gone unrecognized for some time or their significance having been misunderstood.

The developing countries are characterized by the existence of leaders who are determined to bring about radical changes in traditional life and culture, and these leaders both reflect and guide the aspirations, hopes and ideals of their followers. Population is growing rapidly in these countries, in some of them, this constitutes a serious obstacle to economic development. Under the circumstances a return to the old order would only mean starvation and misery for millions. Sociologists from developing countries are therefore forced to take a positive attitude toward social change. Some are also actively involved in the process of development, and an increasing number are likely to be thus involved in the future as these countries become committed to programmes of planned development.

Sociologists may be involved in developmental work, either as regular employees of the government or as members of policy-making committees. In the former role they are like other civil servants except that they continue to be engaged in a sociological activity—the study and evaluation of the work of various developmental agencies and individuals. This is not an easy task as it involves judging, however indirectly, the work of their colleagues in the government. A very tactful report may preserve good relations with colleagues in other departments, but may thereby totally fail in the main task of evaluating developmental work. Pinpointing defects, on the other hand, may not only result in bad relations with particular departments or officials, but may even dry up official sources of information for investigators. The information collected cannot always be used, as it might mean committing a breach of confidence. The work of evaluation thus poses a variety of problems when the evaluating unit is part of the administrative machinery, or even when it is an autonomous organization.

Over the years, sociologists employed by the government are likely to find their expertise becoming blunted and out of date, just as their bureaucratic sense is likely to become keener. The government as well as the discipline might benefit by their spending a few months periodically in universities, attending refresher courses and reading up on the latest developments in theory and method.

The problems of the academic sociologist who serves on government committees are, however, of a different kind. In the first place, he has to decide how much of his time he is going to give to committees, and how much to his teaching, his students and his own reading and research. The pitfalls and dangers attendant on membership of committees are well known. The need to be "practical" and to see the difficulties of government, to present to the people a hopeful view of the future, plus considerations of tact and finally, the desire to rub shoulders with the great of the land, might all make him a pleasant "yes man" who finds himself, as a result, put on more and more committees. Again, the fact that governments now collect vast quantities of data on a wide variety of subjects, and that they have a monopoly over such data, means that committees start with assumptions regarding facts which are not checked by any outside agency.

Perhaps those sociologists most useful to committees are the ones who have had some experience of how the development agencies of the government work and how these agencies actually collect their data. The employment in government of academic sociologists for short periods or for particular assignments, may be desirable from several points of view. It gives the sociologists inside knowledge of how policies are implemented at various levels of the government and of the relations between officials and the people. In other words, it would be a kind of "field experience" of development for them. They would also meet and talk to the men who are gatherers of primary data for the government.

But a most important role of the sociologist is to analyze ongoing social processes in his country. If he is successful in this task he is making a contribution to collective self-knowledge which others, without his training, are ordinarily not capable of making. And knowledge, unless it is suppressed, is likely to lead to action. The sociologist can perform such a function only when he is in a university and it is therefore essential that a sufficient number of able sociologists teach in universities. The higher salaries and attractive perquisites and even the greater prestige, attached to government employment in some developing countries operate against the best men continuing in universities. And the situation is likely to get worse when firms and factories begin to compete with the government in luring sociologists away from teaching and fundamental research.

Underlying his role as teacher and as analyst of social processes, however, there is a commitment to the discipline as well as to his country. As a sociologist he is a member of an international, scholarly community, each member of which is striving to teach the subject and also advance its frontiers. It is well to remember that his other commitment is to the country as a whole and its development, and not to the government of the day, a political party or the establishment. It is true that all developing countries are passing through a strong nationalist phase, and that occasionally this may express itself in chauvinism; but while rejecting the latter we should be careful not to also reject nationalism, which provides a strong motive force for social reform and development. But as a student of social evolution the sociologist should also see that wider political entities than the nation-state are emerging, and that the best hope for the survival of his country (and himself) is a world in which a supranational order has outlawed war and the sources of war, between nations.

The sociologist's commitment to democratic processes is fundamental and is derived from his commitment to his discipline, for unfettered social inquiry cannot exist and flourish in totalitarian systems. This is particularly true in regard to a sociologist studying his own society. Commitment to democratic processes results in the sociologist having a deep concern in national development; the expectations of ordinary people have risen everywhere and they can only be satisfied by swift development as well as by a swift and sharp reduction of existing inequalities. Development which only makes the rich richer and leaves the condition of the masses of the poor unchanged is likely to produce chronic political instability which, in turn, will hamstring development. Commitment to development is therefore also a commitment to the reduction of economic and social inequalities.

I have listed some of the qualities I regard as desirable if not necessary in sociologists coming from developing countries. I would like to add to these an occasional ability to see the absurd side of things and to laugh at themselves. Otherwise they will be pompous and opinionated, and apt to regard themselves as infallible.

NOTES

1. A.R. Radcliffe Brown, foreword to M.N. Srinivas, *Religion and Society Among the Coorgs of South India*, Oxford, 1952, p. v.
2. *Times Literary Supplement*, September 6, 1952.
3. E.R. Leach, *The British Journal of Sociology*, vol. XIV, no. 4, December, 1963, pp. 377–378.
4. M.N. Srinivas, *Marriage and Family in Mysore*, Bombay, 1942.
5. *Ibid.*, p. 126.
6. M.N. Srinivas, see *supra* note 1, p. 225.
7. M.N. Srinivas, see *supra* note 1, p. 73.
8. H.A. Gould, "Sanskritization and Westernization, a Dynamic View", *Economic Weekly*, vol. XIII, no. 25, June 24, 1961, pp. 945–950.
9. L. Dumont and D.F. Pocock, "Village Studies", in *Contributions to Indian Sociology*, no. 1, April, 1957, p. 27.
10. N. Rama Rao, *Kelavu Nenapugaḷu*, Bangalore, 1954, *passim*.
11. Bernard Shaw, preface to "Saint Joan", p. 16 (Penguin edition).
12. E.E. Evans-Pritchard, *Anthropology*, Glencoe, Ill., 1954, pp. 64–85.
13. W. F. Whyte, *Street Corner Society*, Chicago, 1953, pp. 279–360; see also J.A. Barnes, "Some Ethical Problems in Modern Fieldwork", *British Journal of Sociology*, vol. XIV, no. 2, June, 1963, pp. 118–134 and G.D. Berreman, *Behind Many Masks*, Ithaca, 1962.
14. Whyte, *op. cit.*, p. 321.
15. W. Stark, *Revue Internationale de Philosophie*, Brussels, no. 13, July, 1950, p. 19.
16. See in this connection, "Village Studies and Their Significance", in *Caste in Modern India*, pp. 120–135.
17. E.R. Leach, *Political Systems of Highland Burma*, London, 1954, p. 7.

Appendix

CHANGING VALUES IN INDIA TODAY

1

BEFORE I proceed further, I would like to provide a brief and tentative idea of what I mean by "values". I have in mind those ideals of conduct the practice of which is admired by a people. Implicit in such admiration is a recognition that the ideals are difficult to practise, and that those who succeed in doing so are regarded as exceptional individuals, providing models for others to emulate.

However, my aim here is not so much to provide a satisfactory definition of "values"—that I leave to philosophers—but to convey a rough and ready idea of what I mean so that I can proceed with my main task, which is to discuss the changes in ideals of conduct (values) which have taken place (and are taking place) in India today.

Values are a difficult subject to discuss with respect to any people but the difficulty increases enormously when dealing with a country as vast, diverse, stratified and complex as India. Values vary from one section of the people to another on the basis of region, language, religion, sect, caste, class and ethnicity. There are also significant differences between villagers and city-dwellers. Indeed, the complexity is so great that one is tempted to abandon the task as hopeless but then valour is sometimes, though very rarely, better than discretion.

Reprinted from the *Economic and Political Weekly*, vol. XXVIII, no. 19, May 8, 1993.

Values ought to be distinguished from norms governing actual behaviour.[1] For instance, monogamy is a value for men and women in certain sections of Indian society, and this has to be distinguished from norms which govern the behaviour of husbands and wives. Thus a husband in a traditional marriage is expected to provide for his wife and children, while the wife has to cook and serve food and perform other domestic chores. She is also expected to obey her husband, who has the right to chastise her when he thinks that her conduct is not "wifely". But the norms are not very clear when two educated members of the middle classes get married and both of them are earning.

Even at the level of norms, there is a distinction between what may be called "statistical" norms and "ideal" norms. The norm may be mutual sexual fidelity on the part of husband and wife. However, local opinion may recognize that very few men are actually faithful to their wives and breaches of the fidelity norm by men may be viewed leniently, while unfaithful wives may be treated harshly. Again, in a stratified society, the fidelity norm may be regarded as more binding in some strata than in others.

While values and norms varied from group to group, the locally dominant caste or other ethnic group provided a model for emulation for the non-dominants. But this operated in a circuitous way: since the dominant castes were wealthy, powerful and enjoyed high status, lower groups were not permitted to take over their customs, manners and life-styles. Any attempt on their part to emulate the dominants invited punishment, but over a long period of time some of the customs and manners of the dominants gradually percolated to the others. Incidentally, since the 1950s the power of the dominants to enforce their will on the others has been eroded due to legislation, education, improved communications and other modernizing factors.

However, the dominants were not always Hindus: Jains, Sikhs, Christians and Muslims enjoyed dominance in particular parts of India at different periods of time, and their culture influenced the culture of the area in which they were dominant. Some groups were particularly susceptible to the influence of the dominants: thus some Kāyastha groups in parts of North India were influenced strongly by the local Muslim aristocracy, and in South India, the culture of the omnivorous, martial Coorgs was influenced by the puritanical, vegetarian and non-martial Lingāyat rulers. During colonial rule, however, the better-off

Coorgs were influenced by the culture of the British coffee planters in Coorg.

In considering the values, norms and behaviour of people in a country such as India, one cannot ignore the influence of the scriptures and the epics. It is possible that the influence of some scriptures such as the *Manudharmashastra* on the conduct of Hindus has been greatly exaggerated, especially by reformers, but that is no reason for ignoring the influence of the sacred books. The only point is that such influence varies from region to region and group to group, and is therefore difficult to generalize. In this connection, the proximity or otherwise of a great temple, monastery, pilgrimage centre, or the capital of the kingdom, radically affected the values and behaviour of the people. For instance, given the lack of roads in pre-British India, people living even 25 miles from the capital of a Hindu king might be guided entirely by the norms of their caste or tribe, unless a great temple or monastery was located close by. At the same time, the popularity of the epics and of institutions such as *harikatha* (narration of religious tales in prose or verse), helped to spread certain values, norms, ideas and beliefs of all-India Hinduism among people living in different parts of the country. The two points I have just made run counter to each other, but then the interplay of contrary forces must be accepted as a basic characteristic of our field of study.

Contrary to the popular belief that Indian society is rigid and immutable, it has been subject to continuous change. The fluidity which characterized the pre-British political system, particularly at the lower levels, was a source of dynamism in the sense that dominant castes often acquired political power at local levels and sought to legitimize power by claiming to be Kshatriyas, employing genealogists to provide them with lineages which would be regarded as noble, and by Sanskritizing their rituals, customs and life-styles. This in turn gave rise to local caste systems which differed in some ways from similar systems elsewhere. (This was specially true of frontier areas.)

While caste has been studied in some depth, the Bhakti movement, which surfaced in almost all parts of the country though at different times, and which was anti-caste, anti-Brahmin, anti-ritual and anti-patriarchal, has not been studied in sufficient depth or seriousness by sociologists. What was the effect of the Bhakti movement on the caste system and on the ideology of gender relations? Has the Bhakti movement facilitated the acceptance of human equality? Considering that the Bhakti movement goes back to the 7th century A.D., even if we ignore the Jain-Buddhist questioning of the pre-eminence of the Brahmins, does protest against caste and gender inequalities form a main strand of Indian culture instead of being a marginal phenomenon?

The establishment of British rule resulted in shutting the doors on group mobility through the well-known route of capturing political power at local levels, and the picture of Indian society as extremely rigid, bigoted, divided and characterized by untouchability, *suttee* and the inhuman treatment of widows, painted by some British administrators and evangelizing missionaries, was accepted by Indian reformers early in the 19th century. This picture continues to persist though recent sociological research has pointed out serious shortcomings in it.

Changes in values and norms are frequently discussed at the individual level, and without reference to the wider society of which individuals are members, and to the forces operating in the wider society. In this brief chapter, however, some of the changes in the wider society are emphasized, as they are essential to understanding changes in values and attitudes in India today. In section 2, I describe briefly a few major changes that were initiated during the early years of Independence, and they in turn are responsible for some changes in the values and attitudes of individuals.

2

Soon after Independence, the new rulers set themselves the task of producing a constitution committed to bringing about a change from a caste and feudal society to a "casteless and classless" society through the means of parliamentary democracy based on adult franchise. This was a revolutionary decision, in particular the introduction of adult franchise, considering the fact that only 16.6 per cent of the population was then literate,[2] and that over 80 per cent of the people lived in villages which lacked roads and were isolated, particularly during the rainy season. Unlike other known revolutions in history, the Indian one was slow to pick up, and was by and large non-violent till the 1970s, when it turned increasingly violent. Violence of all sorts is now widespread, and in some parts of the country, endemic.[3]

The elite which came to power with Independence wanted the constitution to bring about fundamental changes in Indian economy, culture and society. The constitution provided not only a charter for ushering in a revolution but the instruments for achieving it. As already mentioned, adult franchise was the principal means for bringing about the revolution, while other measures such as the outlawing of untouchability, and its practice in any form declared a criminal offence, the reservation of seats in legislatures for SCs and STs, and jobs in the government were also important. It must be mentioned, however, that these were intended as temporary measures in order to enable the SCs and STs to catch up with the forward sections of society. Provision was also made for the states to take steps to advance the interests of the "Socially and Educationally Backward Classes" (SEBC), also called the "Other Backward Classes" (OBC). The states were asked to prepare lists of such "classes" on the basis of objective criteria: caste was chosen as a major criterion by several states, on the basis of the level of education of its members and their representation in the government services, as compared with the average levels for all the castes in the state.

The southern states have been active since the 1920s in the promotion of the welfare of the OBCs, and this has resulted in the latter making substantial gains. But states such as West Bengal and Orissa have not even prepared lists of OBCs. The Mandal Commission, established by the Janata government in 1978 to suggest suitable measures for increasing the access of the OBCs all over India to education and employment in the government, recommended, among other things, the reservation of 27 per cent of government jobs, both at the centre and in the states for the OBCs. In August 1990, V.P. Singh, then prime minister, decided to implement the Mandal recommendation regarding job reservation. This led to violent protests from college students all over the country, many of them committing suicide by setting fire to themselves. There were writ petitions against the government's decision in the Supreme Court. In a recent judgment (November 1992), however, the Supreme Court has upheld the decision to reserve 27 per cent of government jobs at the centre and in the states for the OBCs, but they have also imposed a few new conditions.

3

It is indeed impressive that India has been able to practise democracy since 1947, except during the emergency years 1975–77. The task of holding periodical elections for electorates running into a few hundred millions, is indeed a Himalayan one, and what should be surprising is not that the elections are marred here and there by violence, booth-capturing and "rigging" but that the bulk of the people in this vast, poverty-stricken, backward and hierarchical country should not only practise democracy but make attempts to deepen, extend and cleanse it.[4] Democracy enables every tension to surface, and with increasing numbers of hereditary groups competing to obtain access to resources which are getting more scarce, the government is continually under such pressure that its survival occasionally appears precarious. But even such a situation is better than that under totalitarian regimes, where everything appears smooth on the surface, only to collapse suddenly and irrevocably. Further, democracy is also an invaluable information system in a large, diversified and poor country like India. Democracy is a necessity for India, and it is likely that India's survival as a single entity is due to its adherence to democracy. Contrast in this connection the sudden collapse of countries to its north and west. India's success with democracy is far more relevant for developing countries than its success in the U.S. or U.K.

Another achievement is the manner in which India has increased its food production from about 52 million tonnes at the time of Independence to over 170 million tonnes today. Of course production must continue to increase if the growing population has to be fed, let alone a surplus created for export. It is also remarkable that India has not had a famine after Independence, whereas China had disastrous famines during the years of the Cultural Revolution (1954–1956) when millions of people died, estimates varying between 16 and 30 million.

As a result of economic development since Independence, the proportion of the population below the poverty line has come down to about one-third.[5] But the country is far from abolishing poverty and from assuring the poorest that their basic needs will be met.

Substantial improvement has occurred in the position of women but it is as yet confined largely to urban middle-class women.

However, women's movements have gained strength in the last three decades and they are aimed at combating specific evils such as dowry and *suttee*, and in achieving eventual gender equality. But I do not discuss this here.

4

No discussion of changing values can avoid referring to pervasive corruption and violence in political and social life. Corruption has grown phenomenally during the last 30 years and no area of life is free from it. Over the years corruption has come to be accepted as a fact of life and it is widely known that the citizen has to pay officials and politicians for permits, licences and other favours. Government officials have to pay bribes, for instance to be transferred out of a place, or to stay where they are. Transfers appear to be a major source of income for higher officials and their bosses, the ministers. This means that transferable officials must collect enough money in the course of their official work to be able to get or avoid a transfer. The net result is that the citizen is compelled to pay a bribe for anything he wants from the government. Corruption has penetrated so deep that a former chief minister of Karnataka once remarked that only a powerful social movement could put an end to it. Apart from the *fact* of corruption, there exists a *mythology* of corruption which is even more destructive of public morale; ordinary people talk gaily of chief ministers who made a few hundred crores in the course of two or three years in power.

There has been a tremendous increase in all kinds of violence, organized violence against the state, inter-group violence, intra-familial violence, an increase in the general climate of violence, and finally, as in the case of corruption, a tacit acceptance of violence and a growing insensitivity to murder, bloodshed, gang wars and rape. Some of the violence is directly related to the politico-economic system if it does not stem out of it, as for instance in "booth-capturing" during elections.

Since the acquisition of political power opens the doors to wealth, influence and status, all sorts of people, including smugglers, black marketeers and mafia dons want to become MLAs and MPs. Political scientists and journalists have written at length about the "criminalization of politics" in recent years but nothing has been done so far to tackle it.

Another prime though indirect source of continued violence and frustration is the excessive concentration of power in the centre (union of India) as compared with the constituent states. Such concentration has been compounded by the Planning Commission, which has become a powerful arm of the centre allocating resources to the states, and also in monitoring the implementation of the projects it funds. This has resulted in a feeling of helplessness on the part of the people in some states, which ultimately leads to violence. The remedy is to give more powers to the states but the centre is dragging its feet on this issue as also on the issue of forming smaller states, which will enable some ethnic groups and areas to shape their own futures. The agitation for the formation of a tribal state, Jharkhand, out of parts of Bihar, West Bengal, Madhya Pradesh and Orissa could have been prevented from assuming the violent forms which it has taken if remedial action had been taken earlier. That smaller states make for greater democracy and better administration, is another argument in their favour.

I do not wish to discuss in detail the phenomenal increase in violence, particularly inter-group violence since Independence, but would like merely to point out that the abolition of untouchability, punishing its practice in any form, the reservation of seats in legislatures, jobs in government and other concessions for the SCs and STs, have angered large numbers of others and, in particular, the rural dominant castes. Clashes between the dominant castes and SCs are frequent and bloody, and are likely to increase with SCs becoming more assertive of their rights.

In urban areas, which are invariably multi-ethnic, economic conflict between groups might assume the form of a struggle between the "sons of the soil" and "outsiders", even when the former are only earlier immigrants. This kind of situation is often exacerbated by politicians, businessmen and the film industry, who may use such conflict to further their own ends. The presence of a large number of unemployed, low-skilled and uneducated youth provides the requisite muscle-power to fight the battles of politicians and businessmen.

No account of inter-group violence can afford to ignore clashes between members professing different faiths, which have become frequent in recent years. The causes are many and tangled but an important factor has been the rise in the post-war world of religious fundamentalism everywhere and in particular, in West Asia. In the South Asian region, relations between Hindus and Muslims came under tremendous strain during the closing years of British rule, and the departure of the British was marked by the partition of India into Pakistan and India, and by the most violent carnage in the region's history, in which nearly half-a-million people were massacred. However, independent India opted for a secular, democratic constitution which guaranteed the protection of the culture, language and religion of the minorities, while Pakistan declared itself an Islamic republic. But in the last few years India's secularism has come under strain, the Bharatiya Janata Party (BJP) and its allied organizations such as the RSS, Vishwa Hindu Parishad and Bajrang Dal, charging the ruling Congress Party with practising "pseudo-secularism" and "minorityism" to the detriment of the interest of the Hindus who constitute 80 per cent of the population. The recent destruction of the Babri Masjid by the followers of the VHP and allied organizations in order to erect a temple to Rāma in its place, was followed by violent riots all over the country, in which over 1,100 people died, and it has greatly exacerbated relations between Hindus and Muslims. The destruction of Hindu and Jain temples and churches in Pakistan, and Hindu temples in Bangladesh in retaliation for the destruction of the masjid have added fuel to the fire. The net result is that India's political system and social order are facing a severe crisis.[6]

With the rapid spread of dowry among the people cutting across not only caste but sect, religion, class and region, intra-familial violence has increased enormously. Harsh economic calculations enter into all traditional marriages, the main aim being to become rich at the expense of the bride's family, and huge sums of cash, gold and consumer durables are extracted by the groom's family. The size of the dowry has become an indication of the status of the groom's family. Greed and crass materialism mark marriage negotiations and dowry demands often pursue the wretched wife even after she has given birth to one or two children. Many women choose to escape torture and humiliation from their affines by committing suicide by the horrible though well-known method of dousing their saris with kerosene and setting fire to themselves.

One cannot fail to mention the part played by the media, the films and TV in particular in fomenting a climate of violence.

Violence, sex and drugs seem to be the staple of films, both foreign and Indian, and the TV brings all this into the living room. Violence, sex and drugs are now a world-wide problem with the invasion of the skies of the developing countries by satellite and cable TV. This is one of the consequences of the world becoming a global village.

5

Since Independence, there has been a visible improvement in the living standards of large numbers of people, who eat better, dress better, invest sizeable portions of their income in the education of their children, live in better housing, and spend sizeable sums in buying such consumer durables as refrigerators, TV sets, washing machines, food-processors, two-wheelers, cars and VCRs. The market for these commodities comprises the middle class and the top 10 per cent of the population, both together amounting to 340 million in 1987–88.[7] It is a huge and growing market, and it is no wonder that multinationals appear to be keen to enter it. It may be noted that buyers of consumer durables are not confined to urban areas, the better-off in rural areas also going in for them. It is not unlikely that the status component in the buying of consumer durables is even higher in villages than in cities, those who own the durables being a small proportion of the local population and the possession of durables being a clear mark of social distance between the haves and have-nots.

Improvements in living standards is usually, if not invariably, followed by an attempt on the part of the upwardly mobile individual to improve the social standing of his family if not of the larger kin-group. A key element in upward mobility is education, for without it good jobs will not be available, living standards cannot be improved, good marriages cannot be contracted and access to other elements of high status denied. But there is severe competition for obtaining admission to good schools which means, by and large, from the point of view of the parents, English-medium schools. (This preference has also spread to rural areas.) The tremendous demand for admission to good English-medium schools has led to the latter charging high fees and, in addition, to the payment of sizeable amounts of money as admission fees. The government has no control over private schools in such matters. This practice is confined at present to some parts of the country, but all over India urban parents experience acute anxiety over the admission of their children to good schools.

Parental anxiety reaches its apogee, however, at the time of their offspring seeking admission to college, in particular to medical, engineering, technical and other professional colleges. The question of admission is further complicated by reserving a proportion of seats to SCs/STs and OBCs. Such reservation is probably highest in Karnataka, where not more than 30 per cent of the seats are allotted on the basis of merit as measured by marks obtained at the qualifying examination, and at the entrance test. The net result is that a large number of "good" students from the "forward" castes are rejected, while those getting lower marks but hailing from the SC/ST and OBC categories obtain admission. This causes much heartburn, and the parents of at least some of these students will try their hardest to obtain seats for their offspring in professional colleges. There is also another and perhaps more prolific source seeking admission to such colleges, namely the rich and influential parents of mediocre students. What are labelled as "capitation fee" colleges meet this demand. "Capitation fee" colleges are Karnataka's contribution to the cause of higher education in India.[8] The Supreme Court has recently condemned the institution of charging capitation fees for admission but unless the causes underlying the demand for them are removed, I am afraid they will continue in one form or another. Many politicians have a vested interest in them.

It is well known that many of those who obtain admission have neither the ability nor the interest to pursue exacting courses of professional study even when the institutions are well-equipped and have competent teachers. The question then arises, why do so many parents want to admit their offspring to such tough and demanding courses of study? The apparent answer that the possession of professional degrees provides the road to economic security is not true, for newspapers recently (1992) reported that in Karnataka alone there are over 18,000 unemployed engineering graduates. And there are also dozens of unemployed doctors. But society continues to place a high value on professional education, and a doctor or engineer son fetches a big dowry which not only improves the family's finances but also its social standing. In some parts of the country, however, there is a caste component to the demand for professional education; the earlier entrants to professional education were from the higher castes and their success and prosperity stimulated large numbers from the backward classes to emulate them.

It is surprising that parents—I am now thinking of *educated parents*—do not seem to pay any attention to the talents and inclinations of their children in choosing careers. The main motive in choosing a professional career for a son or daughter is to boost the latter's image and their own among their relatives, friends and neighbours. The idea that a person should pursue a career which would allow his innate talents to develop so that work not only gives an income but a sense of satisfaction, does not seem to obtain even among the middle classes. A surer and more expensive way of producing educated misfits cannot be imagined and the country has been doing this for over 50 years.

The government of India had a constitutional obligation (Article 45) to make education compulsory for all children in the age-group 5–14 within a period of ten years from 1951, but this has not been met even 45 years after Independence. Further, the national literacy rate is only 52 per cent and there are regions where literacy, particularly female literacy, is abysmally low. However paradoxical it may seem, higher education continues to be highly subsidized, and there is the proud boast that India is the third-largest producer of scientific and technological specialists in the world.

The IITs enjoy great prestige as institutions and they are highly subsidized by the government. Admission to them is eagerly sought after and highly competitive, but how many of those who graduate from them stay in India? Indeed, the question needs to be asked, how many of those who benefit from studying in the elite institutions of higher education in India seek careers in the country? Our most successful exports are our best and brightest men and women!

In contrast to Indians who went abroad in the 1940s and 1950s for higher studies, those who go abroad nowadays do not seem to want to return home to seek careers. Excited parents are heard saying, "My son (daughter) does not want to come back. What is there to come back to?" And they are right. Many if not most of our universities and other centres of higher learning have become cockpits for caste, regional and linguistic conflict and intrigue, and both teaching and research are in a deplorable condition.

Appointments are made frequently on grounds other than merit. In fact "merit" has become a dirty word in the lexicon of the advocates of caste quotas and the "progressives". There is no surer way of being dubbed a "reactionary" than by advocating merit as the main criterion in selection to an important post.

Until recently, some concern was expressed about the "brain drain" from India to the developed countries, and the need to "reverse" the flow. But such concerns seem to have evaporated quietly, and the expatriates have become NRIs, whose dollars seem to be more important to the country than their skills, qualifications and experience. The irony of this situation seems to be lost on everyone. Greenbacks are preferred to grey cells.

The foreign bug has bitten not only the young but older men and women too. Middle-aged Indian women now travel to the U.S. or U.K. to oversee the pregnancies of their daughters, reversing the traditional custom of pregnant daughters going to their natal homes for confinement. Middle-aged women love to talk to their relatives and friends about their stay abroad, the air-conditioned houses and cars, the gadgetry, the glories of the American supermarket, and the conveniences and wealth their offspring command. Back home, the middle class family has shrunk, elderly parents living by themselves and receiving dollar cheques from their offspring. Very soon it will not be untrue to define an urban middle-class family as one which has at least one person earning abroad.

I shall now return to the phenomenon of consumerism, indeed galloping consumerism, for no account of changing values can be complete without reference to it. This is a fairly recent phenomenon but it is making up for lost time by the speed with which it is spreading. Consumerism is heavily dependent on advertising, and the advertising business is not only booming, but attracts many talented people. Indian newspapers and journals nowadays regularly bring out lush supplements with multi-coloured illustrations on glossy paper but with hardly any worthwhile reading matter. Looking at them one wonders whether India is a poor country. Advertisements figure on the TV with glamorous film, sports and athletic stars urging the viewer to buy this or that variety of TV set, refrigerator, washing machine, shaving soap, mouthwash, toothpaste, textiles, shoes and so on. It is safe to assume that as far as the TV is concerned, India is only witnessing the beginning of the exposure. TV-watching has become an addiction with large numbers of people and I learn that even in a remote, small temple town like Melkote (in south Karnataka) over two hundred houses have satellite TV connections. It is alleged that priests hurry through their worship in the temples to go home to watch their favourite programmes!

A distinct teenage culture is emerging, or has already emerged, as a result of the emergence of a sizeable middle class whose youth offer a tempting market for a variety of goods which can be advertised in the newspapers and on TV. The teenagers are recognizable by their distinctive dress, hair-style, lingo, habits and life-style. Their heroes and heroines are usually sportsmen, athletes, film stars, rock musicians and models. The better-off among them visit pubs, Bangalore being a trend-setter, go disco-dancing and smoke pot. They are more subject to peer group pressures than to family influence. Older people seem to be bewildered at the attitudes and behaviour of their teenage relatives. Or perhaps it would be more accurate to describe the situation as one of mutual incomprehension. There is an urgent need for sociologists to study teenagers in the same way as they study the culture and behaviour of far-away tribes and ethnic groups.

An inevitable consequence of growing consumerism is the pressure to buy goods which are not needed. Housewives and teenagers are likely to feel the pressure even more than elderly people. Hire-purchase schemes, chit funds, the organization of periodic sales by big firms, and the use of credit cards are an inevitable consequence of consumerism. Having a lot of goods enhances one's status and one is judged by what one has and not by what one is.

When the rich and the middle classes go in for consumerism, the gulf between them and the poor will widen even further. Since the richest villagers are also victims of consumerism, the rich-poor divide will sharpen in rural areas too. Given the tensions which already exist, namely caste, religion, language, region and low status, consumerism might prove to be the last straw on the backs of the poor. Given an opportunity, the poor might do in Indian cities what the American Blacks did some years ago in Watts and New York. The situations are not all dissimilar.

6

A major change that has occurred with independence and adult franchise is the emergence of political power as more or less the supreme value for a very large number of people. Translating this into traditional terms, it is as though *artha*, the politico-economic realm, has become sovereign, cutting itself loose from *dharma*, the moral realm.[9] Even within the realm of *artha*, power has emerged as superior to wealth, for power can confer wealth and much else besides. The ease and swiftness with which politicians become extremely wealthy is a very familiar phenomenon. But it is also true that businessmen who are very wealthy can use their wealth to manipulate governmental decisions in their favour. In the process the politician and administrator also benefit, the only ones to lose being the people. That wealth is also used to atone for sins and increase one's stock of merit by doing works of charity and contributing funds to temples, mosques and churches, is the other side of the coin. This idea has not lost its hold; indeed, if anything, the contrary, thanks to the fact that a great many people have had access to wealth in recent years.

But it is important to note that power does not only have an instrumental value but is also endowed with glamour. The trappings and perquisites of power, uniformed sentries, resplendently dressed servants, government cars, telephones, PAs, the hundreds of favour-seekers who throng the compounds of ministers and the obsequiousness of these favour-seekers, all serve to proclaim the magic of power. No wonder so many people want it.

Finally, power has emerged as the legitimizer of all achievement and, indeed, of all activity, especially public activity. Ministers are asked to open, inaugurate, release, preside over, chair and grace all kinds of functions—sometimes half the cabinet attends a function and those ministers who do not oblige the organizers are dubbed arrogant. How much of his time a minister spends in attending to his ministry's affairs and in attending to the problems of his constituents and how much on ceremonial and public relations exercises is a matter deserving serious examination.

A recent and significant development is the coming together of the politician and the "renouncer", or man in ochre robes. (The politician is indeed versatile: he moves from the company of criminals of all kinds at one end to that of "godmen" and *sanyasis* at the other.) Here, a distinction needs to be made between different kinds of "renouncers": renouncers who engage themselves in welfare activities, renouncers who are reputed to possess "powers" to effect cures and perform other miracles, and finally, pure contemplatives (like the late Sri Ramakrishna and Ramana Maharishi). Those who are engaged in welfare activities such as starting schools, colleges, hostels, orphanages, hospitals and old people's homes need to cultivate politicians to obtain grants of land and money, and various kinds of permits, even favours. Politicians know that it is good for their image to be seen close to renouncers, and there is always the hope that at some point closeness might yield votes. "Godmen" command large followings and their support is not only politically beneficial, it also provides a shield against the insecurities of the high-risk profession of politics. Finally, the reclusive renouncer is contacted only rarely, for his "blessings". It is in the Indian tradition that the temporal realm acknowledges, though only rarely, the supremacy of the spiritual.

An inevitable result of enhanced opportunities for a large number of people and the prevalence of acute competition for obtaining access to resources such as education, employment and a comfortable standard of living, is the spread of stress and stress-related ailments among the people. High blood-pressure, nervous tension, hyperacidity and insomnia are becoming indicators of middle- and upper-class status. When neglected, they may lead to inefficiency at work, inability to cope with the many demands made on one and, in extreme cases, nervous breakdown. Not only are there not enough psychiatrists to cope with these maladies, but the culture of going to psychiatrists and counsellors is simply not there. Under these circumstances, prayer and meditation, and visits to temples and pilgrimage-centres offer some relief to people, though rationalists may scoff at such practices. People in all walks of life consult astrologers, though it is likely that the middle and upper classes nowadays resort to them more than the others, as their lives are coming under increasing strain. (It is not that the lives of the poor are stress-free but they also have their temples, oracles, amulets, exorcists and holy men.) Incidentally, consulting astrologers is not peculiar to Indians or Asians for that matter. It is prevalent in the West too; the Reagans consulted three astrologers, Princess Diana has an astrologer and we do not know about the other VIPs in the West who consult astrologers.

While consulting astrologers is wide-spread in India, there is a reluctance to acknowledge the fact, particularly among the educated. Intellectuals do not hesitate to pour scorn on astrology, though it is not certain that they themselves do not consult astrologers when in trouble. Politicians do not have a monopoly on hypocrisy.

To recapitulate, in discussing changing values in India today, my approach has been that of an empirically-minded sociologist. But I am also a citizen, and an individual with my own preferences, values, if you like. On the institutional side, I think that people's movements are essential to set right the many ills that infest the body social, of which the body politic is a vital part. People's movements are indispensable to lessen corruption in Indian public life, to see that development plans do not destroy the environment, to ensure gender equality, to promote decentralization of power and to combat growing consumerism. People's movements are needed particularly to teach elected representatives that real power in a democracy rests with the people, and that errant, corrupt or perverse governments will not be tolerated. The tendency to autocracy is so deep at the state and lower levels that periodical elections are not enough to curb it. People's movements might provide the necessary curb but they need time to build up, given the fact that the electorate is poor and uneducated, and that local leaders are bribable. Perhaps institutions such as recall may be necessary to make leaders more responsive to public opinion.

There is also a need to cut down the role of the government and to encourage people to develop their own initiatives. To this end, voluntary associations need to be encouraged, particularly in the execution and monitoring of development and welfare work. On the individual plane, there is need to spread the message that happiness consists not in the senseless accumulation of goods which one can do without but in doing work which not only gives money but also satisfaction. It is also necessary to realize that those who are gifted have an obligation to use the gifts they have inherited and which a favourable environment in early years developed, for the good of society, for the benefit of those who are weaker, and not for self-aggrandizement and self-glorification. Gandhi's idea of trusteeship should not be confined to the wealthy but extended to include the gifted too.

NOTES

[This essay is a revised version of the author's Surya Prakash Memorial Lecture delivered at the Indian Institute of World Culture in Bangalore on September 12, 1992. I thank B.V. Raman for doing me the honour of inviting me to deliver the lecture. Thanks are also due to V.S. Parthasarathy for help in the preparation of the lecture, and P. Ramachandran and R. Krishna Chandran who have typed patiently several versions of the lecture. I have also to acknowledge my indebtedness to the National Institute for Advanced Studies, Bangalore, where I am the J.R.D. Tata visiting professor, for providing me with the leisure and freedom to pursue my studies.]

1. "Values are not the same as norms for conduct. Norms are rules for behaving: they say more or less specifically what should or should not be done by particular types of actors in given circumstances. Values are standards of desirability that are more nearly independent of specific situations. The same value may be a point of reference for a great many specific norms; a particular norm may represent the simultaneous application of several separable values. Thus the value premise of 'equality' may enter into norms for relationships between husband and wife, brother and brother, teacher and student, and so on. On the other hand, the norm 'a teacher must not show favouritism in grading' may, in a particular instance, involve the values of equality, honesty, humanitarianism and several others. Values as standards (criteria) for establishing what should be regarded as desirable, provide the grounds for accepting or rejecting particular norms. Thus achievement values, stressing active instrumental accomplishment against a standard of excellence, may be reflected in norms for sports, games, occupational activities, community service, political life, education, science and so on. The same principle holds for values considered as desirable objects or states. For example, a high positive education of 'freedom' or 'authority' may be one of the grounds for a great many specific norms in various areas of society, culture and personality. On the other hand, many norms are multi-valued, relating simultaneously, for example to hedonic criteria, considerations of efficiency, and values of social integration. A minor but clear case in point might be norms of etiquette for social dining." (Robin M. Williams (Jr.). "Values: The Concept of Values", in *International Encyclopaedia of the Social Sciences*, vol. 16, Macmillan and The Free Press, 1968, p. 283.)
2. See *Statistical Abstracts of India*, 1987, Government of India, Central Statistical Organisation, New Delhi, pp. 542-543. The figure of 166 literates out of 1,000 is based on figures for India excluding Jammu and Kashmir, and NEFA.

3. See in this connection my *On Living in a Revolution and other Essays*, Oxford University Press, Delhi, 1992.
4. The Indian parliament has passed two bills, Panchayati Raj and Nagarpalika, providing for decentralization of power to the people. Two constitution amendment bills, 72 and 73, have been passed, the 72nd amendment providing for decentralization of power to the rural areas, while the 73rd amendment provides for decentralization of power to cities and towns. The bills make it mandatory to hold elections to these local self-governing bodies. See *The Times of India*, December 23 and 24, 1992.

   During the last few months, municipal and panchayat elections have been held in the Punjab, with voter turnout exceeding 60 per cent. Elections have also been held successfully in Meghalaya, Nagaland, and most recently, in Tripura.
5. Attention needs to be drawn in this connection to the perceptive statement of M.Y. Ghorpade, "The poverty line today is defined in a particular way but the nature of poverty has undergone a change and is not so hopeless and helpless as it used to be." ("Whither Economic Policy and Performance?", Rajyotsava Lecture, Institute for Social and Economic Change, Bangalore, November 23, 1992, p. 3.)
6. In the modern world, violence within a country is frequently linked to the ramifications of international politics, to religious fundamentalism, to drug-trafficking, mafia dons, and to the existence of close links between all these factors. In this connection see the excellent article of Jasjit Singh, "Means of Terrorism: From Transistor Bombs to RDX" in *The Times of India*, April 3, 1993.
7. *The Report of the National Council of Applied Economic Research*, New Delhi, quoted in R. Venkatachary, "The Emergence of a New Middle Class" in *The Sunday Times*, November 1, 1992, p. 14.
8. See in this connection, Nupur Basu's article "Capitation Fees: Money *vs*. Merit?" in *India Abroad*, August 21, 1992, p. 29.
9. *Moksha*, the ultimate value, is far too distant to be able to influence people directly, but its indirect influence may be seen in such activities of the elderly as performing daily *puja* and meditation at home, visiting temples and pilgrimage-centres, performing *bhajans*, reading religious literature and leading a life-style characterized by attention to things spiritual and indifference to things material.

READING LIST

I. SANSKRITIZATION AND WESTERNIZATION

Bailey, F.G. *Caste and the Economic Frontier*, Oxford, 1958, pp. 188 ff.

Barnabas, A.P. "Sanskritization", *Economic Weekly*, vol. XIII, no. 15, April 15, 1961, pp. 613–618.

Berreman, G.D. *Hindus of the Himalayas*, Berkeley and Los Angeles, 1963.

Chanana, Dev Raj. "Sanskritization, Westernization and India's North-West", *Economic Weekly*, vol. XIII, no. 9, March 4, 1961, pp. 409–414.

Gould, H.A. "Sanskritization and Westernization, A Dynamic View", *Economic Weekly*, vol. XIII, no. 25, June 24, 1961, pp. 945–950.

Kalia, S.L. "Sanskritization and Tribalization", *Bulletin of the Tribal Research Institute*, Chindwara (M.P.), April 1959, pp. 33–43.

Mahar, Pauline M. "Changing Religious Practices of an Untouchable Caste", *Economic Development and Cultural Change*, vol. VIII, no. 3, April 1960, pp. 279–287.

Marriott, McKim. "Changing Channels of Cultural Transmission in Indian Civilization", in V.F. Ray (ed.), *Intermediate Societies*, Seattle, Wash., 1959.

——. "Inter-actional and Attributional Theories of Caste Ranking", *Man in India*, vol. 39, no. 2, June 1959, pp. 92–107.

Marriott, McKim (ed.). *Village India: Studies in the Little Community*, Chicago, 1955.

Mayer, A.C. "Some Hierarchical Aspects of Caste", *Southwestern Journal of Anthropology*, vol. 12, no. 2, Summer 1956, pp. 117–144.

Orans, Martin. "A Tribe in Search of a Great Tradition: The Emulation-Solidarity Conflict", *Man in India*, vol. 39, no. 2, June 1959, pp. 108–114.

Raghavan, V. "Variety and Integration in the Pattern of Indian Culture", *Far Eastern Quarterly*, vol. 15, no. 4, August 1956, pp. 497–505.

Sahay, K.N. "Trends of Sanskritization Among the Oraon", *Bulletin of the Bihar Tribal Research Institute*, Ranchi, vol. IV, no. 2, September 1962, pp. 1–15.

Singer, Milton. "The Social Organization of Indian Civilization", *Diogenes*, vol. 45, Winter 1964, pp. 84–119.

Singer, Milton (ed.). *Traditional India: Structure and Change*, American Folklore Society, Philadelphia, 1959.

Staal, J.F. "Sanskrit and Sanskritization", *Journal of Asian Studies*, vol. 22, 1963.

Vidyarthi, L.P. *The Sacred Complex in Hindu Gaya*, Bombay, 1961.

Vidyarthi, L.P. (ed.). *Aspects of Religion in Indian Society*, Meerut, 1961.

II. THE BACKWARD CLASSES MOVEMENT

Beteille, A. *The Future of the Backward Classes*, Supplement to *Indian Journal of Public Administration*, vol. XI, no. 1, January–March 1965, pp. 1–39.

——. "Caste and Politics in Tamilnād" (to be published).

Brass, P.R. "Regionalism, Nationalism and Political Conflict in Uttar Pradesh", paper read at a meeting of the Association for Asian Studies, San Francisco, April 2, 1965.

Broomfield, J.H. "An Elite and Its Rivals: Bengal Bhadralok at the Opening of the Twentieth Century", paper read at a meeting of the Association for Asian Studies, San Francisco, April 2, 1965.

Dushkin, L. "The Backward Classes", *Economic Weekly*, Bombay, October 28–November 18, 1961.

Galanter, Marc. "Equality and Protective Discrimination in India", *Rutgers Law Review*, vol. XVI, no. 1, 1961, pp. 42–74.

——. "The Problem of Group Membership: Some Reflections on the Judicial View of Indian Society", *Journal of the Indian Law Institute*, vol. IV, no. 3, July–September 1962, pp. 331–358.

——. "Law and Caste in India", *Asian Survery*, vol. III, no. 11, November 1963, pp. 544–599.

Ghurye, G.S. *Caste and Class in India*, Bombay, 1950.

Harrison, Selig. *India, the Most Dangerous Decades*, Princeton, 1960.

Irschick, E. *Politics and Social Conflict in South India—The Non-Brahmin Movement and Tamil Separatism*, Ph.D. thesis, University of Chicago, 1964.

——. "The Integration of South India into the National Movement." (Mimeographed.)

——. "The Brahmin Non-Brahmin Struggle for Power in Madras", paper read at a meeting of the Association for Asian Studies, San Francisco, April 2, 1965.

Isaacs, Harold. *The Ex-Untouchables*, New York, 1964.

Patterson, M. "Caste and Political Leadership in Maharashtra", *Economic Weekly*, Bombay, September 25, 1954, pp. 1065–1067.

Rao, M.S.A. "Caste and the Indian Army", *Economic Weekly*, Bombay, August 29, 1964, pp. 1439–1443.

Silverberg, James (ed.). *Social Mobility in Caste in India*, special issue of *Comparative Studies in Society and History* (to be published).

Smith, D.E. *India as a Secular State*, Princeton, 1963.

Srinivas, M.N. *Caste in Modern India*, Bombay, 1962.

Wiener, Myron. "The Struggle for Equality in India", *Foreign Affairs*, July 1962, pp. 1–9.

FURTHER READING

Beteille, André. *Studies in Agrarian Social Structure*, New Delhi, 1974.

Dube, S.C. (ed.). *India Since Independence: A Social Report on India 1947–1972*, New Delhi, 1977.

Dumont, L. *Homo Hierarchicus: Caste System and Its Implications*, Chicago, 1970.

Epstein, T. Scarlett. *South India: Yesterday, Today and Tomorrow*, London, 1973.

Gore, M.S. *Urbanisation and Social Change*, New Jersey, 1968.

Mahar, Michael (ed.). *Untouchables in Contemporary India*, Tucson, 1972.

Mandelbaum, D.G. *Society in India*, 2 vols., Berkeley, 1970.

Saberwal, Satish. *Mobile Men*, New Delhi, 1976.

Shah, A.M. *Household Dimension of the Family in India*, New Delhi, 1973.

Singer, Milton. *When a Great Tradition Modernizes*, New York, 1970.

Singer, Milton and Bernard Cohn (eds.). *Structure and Change in Indian Society*, Chicago, 1968.

Srinivas, M.N. *The Remembered Village*, New Delhi, 1976.

——. *Nation-Building in Independent India*, New Delhi, 1977.

Srinivas, M.N., S. Seshaiah and V.S. Parthasarathy (eds.). *Dimensions of Social Change in India*, New Delhi, 1977.

Index